Nigerian Legal Methods

Nigerian Legal Methods

Edited by

C. C. Ohuruogu and O. T. Umahi

CAMBRIDGE SCHOLARS PUBLISHING

Nigerian Legal Methods,
Edited by C. C. Ohuruogu and O. T. Umahi

This book first published 2013

Cambridge Scholars Publishing

12 Back Chapman Street, Newcastle upon Tyne, NE6 2XX, UK

British Library Cataloguing in Publication Data
A catalogue record for this book is available from the British Library

ISBN (10): 1-4438-5126-4, ISBN (13): 978-1-4438-5126-8

DEDICATION

This book is dedicated to the memories of **Mazi Mark Chikere Ohuruogu**, a.k.a "MC" (1932-1995), an educationist par excellence, community leader and disciple of Christ whose exemplary life touched many people, and **Chief William Ikeji Umahi**, a.k.a "Omeluatu I of Mgbowo" (1924-2005) of blessed memory; a community leader, health professional and peace builder. They laid the solid foundation on which we have built.

And to the Alpha, the Omega, the everlasting Father, in whom there is neither variableness nor shadow of turning—GOD.

TABLE OF CONTENTS

TABLE OF CASES

TABLE OF STATUTES

PREFACE

This text is a collection of writings on assigned topics by some scholars and lecturers in the Faculty of Law at Benson Idahosa University and those invited from outside. The idea to write a text for use in the study of legal methods for law students was borne out of the desire to present a range of updated material in this area of study.

The focus of this text is Nigeria. It is written in simple, easy-to-understand language, and meant essentially for law students in the first year of the five year course in Law, as structured by the National Universities Commission (NUC). Nevertheless, persons who have need of information or education on different aspects of Nigerian legal process will also find aspects of the text useful. In addition, advanced students and researchers will find some parts of the text useful, particularly those parts dealing with legal research and writing.

The contributors come from diverse backgrounds and experiences, which is reflected in their styles of presentation. However, each has endeavoured to present the assigned topic in such a form as to enhance comprehension by the primary beneficiaries.

The inclusion of the chapters on advocacy and mooting skills, as well as examination skills and strategies make this text unique, and beyond what existing texts in Nigeria provide. In the course of time, additional topics will be added when we prepare the next edition.

Prof. C.C. Ohuruogu and Dr. T.O. Umahi

ACKNOWLEDGEMENTS

The academic leadership provided by **Professor MacDonald IDUH**, Vice Chancellor of Benson Idahosa University until April 30, 2013 made it worthwhile to embark on this project. We sincerely appreciate him.

The various contributors who had to endure our constant "harassment" and worked day and night to meet tight schedules are worthy of celebration. Kudos.

One person we owe a debt of gratitude is **Peter Ndubuisi MBAH** Esq. LL.B (UEL); LL.M (Maritime & Commercial Law) LASU, MBA; we are grateful for the provision of both moral and financial support for this book.

CHAPTER ONE

LAW IN SOCIAL CONTEXT

LILIAN AKHIROME-OMONFUEGBE[1]

Introduction

In any given society, it is imperative that there should be some set standards or rules to regulate the affairs of people. The ability to make rational choices is one of the major distinguishing features which set men apart from animals. However, where there is freedom of choice, abuse is inevitable. Thus, as far back as biblical days, the need for man to abide by rules so as to avoid chaos and anarchy has always existed. Today even ordinary people regularly make laws for their own circumstances; it is a way of regulating behaviour.[2] Let us look at our everyday life; for example, if you set up a club or a committee which accords its members certain rights and privileges, it becomes a necessity to put in place some form of body of rules or code of conduct to regulate the affairs of the club/committee. An absence of a body of rules or code of conduct will no doubt lead to abuse of the rights and privileges which the members possess.

Looking at this illustration, it is important to note also that this body of rules or code of conduct will not only prescribe a set standard for the members, but will also make provision for some form of sanction or penalty, e.g. payment of fine or loss of membership, in the event that any member does not abide by them. This is important because a code of conduct/body of rules brings about rights and privileges as well as duties. Where there is no means of enforcing the body of rules/code of conduct, these rights will be abused and duties may never be executed. The

---

[1] LLM (Wales), LL.B (AAU), BL, Lecturer in Law, Benson Idahosa University, Benin City, Edo State, Nigeria.

[2] A. Bradney et al, *How to Study Law,* 3rd ed., (London: Sweet and Maxwell, 1995), 3.

members have to be aware that if they do not abide by the rules, they will be punished; this consciousness brings about obedience and conformity, and suppresses deviant behaviour.[3] The same goes for the society at large. All over the world, no matter how free a society claims to be, there must be laws in existence and a system in place to enforce these laws. Sanctions or penalties must also be put in place as a guide, to protect the interests of the entire society. Therefore where a man possesses rights and privileges, there must be corresponding duties/obligations on his part. In other words, where the law imposes on him a duty, it creates also a right in his favour.

This chapter has so far shown that law is necessary to ensure a free, safe, orderly and progressive society. It is important for the people of a society to live a normal and free life and have commercial, religious and personal relationships with one another in peace, safety and orderliness. This chapter will discuss the nature, definition and functions of law. It will also examine some of the legal concepts which describe the aims and objectives of law—that is, how law serves as a check and balance in society.

The Nature of Law

The nature of law simply means the attributes or features and characteristics of law, not the definition; law does not possess a single or definite attribute. It is diverse, and includes the following:

1. A collection of rules to be obeyed; that is, it can be said to be a collection of do's and don'ts. It prescribes what a person should or should not do.[4]
2. It provides remedies for a person against whom a wrong has been committed, as well as sanction or penalty for a person who has disobeyed the law.
3. In times past, laws evolved from customs. In Nigeria, our customary law is a part of our legal system. In the present day, by contrast, laws are made by legislature or parliament depending on the legal system of the country. In Nigeria, laws/statutes are made by legislature.
4. Laws which evolved from custom are largely unwritten, although these days some are partly written and others have evolved through

---

[3] J. H. Farrar and A. M. Dugdale, *Introduction to Legal Method* (London: Sweet and Maxwell, 1990), 6.

[4] E. Malemi, *The Nigerian Legal Method* (*Lagos*: Princeton Publishing Co, 2010), 8.

judicial precedent. However a major feature of law today is that it is written (codified).

5. Sometimes law and morality are confused. They may be used together in certain situations, but law is not the same as morality. Although law may reflect the morality of a society, the main difference is the existence of sanctions which exist in conjunction with law.

6. Law is fundamental—it covers all aspects of human existence. For everything in life, there is a law.

7. Law can also be seen as the answer/response to societal problems or issues. That is, the law makers make the law to address a particular issue or problem/condition prevalent in a society.

8. The aim of law is fairness and equity. Thus the popular saying "no man is above the law." The law serves to bring about justice. For example, the statue of justice is blindfolded and holds two equal scales; this signifies that law promotes justice, fairness and equality irrespective of your colour, economic or academic status. "Law is not a one way traffic, ... and all persons should be able to approach the seat of justice openly without inhibitions or handicap."[5] However, on rare occasions law may lead to injustice, for example where a strict interpretation is applied.

9. As noted above, sometimes a strict interpretation of the law may lead to injustice and this creates a gap between justice and the law. This can be addressed by amendments. Thus we can say that law is not static; it evolves. Dynamism is one of its distinctive features. It is continually amended to meet societal needs and changes. Justice Benjamin N. Cardozo, Justice of the US Supreme Court put it succinctly thus; "The law, like the traveller must be ready for the morrow. It must have a principle of growth."[6]

10. Law is the last hope of the common man. It helps organize a society. Its existence brings about development, growth, stability and hope in a society. It gives the people a sense of security, and helps to structure a society as well as maintain that structure.

11. Law is territorial:[7] it guides and binds the conduct of people within a given territory. Even though the law of the different places

---

[5] Hon. Justice P. A. Onamade, *Guide to Words and Phrases in Nigerian Law,* Vol. 2 (Lagos: Philade Company Ltd, 2003), 649 para. 1469.

[6] Justice B. N. Cardozo, *The Growth of the Law*, (New Haven: Yale University Press; 1924), pp. 19-20. See also the case of *Wood v. Lucy* 222 N.Y 88, 90-91 (1917).

[7] A. O. Sanni, *Introduction to Legal Methods* (Ile-Ife: Obafemi Awolowo University Press Limited, 2006), 7.

might be similar; there will always be differences which distinguish one town from another.

What Is Law?

Over the years, there have been several attempts at a definition of this concept. However numerous the definitions are today, none is free from criticism. There cannot be said to be any authoritative, complete or absolute definition of law. Nevertheless, the overall attempt to define the concept has succeeded in one way or another to capture the essence of what law ultimately is.

The difficulty in achieving an absolute definition may be due to the dynamic and evolving nature of the law. Thus everyday new features of this concept are discovered, such that the definitions of previous years become limiting and do not completely or sufficiently describe law. Some of the definitions attributed to law include:

- A rule of behaviour; a code of conduct. It is the rules and regulations of a particular country, usually made by the legislative arm of government which orders the way persons, bodies and society should behave.[8]
- The whole reservoir of rules from which judges draw their decisions.[9]
- The rule of action which is prescribed by a superior person or body and which an inferior person or body is bound to obey.[10]
- A body of rules made by institutions, bodies and persons vested with the power to make such rules which are binding and enforced among the members of a given society.[11]

Some schools of thought however believe that the definition of law is only complete when it includes the presence of sanctions; following this understanding, law is therefore defined as rules whose obedience is

---

[8] E. Malemi, *The Nigerian Legal Method* (Lagos: Princeton Publishing Co, 2010), 7.

[9] See L. B. Curzon, *Basic Law: An Introduction for Students*, 1990, cited in E. Malemi, *The Nigerian Legal Method* (Lagos: Princeton Publishing Co, 2010), 7.

[10] Sir William Blackstone (1923-1980), cited in E. Malemi, *The Nigerian Legal Method* (Lagos: Princeton Publishing Co, 2010), 7.

[11] B. A. Garner, *Black's Law Dictionary* 9th ed. (St. Paul, Minnesota: West Group; 2009).

secured by sanctions;[12] that is, a body of rules made by the Sovereign, to be obeyed by the people, disobedience of which would attract sanctions. John Austin (1954),[13] who propounded the Command Theory of Law, put it succinctly thus: "That law is a command set by a political superior for a political inferior, which the inferior has to obey or suffer sanction."[14] This definition, though clearly applying to criminal law with regard to sanctions (punishment of offenders), has however been criticized as it has been argued by scholars that law is not always couched in the form of a command. Some laws are only procedural e.g. the Marriage Act[15] in Nigeria which regulates statutory marriages, or the Civil Procedure Rules of the various state high courts in Nigeria.

Another criticism is that in modern democratic countries today, there no longer exists a "political superior" who has unlimited powers. For example, in Nigeria, the Constitution[16] posits that the people of Nigeria made and adopted the Constitution as their supreme law and appointed the government into power through their vote. In essence, the government and the people work hand in hand and the leaders are not to be seen as "uncommanded commanders."[17] In the case of *IGP v. All Nigerian Peoples Party & Others,*[18] the respondents had contended in court that the Public Order Act[19] was unconstitutional, as its provisions constituted a breach of fundamental rights to peaceful assembly and association provided in the Constitution.[20] The Federal High Court, Abuja held that the Public Order Act was unconstitutional and in breach of the rights of the respondents to freedom of peaceful assembly. On appeal, the Court of Appeal affirmed the judgment of the trial court. This example clearly shows why the command theory does not give a very good definition of law as it stands today.

---

[12] A. O. Obilade, *The Nigerian Legal System* 3rd ed. (Ibadan: Spectrum Books Ltd, 2005), 3.

[13] John Austin (1954) of the Positive Theory school of thought, cited by L. B. Curzon, *Jurisprudence* 2nd ed., (London: Cavendish Publishers Limited), 99-110.

[14] John Austin of the Positive Theory school of thought.

[15] CAP M.6, Laws of the Federation of Nigeria (LFN) 2004.

[16] The preamble to the 1999 Constitution as amended 2011; see also Chapter 1 of the Constitution.

[17] E. Malemi, *The Nigerian Legal Method* (Lagos: Princeton Publishing Co, 2010), 61.

[18] (2009) 18 NWLR (Pt. 1066) p.457.

[19] 1990 (now 2004).

[20] Section 40, 1999 Constitution as amended 2011.

All of these definitions have attempted to capture the meaning of law. Similarities run through all the various definitions. In essence, therefore, law can be understood to mean a set of rules which prescribe the standard by which persons or bodies should behave/conduct themselves in society.

Functions of Law

1. Law provides a structured framework for a society, guiding and regulating all aspects of human existence and relationships. In other words, it stipulates what a good, orderly, safe, peaceful and organized society should look like, such that any behaviour, relationship or institution that promotes or creates anything outside that stipulated framework will be seen as contrary to the law or illegal.
2. Law serves to guarantee and streamline the freedom, rights and duties of the members of a society. Therefore, though an individual may possess "absolute" freedom, the law puts a limit to such freedom[21] in order to protect the interests of other members of society.
3. Law serves as a medium for resolving disputes or conflicts. It follows therefore that there exist the necessary institutions like law courts, tribunals, etc, to carry out these functions. Law also seeks to provide remedies and justice to people who have suffered negatively[22] by the action or inaction of another. The most obvious way in which law contributes to the maintenance of social order is the way in which it deals with disorder or conflict.[23]
4. Law can also be put in place specifically to address or respond to a particular societal problem or issue.[24] For example, the increase in child abuse and child trafficking in recent times have made it necessary for laws prohibiting and punishing such offences to be put in place.[25]
5. For there to be social order and balance in a society, there has to be well-formulated law and institutions or systems put in place to enforce such law. Thus law serves as a formal mechanism of social control. It plays a major role in ensuring the existence and maintenance of order in a society. "… When the law curbs the excesses of the strong

---

[21] Section 45 of 1999 Constitution as amended 2011.
[22] *INEC v. Oshiomohle* (2008) WRN 24, where the gubernatorial aspirant (Oshiomohle) contested the INEC election result in court and judgment was given in his favour; he was returned as the legitimate governor of Edo state of Nigeria.
[23] G. Slapper and D. Kelly, *The English Legal System*, 12th ed. (Essex: Pearson Education Limited, 2012), 2.
[24] *Ibid*, p. 2.
[25] See Child Rights Act, 2003.

and balances their rights and duties as well as powers… then we can say the law has dominion…"[26]

6. Finally, law constitutes and regulates the principal organs of power in a society.[27]

This chapter has looked at the nature, definition and functions of law. A good question to ask at this stage is what the main aim or objective of the law is particularly in relation to its functions, what does the law aim to achieve as its end result?

Aims and Objectives of Law

In summary, the law serves as a check and balance in society. It ensures that every individual is accorded certain rights and privileges as a human being, but stipulates that individuals must exercise those rights in such a manner that will not interfere with the rights and privileges of others in society.

Some of the legal concepts describing the aims and objectives of law are as follows:

1. Law and Order

According to Gary Slapper and David Kelly,[28] "law plays an important part in the creation and maintenance of social order."[29] The major aim of any government is to maintain law and order within its territory. In order to achieve this, laws are usually put in place and institutions/bodies set up for the enforcement of these laws. This is because the law would no doubt be useless if there was no means of enforcing it.

A. O. Obilade[30] in defining law explains that, in the absence of law, there would be chaos and anarchy. Imagine a society in which people were allowed free reign, with no rules and no code of conduct—disaster would be prevalent in such an environment. Therefore, the law is an instrument

---

[26] O. N. Ogbu, *Modern Nigerian Legal System* (Enugu: CIDJAP Publishers, 2002), 7.

[27] J. H. Farrar and A. M. Dugdale, supra note 3.

[28] G. Slapper and D. Kelly, *The English Legal System*, 12th ed., (Essex, United Kingdom: Pearson Education Limited, 2012), 2.

[29] *Ibid*, p. 2.

[30] A. O. Obilade, *The Nigerian Legal System*, 3rd ed., (Ibadan: Spectrum Books Ltd, 2005), 3.

of social control to promote order in society. This is the main reason for the creation of a government and governing bodies in any society. For example, in Nigeria, the Constitution provides that "the promotion of the welfare and the good of the people shall be the primary purpose of the government."[31]

Similarly, in the international scene, where countries interact with each other, different rules (treaties, conventions. etc) are put in place to regulate the relationships between them.[32] Even during war, when it may seem as if there is no order, law comes into force and ensures that the war is fought according to the laws of war. For example, international humanitarian law (IHL) deals with law applicable during armed conflict (all cases of declared war).[33] One of the main provisions under IHL is that combat must be restricted between combatants only and civilians should not be attacked. Thus, the elderly, women and children are protected at times of war.[34] Breach of law of war is a 'war crime;' for example, Charles Taylor, former president of Liberia, was sentenced to fifty years in prison for war crimes. There are numerous other examples of people punished for war crimes by United Nations tribunals. Finally, for order to be maintained through law, the enforcement and administration of law has to be done without fear of favour to anyone, else this aim will be defeated.

2. Law and Justice

Some authors have defined justice as, "fairness, rightness, right, just, good, reasonable."[35]Justice is ultimately the correct application of the law.[36] Hence, we can say that justice simply means what is good, fair and right. Justice seeks to promote equality. As discussed earlier on in this chapter, the law is the last hope of the common man. The fact that the law aims at promoting justice is the reason why a man cannot do wrong to his

---

[31] Section 14 (2) (b) of the, 1999 Constitution of Nigeria as amended 2011.

[32] For example, trade-related aspects of intellectual property rights agreement.

[33] W. Kälin et al, *Law of International Human Rights Protection* (Oxford: Oxford University Press, 2009), 108.

[34]*Ibid*, p. 81. See also M. Sassòli *et al*, *How Does Law Protect in War? Cases, Documents and Teaching Materials on Contemporary Practise in International Humanitarian Law*, Vol. 11, 2nd ed. (Geneva: ICRC, 2011), 128, 132.

[35] E. Malemi, *The Nigerian Legal Method (*Lagos: Princeton Publishing Co, 2010), 114.

[36] A. O. Sanni, *Introduction to Legal Methods* (Ile-Ife: Obafemi Awolowo University Press, 2006), 32.

fellow man and not receive a penalty. This serves as a deterrent to other members of society.

Justice seeks to balance the conflicting or competing interests of people in society. There are two main types of justice:

a. Formal justice
b. Substantive justice

a) Formal justice

This is when the law is applied strictly and mechanically by the court. In this case, the judge will interpret the law as it is, without regard or recourse to any external factors or influence (how he feels or what he thinks). One of the arguments in favour of formal justice is that it does not see anything wrong with the law as it is and as such can be applied the way it is without fear or favour. Proponents of this type of justice also posit that it promotes clarity and certainty of the law, since everyone will know what the law is and follow it as it is without allowing external considerations to affect the interpretation or application. This is the type of justice achieved when the literal rule of interpretation of statutes[37] are applied by judges. See the case of *PDP v. INEC,*[38] where the court held that if the wording of a statute is clear and unambiguous it should be given its clear and literal meaning. It was also held in that case that if there is a gap in statutory provisions, it is the job of the legislature to correct it, not that of the judges. Thus the judges should interpret the law as it is without modification.

Nevertheless, a major demerit of this type of justice is that since it does not see anything wrong with the law, it does not encourage improvement, change or development of the law. Considering the fact that one of the major features/attributes of law is its dynamism and ever-evolving nature, this is a big minus for the theory of formal justice. Law should not be static; it has to constantly improve and develop to suit the ever growing and changing needs of society.

[37] This is when the judge gives the words of statute their literal and ordinary meaning.
[38] (1999) 11 NWLR (Pt. 626) p. 200 SC.

b) Substantive justice

This is when the court adopts a more liberal approach in the application of law. Here, the judge will consider some external factors especially if a strict application of the law will lead to manifest hardship. It is the need to do substantive justice that led to the existence of the doctrine of equity in the history of English law.[39] Common law, which had already been in existence, was found to be too strict and inflexible and caused manifest hardship on the people.[40] Thus the Chancellor or Judges of the Chancery Court interpreted the law liberally to achieve substantive justice[41] and fairness. Substantive justice is also known as judicial activism.

This type of justice is more predominant today as judges are now more interested in achieving justice than strictly interpreting the law. For instance, technicalities during court proceedings are no longer a ground for striking out cases in court. Previously, the fact that a court process was not properly endorsed, or if the heading bore the wrong name of court or wrong section of the law under which it was brought, was usually enough grounds to strike out the matter. However today the case is different as courts are encouraged to promote justice and lean less on technicalities.[42]

3. Law and Freedom

Freedom is a state of being free. It means liberty, right to do what one wants to do, or right to refrain from what one does not want to do.[43] Man has an innate desire to be free at all times. The history of mankind is replete with stories of how man has pursued this desire from time immemorial. This accounts for the various wars and protests that man has waged in a bid to counter domination and intimidation.

---

[39] G. Rivlin, *Understanding The Law*, 4th ed. (Oxford: Oxford University Press, 2006), 26, 27.

[40] C. Elliott and F. Quinn, *English Legal System*, 12th ed. (Essex: Pearson Education Limited, 2012), 117.

[41] *Ibid*, p. 27.

[42] See the case of *Famfa Oil Limited v. Attorney General of the Federation.* (2003) 18 NWLR (pt 852) 453; see also *Muyiwa Inakoju and Ors v. Hon. Abraham Adeolu Adeleke and Ors-* [2007] All FWLR (Pt. 353) 3 p. 97 where Niki Tobi JSC asserted that justice should prevail over technicalities.

[43] E. Malemi, *The Nigerian Legal Method* (Lagos: Princeton Publishing Co, 2010), 117.

Law recognizes that all men are free and seeks to regulate this freedom vis-à-vis the interests and rights of others in society. For example, in Nigeria, Chapter Four of the Constitution outlines "Fundamental Human Rights of Individuals." In other words, a man's exercise of freedom should not infringe or limit the rights and freedom of another man. This being the case, a person's freedom is curtailed by his duties/obligation to the state and to others in society. However, the state/government cannot restrain a man from exercising his freedom.[44]

Examples of some kinds of freedom are freedom of assembly,[45] freedom of association,[46] freedom of movement,[47] freedom from discrimination, etc; see generally Sections 33-43 of the 1999 Constitution as amended, 2011. However, as earlier noted, the law restricts and limits the rights of individuals in the interest of society at large.[48] The law serves as a check on the people's exercise of freedom in the following ways:

a) Freedom of Assembly/Association

Every individual is free to belong to any assembly or association[49] of his choice and is also free to decide not to belong to any association if he so chooses. Thus, people belong to different associations for the furtherance of their personal or group goals; some examples include membership of churches,[50] political groups, town meetings, etc. However, the law forbids the formation or belonging to any association whose objective is unlawful, illegal or prohibited, such as a secret cult.[51] In addition, any association that will aid unlawful or illegal transactions is forbidden by law.

b) Freedom of Contract

Any person has a right to enter into any contract he chooses with another person, within the confines of the law. He can also refuse to enter

---

[44] *IGP v. All Nigerian Peoples Party* (2009) 18 NWLR (Pt.1066) p. 457.
[45] Section 40 of the 1999 Constitution of Nigeria as amended 2011.
[46] *Ibid* at Section 40 of the 1999 Constitution of Nigeria as amended 2011.
[47] *Ibid* at Section 41 of the 1999 Constitution of Nigeria as amended 2011.
[48] Section 45 of the 1999 Constitution of Nigeria as amended 2011.
[49] *Ibid* at Section 40 of the 1999 Constitution of Nigeria as amended 2011.
[50] Section 38 specifically provides that a person is entitled to have any religion of his choice, and has the freedom to worship with others or alone in public or in private.
[51] Section 38 (4) of the 1999 Constitution of Nigeria as amended 2011.

into a contract if he so desires.[52] This is the basis of the "free enterprise philosophy" which is believed to be the fastest route to economic growth and societal development. However, the law places certain limitations on this freedom. For example, a contract to facilitate the commission of a crime, or a contract that is unlawful or prohibited will be void.

c) Political freedom

In Nigeria, every citizen who is over the age of eighteen and is resident in Nigeria is entitled to register and vote at elections.[53] Thus a person has a right to vote and be voted for or can decide not to even vote at all. However, this political freedom is restricted by law in several ways. For example, people under the age of eighteen, people of unsound mind, etc. cannot vote. The constitution also stipulates certain criteria for the formation and conduct of political parties.[54]

4. Law and the State

The concept of the state has been subject to several definitions. One such definition is as follows:

> A state is a territorial unit, containing a stable population under the authority of its government and recognized as being capable of entering into relations with other entities…[55]

Therefore the four basic features of a state are as follows:[56]

1. A defined territory
2. Stable population
3. Government exercising authority
4. Ability to enter into relations with other states.

The fact that there is a dispute as to the extent of a state's boundaries does not stop it from being referred to as a state.[57] Some countries

---

[52] A. O. Sanni, *Introduction to Legal Methods* (Ile-Ife: Obafemi Awolowo University Press, 2006), 36.
[53] Section 77(2) and 117(2), 1999 Constitution of Nigeria as amended 2011.
[54] *Ibid* at Section 222.
[55] D. W. Greig, *International Law* (London: Butterworths, 1976), 93.
[56] K. G. Richard, *International Law* (Essex: Pearson Education Ltd, 2003), 168.

comprise of a single state with a single race and ethnic group; for example, Japan, Switzerland, etc. Some others are multi-ethnic and contain people of diverse races; for example, Nigeria, the United States of America.

Law is used to define and establish the structure and organization of a state. In Nigeria, the constitution establishes Nigeria as a federation, an indivisible state, consisting of states and a federal capital territory.[58] Presently Nigeria has 36 states and a federal capital territory, Abuja.[59] We have an estimate of two hundred and fifty (250) ethnic groups and languages.[60] It operates a federal system of government; that is, it is made up of a central governing body and other smaller independent divisions which are self-governing but derive their powers from the central governing body. Law defines the scope of the powers of the government; it also regulates the relationship between the government and the people.

The state is an entity conferred with rights and duties by the law.

In a federal state such as Nigeria, where there is separation of powers, we have various arms of government, i.e. the legislative which makes the laws, the executive which enforces and executes the laws, and the judiciary which interprets the law. Law ensures that each arm acts within the confines of its powers,[61]and it defines and limits the extent of their powers.[62] The law prescribes the aims and purpose of government; for example, in Nigeria, Section14 (2) (b) of the Constitution stipulates that "The security and welfare of the people shall be the primary purpose of government."Law seeks to protect the state and the individuals therein, and is therefore essential for their co-existence.

---

[57] N. S. Malcom, *International Law* (Cambridge: Cambridge University Press, 2005), 179.

[58] Section 2, 1999 Constitution of Nigeria as amended, 2011.

[59] Section 3, 1999 Constitution of Nigeria as amended 2011.

[60] Anonymous, http://www.britannica.com/EBChecked/topic/414840/Nigeria/55288/people, Accessed on 08/10/2012.

[61] See T. A. Aguda, *The Judiciary in the Government of Nigeria* (Ibadan: New Horn Press, 1983), 1.

[62] See Chapter V for Legislature, Chapter VI for the Executive and Chapter VII for the Judiciary of the 1999 Constitution of Nigeria as amended 2011.

5. Law and legitimacy

Legitimacy is a state of being legal, valid or permitted by law.[63] It is a state of conforming to law and legality.[64] It describes something which is genuine and valid.[65] Thus if something is illegitimate, it is unlawful or illegal. It is the law that prescribes what is lawful and what is unlawful; we can only say something is a crime after having enquired from the law, and we discover that it is prohibited by law.[66] The Nigerian Constitution defines an offence or a crime as an offence which is defined by law and its penalty is prescribed in written law. Thus a person cannot be convicted of a crime except if that crime is defined in law and its punishment also prescribed by law.[67] We can therefore say that any act done in accordance with the law is called legitimate or legal, while that done in contrast to the provisions of the law is illegal or unlawful. Another instance where the word 'legitimate' is frequently used is in reference to a child who is born during the subsistence of his or her parent's marriage; such a child is called 'legitimate', while a child born out of wedlock is usually referred to as an 'illegitimate' child. The 1999 Constitution as amended in 2011 provides that any person or group of persons who take control of government by means which are not in accordance with the constitution shall not be recognized.[68] What this provision is saying in essence is that a legitimate government is one that is created in accordance with the Constitution's provision. Consequently a government that assumes power by means contrary to the provision of the Constitution will be illegitimate or illegal. This is why anyone caught attempting a coup is charged with treason and the punishment is death.[69] We do know from history however that despite this provision, the history of the Nigerian government is replete with occurrences of coups, some of which had even been successful.

---

[63] B. A. Garner, *Black's Law Dictionary*, 9th ed. (St. Paul, Minnesota: West Group, 2009).
[64] J. H. Farrar and A. M. Dugdale, *Introduction to Legal Method* (London: Sweet and Maxwell, 1990), 11.
[65] B. A. Garner, *Black's Law Dictionary*, 9th ed. (St. Paul, Minnesota: West Group, 2009).
[66] C. O. Okonkwo, *Okonkwo and Naish: Criminal Law in Nigeria* (Ibadan: Spectrum Books limited, 2002), 20.
[67] Section 36 (12), of the 1999 Constitution of Nigeria as amended 2011.
[68] *Ibid* at Section 1(2).
[69] See Section 37 and 38 of the Criminal Code Act, CAP 42.

6. Law and sovereignty

Sovereignty means having supreme authority that is not subject to any other authority.[70] It is the supreme authority in an independent political society.[71] It can also be used to describe the political power and independence of a person who is a ruler. In previous times, before the formation of states/countries—which have either federal or unitary systems of government[72]—what existed were single independent authorities governed by lords, kings, etc. In Africa, kings were regarded as gods who wielded absolute power and authority and were not subject to challenge. In modern times, this kind of "almighty ruler" is now a rare occurrence. Even where there is a single head/ruler, e.g. a monarch, like the Queen of England, their powers are no longer absolute; they are limited by the provisions of the laws of the land.

Thus, law restricts and limits the powers of the ruler of a state, nation or country vis-à-vis the rights of the people he or she is ruling. Sovereignty today is used to refer to a system of government which reflects the preference of citizens in its policies. In the present day therefore, sovereignty rests in the people of the land. In Nigeria for example (and with other democratic countries), the sovereign power is vested in the people. Section 14(2) (a) of the 1999 Constitution as amended in 2011 provides that: "Sovereignty belongs to the people of Nigeria from whom government through this constitution derives all its powers and authority." The preamble of the Constitution provides that the people of Nigeria have agreed and adopted the Constitution as the supreme law of the land.[73]

The people also exercise their sovereignty by voting. This means that the people are the highest authority and the government should derive its powers from them. The will of the people is supreme and supersedes that of any individual ruler. The people's wishes are reflected in the valid laws made by their representatives in the legislature (that is, the people in the legislature have been put there by the people of the society through their votes, so they are there to serve the people). This is the underlying principle of democracy, which is usually described as "government of the people, by the people and for the people."

---

[70] B. A. Garner, *Black's Law Dictionary*, 9th ed. (St. Paul, Minnesota: West Group, 2009).

[71] *Ibid.*

[72] A federal system has a central government and several individual independent entities, while a unitary system has power in a single central unit.

[73] This means that though the Constitution is the supreme law of the land, it expresses the will of the people.

The government in power is there to serve the people and rule in the people's interest. The people exercise the power to change and vote in leaders of their choice. This is done through elections, protests, rallies, calls for international sanctions, etc, in any situation whereby they feel that the government is no longer representing their interest.

CHAPTER TWO

ASPECTS OF LAW

THEOPHILUS CHINEDU NWANO[1]

There are a number of possible approaches to the study of law, of which one is the traditional or formalistic approach. This approach to law is posited on the existence of a discrete legal universe as the object of study. It is concerned with establishing knowledge of the specific rules, both substantive and procedural, which derive from statute and common law and which regulate social activity.[2]

This chapter will introduce some fundamental aspects of law that will underpin an understanding of our legal system. This will be done by introducing you to the different aspects of law that a student will become familiar with as he or she goes through this book.

Defining law itself may seem at first glance to be very simple, but in reality is not easy. As strange as it may seem to ask the question of what law is, it is important to note that philosophers and legal theorists have expended many pages trying to answer the question in different ways. Some of the answers given by philosophers and theorists have reduced law to its most basic forms; for example, Dennis Lloyd, in his book 'The Idea of Law' stated that "Law is one of the institutions which are central to the social nature of man and without which he would be a very different creature."[3] Another theorist propounded that law is the cement of society and also an essential medium of change.[4] So many definitions have been ascribed to law; for instance, law has been said to be a system of rules laid down by a body or person with the power and authority to make law; also

---

[1] LL.M (LASU), B.L, LL.B (LASU), Lecturer, Department of Public Law, Benson Idahosa University, Benin City. Email: tnwano@biu.edu.ng, tnwano@gmail.com.

[2] G. Slapper & D. Kelly, *The English Legal System*, 11th ed. (London: Rutledge Taylor and Francis Group, 2010-2011), 1.

[3] D. Lloyd, *The Idea of Law*, (London: Penguin Books Ltd, 1991), 7.

[4] G. Williams, *Learning the Law* (London: Stevens and Son Ltd, 1982), 1.

it has been said elsewhere that law is what legislators, judges and lawyers do.[5] Others have argued that law is a tool of oppression used by the ruling class to advance its own interest.[6] Law can also be understood to mean a system of rules grounded on fundamental principles of morality.

Each of these characterizations has the capacity to tell us something useful about the nature of law and how it operates. Nevertheless, to achieve a perfect understanding it is apt at this point in the chapter to characterize law into different aspects or classifications. It must be noted that there is no special and authoritative classification of law but in this chapter we will consider the following:

1. Eternal and Divine law
2. Public and Private law
3. Criminal and Civil law
4. Substantive and Procedural law
5. Unwritten and Written law
6. Common law and Equity
7. Customary law

Eternal Law

According to Thomas Aquinas,[7] who was a leading protagonist of his period,[8] eternal law is "God's law for the governance of the universe."[9] "The eternal law is nothing else than the plan of the divine wisdom considered as directing all the acts and motions of creatures"[10] to the attainment of the ends. Man, however, unlike the rest of creation, is free and rational and capable of acting contrary to eternal law. Therefore, this law has to be promulgated to him through reason. There is no need of promulgation to other created things, for they lack the intelligence of man.[11] It may conceivably be argued that it is only the faculty of appreciating order, implanted in the mind that should be ascribed to the

---

[5] A. O. Obilade, *The Nigerian Legal System* (Lagos: Spectrum Books Ltd, 2005), 3.

[6] K. Marx, selected writings in *Sociology and Social Philosophy*, as cited by A. W. Wood, *Karl Marx,* 2nd ed. (Abingdon: Routledge Publishers, 2004), 2.

[7] 1224-1274 A.D.

[8] Other protagonists include Hugo Grotius, Thomas Hobbes, Jean Jacques Rousseau and Thomas Paine.

[9] S. Ofei, *Law and Philosophy* (Benin City: Idodo Umeh Publishers Ltd, 1987), 33.

[10] R. W. M. Dias, *Jurisprudence*, (London: Butterworths Publishers, 1985), 472.

[11] *Ibid*, p. 473.

deity. On that supposition eternal law would be what man creates to it and comprehensible by reason. This question, of course, strikes at the root of religious beliefs and as such, is too large a matter to be debated at this juncture.[12]

Furthermore, eternal law borders on what God has ordained, that which is above the creation by man or instruction by man, e.g. the rising and the setting of the sun; the coming of rainy and dry seasons in tropical countries or the coming of autumn, winter, spring and summer in temperate countries annually; the fact that a male and female have to mate for procreation. It is immaterial if the product of procreation is a test tube baby because the by-products that gave rise to the baby originate from a male and a female.[13] Aquinas concluded that eternal law is the law of God who controls all creation, i.e. the rational guidance of created things on the part of God as the prince of the universe which has the quality of law.[14]

Divine Law

According to Aquinas, law is revealed through the scriptures,[15]and directs human beings to their supernatural end (the vision of God).[16] The Judaic view of law was that it represents God's will on earth. The early Christians however were taught to despise the things of this earth and to expect the destruction of the world and the ultimate reign of God's kingdom. Hence, while the earthly rules had to be obeyed until they were overthrown by God's decree, earthly laws merely arose out of man's sinfulness, which was derived from the fall of man. Therefore although the early Christians took up stoic belief in the brotherhood of man they were indifferent to the idea of a universal law of reason upon this earth. The impact of Christianity on Platonism is revealed in St. Augustine's work, where he equates the Platonism realm of ideal justice with a conception of the city of God on earth, when Christian justice will at last reign supreme.[17] "Without justice," remarks St. Augustine, "what is a state but a robber-band?"[18] Such justice is really a part of divine law which God has laid down to govern mankind so long as our sinful earthly existence

---

[12]*Ibid*, p. 473.

[13] P. I. Abumere, *Fundamentals of Legal Method*, (Onitsha: Roberts Printers Ltd, 1999), 68.

[14] F. Adaramola, *Jurisprudence,* 4th ed. (Durban: LexisNexis Butterworths, 2008), 18.

[15] R. Dias, *Jurisprudence,* (London: Butterworths, 1985), 472.

[16] S. Ofei, *Law and Philosophy*, (Benin City: Idodo Umeh Publishers Ltd, 1987), 33.

[17] D. Lloyd, *The Idea of Law*, (London: Penguin Books, 1991), 79.

[18]*Ibid.*

endures. It is therefore part of the divine order of things, though inferior to the ultimate divine justice which will reign in the City of God. All human institutions such as law, property and slavery are imperfect on account of sin but still form part of the necessary order of things. Natural law is thus equated with divine law, partly miraculously revealed, and partly ascertainable by reason, but the defects in man's existing nature due to sin call for a natural law which lacks many of the features of ideal justice.[19]

The Ten Commandments are part of divine law and were handed down to Moses of the Christian Bible on Mount Sinai.[20] Moses was instructed to hand over these commandments to the believers in God so that they would know what to do in order for their actions to find acceptance in the sight of God. In addition, Jesus Christ came to this world to rescue man from perpetual destruction by dying on the cross and rising from the dead on the third day[21]. Other religious bodies like Islam and Hinduism also have divine laws embedded in their beliefs.[22] Conclusively, Aquinas explains that divine law is part-and-parcel of the eternal law, being the revelations to man through the holy books.[23]

Public Law

Public law is concerned with the constitution and functions of the many different kinds of governmental organizations, including local authorities, and their legal relationships with the citizen and each other. These relationships form the subject matter of constitutional and administrative law.[24] Public law is also concerned with tackling crime, which involves the state's relationship with the power of control over the individual. Public laws are laws which apply to the general public,[25]And they concern:

1. The structure and organization of the state, country or given geographical entity.

---

[19]*Ibid*, p. 89.
[20] Exodus, Chapter 20 v 2-17, NKJ Version.
[21] Luke 23 v 46, 24 v 6, NKJ Version.
[22] Quran 17: 23. 2 v 224.
[23] F. Adaramola, *Jurisprudence,* 4th ed., (Durban: LexisNexis Butterworths, 2008), 18.
[24] M. Loughlin, *Public Law and Political Theory*, (Oxford: Clarendon Press, 1992), 2-4.
[25] A. B. Garner, *Black's Law Dictionary,* 9th ed., (St. Paul, Minnesota: West Group, 2009).

2. The relationship between the state and the persons who make up the state, and the rights and duties the public offers to the state, to each other and to other persons or bodies in the community or country.
3. The relationship between the constituent parts of the state within a country, or the relations of countries to one another, along with the structure, operations, rights and duties of government, and its relationship with individuals and bodies in society.

A public law is a law that applies to the public or people of a country. It is generally unlike a private law which may operate to affect only an individual or a few people that it concerns, such as contract, tort, succession, wills, trust, and so on. Examples of public laws include constitutional law, administrative law, criminal law, criminal procedure law, civil procedure law, mass media law and law of evidence.

Private Law

Private law is the branch of law which is concerned with the legal relationships of private individuals, associations of persons and corporate bodies, and their rights and duties.[26] Examples of private laws include the law of contract, law of torts, consumer protection law, family law, law of succession, inheritance or wills law, law of property, law of trust and commercial law, that is business law, which is made up of several laws, such as law of business associations, company law, partnership law, sole entrepreneurship and agency, contract, sale of goods, hire-purchase, credit sales, law of insurance, law of money lending and so forth. Private law is concerned with the legal relationships of ordinary persons in everyday transactions. It is also concerned with the legal position of corporate bodies and associations of persons, the former of which are given a special form of legal personality.

Substantive Law

Substantive law is the law which stipulates the rights and duties of individuals. It is also the part of the law which creates, defines, and regulates the rights, duties and powers of parties.[27] Substantive law[28]

---

[26] M. Loughlin, *Public Law and Political Theory*. (Oxford: Clarendon Press, 1992), 2-4.
[27] A. B. Garner, *Black's Law Dictionary,* 9th ed., (St. Paul, Minnesota: West Group, 2009).

includes every law except procedural law.[29] Substantive law means actual law, or law as we know it. It is the law which creates, defines and regulates the rights and duties of persons. It is the law which stipulates what conduct is lawful and therefore permissible or unlawful and therefore prohibited. Substantive law is the law of rights and duties, and is administered by the courts. Examples of substantive law include the law of contract, criminal law, torts, law of wills, business law, constitutional law, administrative law and so forth.

Procedural Law

Procedural law is the law of procedure. It is the law of the process and procedure of enforcing substantive law. Procedural law stipulates the process and methods of proof and specifies how to obtain and enforce remedies for the breach of substantive law. It prescribes how a right or a duty created by a substantive law should be enforced.

Put simply, it enforces substantive law and prescribes how legal action should be instituted in court, conducted and concluded, and how judgment should be obtained and enforced. It is the procedure and machinery for the application or enforcement of substantive law. There are two procedures in law: civil procedure and criminal procedure. Examples of procedural laws are many and include the law of evidence,[30] criminal procedure law,[31] sheriffs and civil process law, law of pleading and jurisdiction, civil procedure rules, such as the High Court (civil procedure), rules of the various State High Courts,[32] and the practice and procedure of all courts, tribunals, etc.

Criminal Law

Criminal law is that law which, for the purpose of preventing harm to society, (a) declares what conduct is criminal and (b) prescribes the

---

[28] Examples of substantive law include constitutional law, administrative law, human rights law, international law, land law, law of trust and trustee, etc.

[29] Examples of procedural law include law of evidence, criminal procedure law, civil procedure law, arbitration law, ADR, etc.

[30] For instance, Nigerian Evidence Act 2011.

[31] For instance, Criminal Procedure Act CAP C41, 2004 and Criminal Procedure Law, Lagos State CAP C18, 2003.

[32] For instance, High Court of Lagos State (Civil Procedure) Rules, Lagos State, CAP 114, 2004.

punishment to be imposed for such conduct.[33] It includes the definition of specific offences such as stealing, robbery, murder, receiving stolen property, etc. Criminal law defines crime, prohibits crime and states the rules of liability and the penalties for breach. It is essentially designed for the purpose of preventing crime and harm to persons, property, and society or state.

Criminal law declares and stipulates the conducts which are criminal and therefore prohibited, and prescribes the punishment or sanction to be imposed for such conduct. Criminal law is codified as statute law, i.e. criminal code and penal code. It is a constitutional requirement in Nigeria for an alleged offender to be tried, convicted and punished accordingly, and such alleged crime and the punishment must be under a law which is written and prescribes a sanction. Thus, Section 36 of the 1999 Constitution which deals with the right to a fair hearing provides in subsection 12 that: Subject as otherwise provided by this constitution, a person shall not be convicted of a criminal offence unless that offence is defined and the penalty therefore is prescribed in a written law; and in this subsection, a written law refers to an Act of the National Assembly or a law of a state, any subsidiary legislation or instrument under the provisions of law.[34]

In criminal law, all crimes or offences may be classified as:

a. Offences against the person[35]
b. Offence against property;[36] and
c. Offences against the state[37]

Crimes may also be classified as: felonies,[38] misdemeanours[39] and simple offences;[40]or summary offences[41]or indictable offences[42], triable either way.

---

[33] Section 36(12) 1999 Constitution of Nigeria as amended 2011.

[34] *Aoko v. Fagbemi* (1961) 2 All NLR 400; *Tofi v. Uba* (1967) 3 NWLR Pt. 62, p. 707 CA.

[35] Section 252 of Criminal Code CAP C38 LFN 2004, *Chukwu v. State* (1992) 7 LRCN 83.

[36] Section 383 of Criminal Code CAP C38 LFN 2004, *Chianugo v. State* (2002) 2 NWLR (pt. 750) 225.

[37] Section 37 and 38 of Criminal Code CAP C38 LFN 2004, *Aje v. State* (2006) 8 NWLR (pt. 982) p. 349.

[38] A felony is an offence which is declared by law to be a felony or is punishable without proof of previous conviction with death or with imprisonment for 3 years or more. Section 3 of Criminal Code CAP C38 LFN 2004.

An offence or crime may be created by a:

a. Federal law
b. State law
c. Local government law, that is, a bye-law, or even a delegated legislation made by a public authority, statutory body, or agency, for instance a subsidiary legislation made by a body like the Central Bank of Nigeria, or the National Agency for Food and Drug Administration and Control, Standards Organization of Nigeria, or Ministry of Health and so forth.

Penalty for Crimes

The penalty for a crime may be one or a combination of any of the following sanctions:

Fine

This is a sum of money which a court orders a convicted person to pay to the government treasury. A sentence for a particular offence may be a fine or imprisonment or both. Where a sentence of fine is to be imposed, the court must have regard to the ability of the accused to pay.[43]

Imprisonment

This may be imposed in nearly all cases.[44] Imprisonment is a punishment for criminal offences and consists of the detention of the

---

[39] A misdemeanour is any offence which is declared by law to be a misdemeanour. It is punishable by imprisonment for not less than 6 months but less than 3 years. Section 3 of Criminal Code CAP C38 LFN 2004.

[40] All offences other than felonies and misdemeanour are simple offences. *Saliso v. Police* (1960) WNLR 213.

[41] Summary offences are offences which may be tried by court having summary jurisdiction. Trial is usually conducted by a Magistrate. Section 2, Criminal Procedure Act.

[42] Indictable offences are more serious offences which carry the risk of imprisonment for a period exceeding 2 years, or which on conviction may be punished by the imposition of a fine exceeding =N=500. . *Johnson v. Lufadeju* (2002) 8 NWLR (Pt. 768), 192.

[43] Section 391 of Criminal Procedure Act.

[44] *Clark v. State* (1986) 4 NWLR pt.35, p.381.

offender in a prison. A punishment of imprisonment is usually coupled with hard labour, except where it this is not specified to be the case.[45]

Death Sentence

The death sentence or capital punishment where prescribed by law is a mandatory sentence. It leaves a judge with no discretion, and the plea of *allocutus*[46] has no relevance here. This penalty does not make room for the correction of the character of the offender and for his rehabilitation back into society. Where the law prescribes it, the death sentence must only be imposed after the scrupulous, painstaking and careful exhaustion of the due process of law as provided in the fair hearing provision of the Constitution and with the greatest caution, for after the sentence has been carried out, no apologies to the family of the executed prisoner by the State are sufficient.[47]

The law must scrupulously guard against the execution of an innocent person, for it is better that ten guilty persons go free for one innocent person to be convicted and punished.[48] The human justice system is not free from error, and increasingly the death sentence has been abolished in many countries, especially in the western world.[49]

Exceptions to the death sentence

(1) Pregnant woman[50]

When a woman convicted of an offence is proved to be pregnant, she shall not be sentenced to death but in lieu thereof a sentence of imprisonment for life shall be imposed.

(2) Children and young persons[51]

The death sentence shall not be imposed on a person who at the time of the commission of the offence has not attained 17 years of age. A young offender is usually ordered to be detained at the pleasure of the

---

[45] Section 377 of Criminal Procedure Act.

[46] A plea for mercy.

[47] *Bello v. A.G. Oyo State* (1985) 5 NWLR Pt. 45, p828. *FMG v. Ken Saro Wiwa & 8 others* Unrep Suit No. OCDT/PH/1/95.

[48] *Ibid.*

[49] For instance, Murder (Abolition of Death Penalty) Act 1965, United Kingdom. *Ukorah v. State* (1977) 4 SC 167 at 171.

[50] Section 368 (2) CPA and Section 270 and 271 (3) CPC.

[51] Section 368 (3) CPA and Section 270 and 272 (3) CPC.

President in respect of Federal offence and the Governor in respect of a State offence.[52]

Caning[53]

Caning may be in addition to or in lieu of imprisonment; it shall not exceed 12 strokes and shall be with a light rod or a cane.[54] It is not to be passed on a woman[55] or on a man who is 45 years and above,[56] or on a man who is under the sentence of death.[57]

Other Types of Sentences

Other types of sentence include binding over;[58] costs;[59] disqualification from holding a public office; removal from office; forfeiture,[60] such as when ill-gotten wealth, fake or unhealthy goods or property are liable to forfeiture, confiscation or destruction under law; refund of stolen money or return of stolen goods,[61] property or ill-gotten wealth; imposition of such social or community service or labour as the court may deem fit; a period of supervision under a law officer as the court may deem fit under a probation order; deportation of a foreigner for certain offences.

Civil Law

Civil law is a comprehensive system of rules and principles usually arranged in codes and easily accessible to citizens and jurists. It is a well-organized system that favours cooperation, order, and predictability, and is based on a logical and dynamic taxonomy developed from Roman law and reflected in the structure of the codes.[62]

---

[52]*Modupeola Johnson v. State* (1986) 4 NWLR pt.35 p. 381.
[53] Section 387 CPA, Section 77 PC.
[54] Section 386(2) CPA and Section 308(5) CPC.
[55] Section 308(4) CPC and Section 385 CPA.
[56] Section 308(5) CPC and Section 385 CPA.
[57] Section 308(5) (b) CPC.
[58] Section 300, Section 309 Criminal Procedure Act and Section 25 Criminal Procedure Code.
[59] Section 255 Criminal Procedure Act.
[60] Section 68 (1) (b) Penal Code CAP 89.
[61] Section 270 Criminal Procedure Act.
[62] Paul M. Hebert Law Centre, www.law.lsu.edu. Accessed on 20/10/2012.

Civil law encompasses the whole of private law and public law, excepting criminal law. Generally, all laws excluding criminal law, military law and martial or emergency law,[63] are civil laws. Criminal law is concerned with legal rules which provide that certain forms of conduct shall attract punishment by the state, e.g. homicide and theft. Civil law includes the whole of private law and all divisions of public law except criminal law. In order to understand the various branches of substantive civil law, it is necessary to distinguish the following:

Contract

A contract is an agreement, made between two or more persons, which is intended to have legal consequences. It can also be defined as a promise or a set of promises which the law will enforce.[64] Thus, if there is a breach of contract, the aggrieved party can go to court and obtain a remedy. It should be noted that the parties to a contract in general enter voluntarily into their obligations; the function of the law is merely to act in an impartial way in order to settle any disputes which arise between the parties to the contract.

It is, however, worth noting that not all contractual obligations are undertaken voluntarily. In order to protect the consumer, certain obligations are implied in some contracts by statute and cannot in some cases be removed, e.g. an undertaking that the goods are of satisfactory quality in consumer sales where the Sale of Goods Act 1979 applies.

Tort

A tort, on the other hand, is a civil wrong independent of contract. It arises out of a duty imposed by law, and not by agreement, and a person who commits a tortuous act does not voluntarily undertake the liabilities which the law imposes on him.[65]

A tort is a civil wrong involving a breach of duty fixed by the law, such duty being owed to persons generally and its breach being redressible primarily by an action for damages.[66]

---

[63] Section 33 (2) (c) 1999 Constitution of Nigeria as amended 2011.

[64] G. H. Treitel, *The Law of Contract,* 9th ed. (London: Sweet & Maxwell, 1997), 1.

[65] *Smith & Keenan's English Law,* 16th ed., (London: Longman Publication, 2010), 4.

[66] S. Borne, *Osborn's Concise Law Dictionary,* 9th ed., (London: Sweet & Maxwell, 2001), 379.

There are many kinds of tort with a common characteristic; injury of some kind inflicted by one person on another. Nuisance,[67] inflicting injury by negligence,[68] trespass,[69] slander[70] and libel[71] are all well-known civil wrongs. The typical remedy in this branch of the law is an action for damages by the injured party against the person responsible for the injury. Such damages are designed not to punish the wrongdoer but to compensate the injured party.

Crimes and civil wrongs distinguished

The distinction does not lie in the nature of the act itself. For example, if a porter at a female hostel is offered a reward to carry A's luggage, and he runs off with it, then the porter has committed a crime, that of stealing, and two[72] civil wrongs, i.e. the tort of conversion[73] and a breach of his contract with A. Again, a railway signalman who carelessly fails to operate the signals so that a fatal accident occurs will have committed one crime, i.e. manslaughter if individuals are killed, and two civil wrongs, the tort of negligence[74] in respect of those who die and those who are merely injured, and a breach of his contract of service with the employer, in which there is an implied term to take due care. It should also be noted that in this case the right of action in tort and the right of action in contract would be brought by different persons.

---

[67] A nuisance is any conduct that is obstructing the public or a section of it in the exercise and enjoyment of a common right. *Adeniran v. Interland Transport Ltd* (1991) 9 NWLR (Pt. 214) p. 155 SC.

[68] "Negligence is the omission … to do something which a reasonable man, under similar circumstances would do or, the doing of something which a reasonable and prudent man would not do." See also *Odinaka v. Moghalu* (1992) 4 NWLW (Pt. 233) p. 1 at 15 SC.

[69] Trespass is an intentional tort that involves interfering with someone else's rights. Rottenstein Law Group LLP, www.rotlaw.com. Accessed on 20/10/2012. An unlawful act committed against the person or property of another. B. A. Garner, *Black's Law Dictionary*, 9th ed., (St. Paul, Minnesota: West Group Publishing, 2009).

[70] Slander is a statement made in a transitory form and not in a permanent form. *Bakare v. Ishola* (1959) WRNLR 106.

[71] A libel is a defamatory statement made in a visible or permanent form, such as written or printed statements. *African Press Ltd. v. Ikejiani* (1953) 14 WACA 386.

[72] Section 383 of the Criminal Code CAP C38 LFN 2004.

[73] *Adewusi v. State* (1963) 1 All NLR 316, *Alake v. State* (1991) 1 NWLR (pt. 205), 567.

[74] Supra footnote 64.

Terminology and outcome of criminal and civil proceedings

In criminal proceedings a prosecutor prosecutes a defendant. If the prosecution is successful, it results in the conviction of what is now the offender. After the conviction the court may deal with the offender by giving him a custodial sentence, e.g. a prison term, or a non-custodial sentence, e.g. a community sentence or fine.

As regards civil proceedings, a claimant sues (brings a claim against) a defendant. If the claimant is successful, this leads to the court entering judgment ordering the defendant to pay a debt owed to the claimant or money damages. Alternatively, it may require the defendant to transfer property to the claimant, to do or not to do something *(injunction)*, or to perform a contract *(specific performance)*. Some of these remedies are legal and others equitable.

Trusts

A trust arises where one or more persons holds property, e.g. shares, for the benefit of other persons. People often wish to provide for their children or grandchildren when they die. They may leave some of their property on trust, particularly where, as in the case of grandchildren, they are minors, i.e. under the age of 18. They can appoint trustees who will take over the ownership of the property but they themselves will not benefit from that ownership, since the capital and/or income of the trust will be used for the benefit of the children or grandchildren, who are called the beneficiaries. It is, however, necessary to include a charging clause in the trust instrument or will, to allow payment of fees where the trustees are professional persons or a trust corporation. Trusts may also be set up by living persons. The characteristics of a trust are that it involves three elements, namely (1) a trustee, who holds the trust property and is subject to equitable duties to deal with it for the benefit of another; (2) a beneficiary, to whom a trustee owes equitable duties to deal with the trust properties for his benefit; (3) a trust property, which is held by the trustee for the beneficiary.[75]

---

[75] A. B. Garner, *Black's Law Dictionary,* 9th ed., (St. Paul, Minnesota: West Group, 2009).

Unwritten Law

Unwritten law is law that is either wholly unwritten or partly unwritten. Unwritten law is law that is not enacted or passed in the form of statute law. Unwritten law is all parts of the law, observed by the people and administered in the courts, but which has not been passed in the form of statute law. Unwritten law may be partly written or wholly unwritten. Examples of unwritten laws include the common law of England, customary law in Nigeria,[76] and judicial precedents, or case law; that is, principles and rules of law as established by courts in judicial proceedings.

Written Law

Written law is commonly known as statute law or legislation. Written law is law which takes its force from express legislative enactment. Examples of written law, statute, or statute law include a written constitution, such as the Nigerian Constitution;[77] Acts of Parliament, such as Acts of the National Assembly;[78] laws of the House of Assembly of a State;[79] decrees[80] and edicts of military governments; treaties made between or among different countries, and so forth.

The Common Law

Common law is the law which grew from the customs common to the people of England and Wales. It is that part of the laws of England which grew from the common customs of the people and which was applied as judicial precedents, that is, decisions of the courts through the ages. Thus, common law is the ancient unwritten law of England. For a treatment of the history of English common law, see *Smith & Keenan's English Law*.[81]

---

[76] See also A. D. Badaiki, *Development of Customary Law*, (Lagos: Tiken Publishers, 1997), 15.

[77] 1999 Constitution of Federal Republic of Nigeria.

[78] E.g. Land Use Act of 1978, Evidence Act 2011, etc.

[79] E.g. the Recovery of Premises Ordinance CAP 176 (Lagos), Recovery of Premises Law CAP 113 (Eastern Region), etc.

[80] Decree No. 1 1966 (Suspension and Modification), Decree No. 13 1990 (Supremacy and Enforcement of Powers).

[81] For a treatment of the history of the English common law see *Smith & Keenan's English Law,* 16th ed., (London: Longman Publishers, 2010), 5.

According to Smith and Keenan,[82] the administrative ability of the Normans began the process destined to lead to a unified system of law which was nevertheless evolutionary in its development. The Normans were not concerned with changing English customary law entirely by imposing Norman Law on England. Attempts were made to ensure a greater uniformity of the General Eyre[83] whereby representatives of the King were sent from Westminster on a tour of the shires for the purpose of checking on the local administration. During the period of their visit, they would sit in the local court and hear cases, and gradually they came to have a judicial rather than administrative function and were called the Justices in Eyre.

Henry II took steps to formalize the jurisdiction of the General Eyre by the Assize of Clarendon[84] and the Assize of Northampton.[85] These provided that in relation to the criminal law there should be 12 men in every country to be responsible for presenting to the sheriff those suspected of serious crimes. The accused were then brought before the General Eyre when it arrived in the area. As regards the civil law, a new civil remedy called the Assize of Novel Dissension (lately dispossessed) was offered to persons who complained that their land had been wrongly seized. From this remedy grew a range of civil actions which were brought before the General Eyre. Thus, royal and more uniform justice began to come to the country as a whole.[86]

The General Eyre disappeared in the reign of Richard II,[87] but a system of circuit judges from what is now the High Court took its place, the first circuit commission having been granted in the reign of Edward III.[88] The Justices in Eyre were replaced by more formally trained lawyers over the period 1327-77. By selecting the best customary rulings and applying these outside their country of origin, the circuit judges gradually moulded existing local customary laws into one uniform law "common" to the whole kingdom. Thus, customs originally local ultimately applied throughout the realm. Even so, there was no absolute unification even as late as 1389, and in a case in what is now the High Court in that year, a custom of Selby in Yorkshire was admitted to show that a husband was

---

[82] *Ibid*, p. 6.
[83] 'Eyre' simply means 'a journey.'
[84] 1166.
[85] 1176.
[86] See also O. F. Emiri, *Handbook on Modern Equity,* 1st ed., (Lagos: Jeroilirona Press, 1999), 5.
[87] 1377-99.
[88] 1327-77.

not liable in that area for his wife's trading debts, though the common law elsewhere regarded him as liable.[89]

Furthermore, the right to make a will of personal property, e.g. jewellery, was not universal in England until 1724, when it finally extended to the City of London. Before that time, half of the personality (i.e. property unconnected with land), 'the dead man's part', went to the church and the other half to the wife and children. Land could still not be left by will but descended to the heir by law, though it later became possible, as it is today, to leave land by will.

However, many new rules were created and applied by the royal judges as they went on circuit, and these were added to local customary law to make one uniform body of law called 'common law'. Thus, the identity between custom and the common law is not historically accurate, since much of the common law in early times was created by the royal judges, who justified their rulings by asserting they were derived from the 'general custom of the Realm'. Thus, in *Beaulieu v. Finglam,*[90] it was said that a man who by his negligence failed to control a fire so that it spread to his neighbour's house was liable in damages according to 'the law and custom of the realm', though it is not easy to see which customary rule the court based its decision on.

Equity

Equity means fairness, just or natural justice, moral rightness and good. In legal parlance, rules of equity are the rules of fairness and natural justice, formulated and administered by the court of Chancery to supplement and remedy the hardships of the common law of England. It encompasses the principles of fairness, right, justice, good judgment or good conscience formed and applied by the Lord Chancellor or Chancellors in the Court of Chancery to supplement and ameliorate the hardships wrought by the common law.

Historically the growth of the common law was rapid in the thirteenth century but in the fourteenth century it ceased to have the momentum of earlier years. As the legal profession came into existence the judges came to be chosen exclusively from the profession, instead of from a wider variety of royal officials, as had been the case in the thirteenth century. The common law courts became more self-conscious about what they

---

[89] *Smith & Keenan's English Law,* 16th ed., (London: Longman Publishers, 2010), 8.

[90] (1401) YB 2 Hen 4, f 18, pl6.

were doing and attempted to become more systematic. There was much talk about the proper way of doing things, of not being able to do this or that and much clever reasoning. Reports of cases in the Year Books, the nearest we have to law reports at this time, show a considerable concern for procedural points and niceties, a reluctance to depart from what had become established, a close attention to the observance of proper forms and much less concern for what the circumstances of a particular case demanded if it was to be settled in an appropriate way.[91]

Defects of the Common Law

The inadequacies of the services and the harshness of the common law courts brought in some criticism by the people, including:

1. The inflexibility of the writ system, which led to injustice because matters that were not within the scope of the writs recognized by the common law were dismissed.
2. The common law did not recognise the ownership of property other than by those who were strict legal owners; nor did it recognize security for loans (mortgages) or the right of third parties in general.
3. The common law courts had no power of enforcement and did not allow any form of oral evidence.
4. The only remedies provided by the common law were damages, which were inappropriate in certain cases.

For example, the writ of trespass to land was available. However, trespass is a direct wrong, e.g. actually being on the land. Indirect activity affecting enjoyment of land was not covered, e.g. nuisance from smelly pigs or smoky bonfires. There was at that time no writ to deal with this type of indirect harm. The common law came to expand its writs to cover an action for damages in this situation, but in the meantime equity had carved out a jurisdiction and had an ideal remedy to deal with nuisance,[92] i.e. the issue of an injunction requiring the defendant to cease the activity, pay a fine or be imprisoned for contempt of court. Moreover, writs were expensive, and their cost could deprive a party of justice. In some cases the cost of the writ was more than the amount of the claimant's claim so he did not bother to sue.

---

[91] *Smith & Keenan's English Law,* 16th ed., (London: Longman Publishers, 2010), 8.

[92] *Seager v. Copydex Ltd* (1967) 1 WLR 123; *Woods v. Martins Bank Ltd* (1971) AC 79.

However, a practice grew up under which the clerks in Chancery provided new writs even though the complaint was not quite covered by an existing writ, thus extending the law by extending the scope of the writ system.[93] This appeared to Parliament to be a taking away of its powers as the supreme law-giver. Further, it took work away from the local courts to the Royal Courts, thus diminishing the income of the local barons who persuaded Parliament to pass a statute called the Provisions of Oxford in 1258, forbidding in effect the practice of creating new writs to fit new cases. This proved so inconvenient that an attempt to remedy the situation was made by the Statute of Westminster II in 1285, which empowered the clerks in Chancery to issue new writs in *consimili casu* (in similar case), thus adapting existing writs to fit new circumstances. The common law began to expand again, but it was still by no means certain that a writ would be forthcoming to fit a particular case, because the clerks in Chancery used the statute with caution at first.

Procedure at Common Law

Other difficulties arose over the procedure in the common law courts, because even the smallest error in a writ would avoid the action. Furthermore, some common law actions were tried by a system called 'wager of law,' and the claimant might fail on what was really a good claim if a defendant could bring more people to say that the claim was false than the claimant could get to support it.

The system worked well in local courts where the witnesses (called 'oath helpers') knew the parties and circumstances of the case. However, in cases brought at Westminster, it fell into disrepute because 'oath helpers' who would support any case could be hired outside the court for a few pence.

Relationship of Law and Equity

Although law and equity eventually operated alongside each other with mutual tolerance, there was a period of conflict between them. This arose out of the practice of the Court of Chancery which issued 'common injunctions' forbidding a person on threat of imprisonment from bringing an action in the common law courts, or forbidding the enforcement of a common law judgment if such a judgment had been obtained.[94]

---

[93] *Charles Richards Ltd v. Oppenheim* (1950) KB 616, at 623.

[94] *Neath v. Rydley* (1614) Cro Jac 335; *Courtney v. Glanvil* (1615) Cro Jac 343.

This period of rivalry culminated in the Earl of Oxford's case in 1615 when Lord Coke, representing the common law courts, offered a direct challenge to the Court of Chancery's jurisdiction. The challenge was taken up and James I, on the advice of Lord Bacon, then the Attorney-General and later Lord Chancellor, gave a firm decision that, where common law and equity were in conflict, equity should prevail.[95]

Thus the two systems settled down and carved out separate and complementary jurisdictions. Equity filled in the gaps left by the common law, and became a system of case law governed by the binding force of precedent. However, it also lost much of its earlier freedom and elasticity. It was certainly no longer a court of conscience.[96]

Many reforms were still to come. Equitable and legal remedies had to be sought in different courts, but in due course this was rectified by the Judicature Acts, 1873-75, which brought about an amalgamation of the English courts. Since then both common law and equitable remedies have been available to a litigant in the same action and in the same court.

Before leaving the topic, a final characteristic of equity should be noted, which is that equity never says the common law is wrong, but merely provides alternative solutions to legal problems. This is illustrated by certain cases in the law of contract. For example, the decision in *Central London Property Trust Ltd v. High Trees House Ltd,*[97]shows how modern equity sometimes adopts a different solution from that provided by the common law. Equity is not therefore a complete system of law. It complements the rules of the common law but does not replace them.

Finally, Sections 36-44 of the Judicature Acts[98] settled the issue, by providing that whenever there was a conflict between common law and equity, equity should prevail.[99] This provision of statute has been made part of Nigerian law jurisdictions.[100]

---

[95] This principle now appears in S.49 of the Supreme Court Act 1981, having appeared in a number of earlier Judicature Acts.

[96] J. O. Fabunmi, *Equity and Trusts in Nigeria,* 2nd ed., (Osun: Obafemi Awolowo University Press Ltd, 2006), 35.

[97] (1947) KB 130 All ER 265.

[98] 1873-75 England.

[99] See for instance, Supreme Court Act 2004 s. 17; Magistrate Courts law, Lagos State 2003, s. 23; High Court of Lagos State Law 2004 ss. 13 and 15.

[100] The dispute finally came to a head under James I. It was implicit in the ruling that if in any situation, there was a direct clash between the two systems; the rule of equity would prevail. This was subsequently incorporated into section 25 (ii) of the Supreme Court of Judicature Act, 1925.

Customary Law

Customary law consists of custom which is accepted as binding by people of a certain community. Customary law is the body of customs which from long use have acquired the force of law among a people. It is the way of life, also defined as a rule, which in a particular district has from long usage obtained the force of law.[101]

Customary law is the indigenous law of the various peoples or ethnic groups of Nigeria and Africa from before the advent of foreign laws, in the form of religious law, English law, statute law and so forth. For a custom to be accepted as valid and obligatory in any community in Nigeria it must pass the validity test.[102] The validity test is a legal requirement that a custom must not be repugnant to natural justice, equity, good conscience, and public policy, nor incompatible with any law for the time being in force. When a custom satisfies the above legal requirements or validity tests, a court of law will enforce it as a customary law among the members of the community to which it applies.

Finally, customary law is usually flexible and is either unwritten or partly written. However, a custom must exist at the point in time a party is claiming it, otherwise a court will not apply it. Customary law is often applied by a court as a judicial precedent. A court may take judicial notice of customary law or require its proof.

Judicial Notice of Customary Law

Judicial notice consists of facts, the existence of which a court itself is aware.[103] Section 14 of the Evidence Act is about the rule of custom, which is a question of fact that must be proved by calling credible evidence in support of its existence, unless it has been so frequently proved before the court i.e. notorious enough to be judicially noticed.[104]

---

[101] Nigerian Evidence Act 2011, S. 2.

[102] See for instance Nigerian Evidence Act, 2004 S. 14(3). Supreme Court Act, 2004, s. 17, High Court of Lagos State Law, 2004, s.26. See also *Agbai v. Okagbue* (1991) 7 NWLR Pt.204, 391 SC.

[103] Section 73 of the Nigerian Evidence Act 2011. See also *Commonwealth Shopping Representative v. P. O. Branch Services* (1923) AC 191 at 213; *Aromolaran v. Oladele* (1990) 7 NWLR (Pt. 162), 359.

[104] *Larinde v. Ajiko & Anor* (1940) 6 WACA 108; *Oko v. Nkudiken* (1993) 2 SCNJ 33.

A custom may be judicially noticed or be proved by the alleging party.[105] Rules of customary law are indigenous and must not be imported from a distant region;[106] the persons who are witnesses must come from the same community and evidence of rule of custom ought to be corroborated.

Proof of Customary law

The Evidence Act[107] provides that where a custom cannot be established by judicial notice it may be established by proof. Except when a custom is judicially noticed, the party contending that it exists has to prove it as a fact, or prove its existence by evidence. By virtue of the evidence enactments, native chiefs or other persons having special knowledge of customary law may be called to express their opinion as evidence on a point of customary law where such custom is valid.[108]

Conclusion

The study of law is not just a matter of learning the rules; indeed this is a general misconception. It is our conclusion that critical, analytical thought should inform the work of a good student because studying the law involves considering a fundamental institution in society as a whole.

[105] *Adegboyega v. Igbinosun* (1969) N.M.L.R. 9, S.C.
[106] *Taiwo v. Dosumu* (1966) N.M.L.R. 4 S.C.
[107] Section 14(3).
[108] A custom is valid if; (a) it is not repugnant to natural justice, equity and good conscience, (b) it is not incompatible with any law for the time being in force; (c) it is not contrary to public policy.

CHAPTER THREE

LAW AS AN INSTRUMENT OF SOCIAL CONTROL

CHUKWUMA FAMOUS IKECHUKWU[1]

Introduction

Before considering law as an instrument of social control, two important concepts must be understood. The first is the concept of social behaviour, while the second is the concept of social control.[2]

Social behaviours are those behaviours which directly affect other members of a society. They are distinguished from non-social behaviours, which are behaviours that affect the private life of the person involved and do not have a direct effect on other members of a society. For example, if Mr A wakes up in the morning, his choice of taking breakfast or not is entirely at his own discretion. If he decides to take breakfast, his choice of what to eat or how to prepare it remains also entirely at his discretion. Whatever choice he makes with regard to these scenarios, no other person in society is affected. Hence, those behaviours are non-social behaviours. However, where he decides to take breakfast, and the way and manner he gets his food will involve some form of interaction with other members of society. Whether he buys his food or steals it, he must come into contact with other people. It is thus a social behaviour because other people are affected by it.

Social control on the other hand is the regulation and management of the social behaviours of people, with a view to maintaining order and promoting predictability of actions. There are various instruments used by society to control social behaviours. They include religion, family, education, law etc. However, of all the instruments of social control, law is the most effective because of its ability to enforce rules by the use of sanctions. Law controls social behaviours mainly by the actual or

---

[1]Lecturer, Faculty of Law, Benson Idahosa University, Benin City, Edo State.

[2]These concepts are going to be given only a cursory examination.

threatened use of force, whether physical or psychological, to bring about conformity with its norms and to punish violation of its rules through specialized agencies.

Methods of Social Control through Law

There are a variety of methods used by law to control social behaviours. Professor Robert Summers identified five of them: penal, grievance-remedial, private arranging, administrative-regulatory and public benefit, which Farrar and Dugdale renamed 'the conferral of social benefits technique.'[3] Farrar and Dugdale also added two other techniques: the constitutive and the fiscal techniques.[4] We shall now consider these techniques with other possible alternatives in the following order:

1. Penal technique
2. Grievance-remedial technique
3. Private arranging technique
4. Constitutive technique
5. Administrative-regulatory technique
6. Fiscal technique
7. Conferral of social benefit technique

Penal Technique

This technique controls social behaviours by the use of punishment. It operates mainly in the realm of criminal law. Here, the law specifies certain rules or standards which prohibit deviant behaviours, prescribes sanctions or punishment for the breach of such rules and establishes the appropriate mechanism for the enforcement of such rules. The courts, police force, prisons and other law enforcement agencies are created and maintained to enforce the laws which have been made. The main feature of the penal system is that it punishes deviant behaviours.

---

[3] R. S. Summers, *The Technique Element in Law,* California Law Review 59 (1971), 733. Also reproduced in *Essays in Honour of Hans Kelsen* edited by the California Law Review with a preface by A. A. Ehrenzweig, cited in J. H. Farrar & A. M. Dugdale, *Introduction to Legal Method*, 3rd ed., (London: Sweet & Maxwell, 1990), 13. R. S. Summers was said to have applied his technique analysis to the legal system as a whole in his anthology *Law, Its Nature, Function and Limits* (2nd ed., 1972).

[4] J. H. Farrar & A. M. Dugdale, *Introduction to Legal Method,* 3rd ed. (London: Sweet & Maxwell, 1990), 13.

As an instrument of social control, the penal technique is effective in crime prevention and prosecution. As a preventive measure, it has the proclivity to deter people from engaging in criminal activities. Some people are deterred by the presence of policemen, others by their knowledge of the law, and others by the fear of punishment. Some other people, however, stay away from criminal activities because of their personal convictions and morals, not necessarily because of penal restrictions. The penal technique also controls social behaviours by prosecuting offenders when a crime is committed. When a crime is committed, the matter is reported to the police who will then conduct an investigation and charge the alleged offender to attend court for trial. At the end of the trial, if the accused person is convicted, he or she will be punished. Such punishment inflicts pain on the offender, appeals to the injured party who yearns for justice and engenders confidence in the public to justice from the courts instead of resorting to self-help. It also serves as a deterrent to other people with similar criminal tendencies.

For an act to be termed punishment, it must involve the following:

1. It must inflict pain, hardship or other consequences normally considered unpleasant.
2. The pain inflicted must be for an offence or the violation of a law.
3. The pain must be inflicted on a person who is found guilty of an offence.
4. The pain inflicted must involve some form of moral condemnation and denunciation.
5. The act of punishment must be intentionally administered by human beings other than the offender.
6. It must be imposed and administered by an authority constituted by a legal system against which the offence is committed.[5]

The purpose of punishment has been identified as:

1. Retribution
2. Deterrence
3. Denunciation

---

[5] H. L. A. Hart, 'Prolegomenon to the Principles of Punishment' (*Proceedings of the Aristotelian Society,* N.S. Vol. LX (1959-60)), 21, cited in T. McPherson, *Punishment: Definition and Justification* www.jthomasniu.org/class/stuff/temp/pundefjust1.pdf. Accessed on 08/02/2012. See also J. Garret, *The Concept of Punishment* www.wku.edu/~jan.garret/320/punishment.htm. Accessed on 08/01/2010.

4. Rehabilitation[6] and
5. Incapacitation.

The retributive end of punishment is to render to the offender a just reward for his wrong. Deterrence is used to make both the offender and other members of the society see the need to stay away from such deviant behaviours. Denunciation is society's way of condemning such deviant behaviours in strong terms. Rehabilitation seeks to reform the offender into a more useful, productive and law-abiding member of society. When punishment is used as a means of incapacitation, it seeks to render the offender unable to commit any other offence. This is why offenders are kept in prisons and in some cases sentenced to death.

However, in *State v. Njoku,*[7] Saulawa JCA, quoting Lord Denning, MR stated that:

> The punishment inflicted for grave crimes should adequately reflect the repulsion felt by the great majority of citizens for them. It is a mistake to consider the objects of punishment as being deterrent or reformative or preventive and nothing else… the ultimate justification of any punishment is not that it is deterrent, but that it is emphatic denunciation by the community of a crime and from this point of view, there are some murders which, in the present state of public opinion, demand the most emphatic denunciation of all, namely the death penalty.

Alternatives to Penal Method

Apart from penal technique, people may apply other methods to deal with deviant behaviours. First, by non-interference; although it is desirable for society to punish some kinds of behaviour, the extent to which it can go is debatable. There are some behaviour that may be considered morally reprehensible yet cannot be punished by law, probably because they are private in nature; hence society would rather not interfere with them. For example, private sexual behaviours such as adultery are left unpunished under the criminal code.[8] Such behaviours may also be left unpunished because it is not practicable to do so or because society is not directly

---

[6] Law Reform Commission, New South Wales, "Purpose and Principles of Sentencing Law" *Discussion Paper 33 (1996)-Sentencing* www.lawlink,nsw.gov.au/irc.nsf/pages/DP33CHP3 Accessed on 08/01/12.

[7] (2010) 1 NWLR (Part 1175) 243.

[8] Although under Sections 387 and 388 Penal Code, applicable in the Northern part of Nigeria, adultery is punishable.

affected. Another alternative may be a warning. Rather than going through trial for some minor offence, or putting offenders like children on trial, those offences or offenders may be dealt with by a simple warning.

Another alternative is the use of force or self-help. This way, people take the law into their own hands and serve their offenders what they feel is their just recompense, without any recourse to legal institutions. This method of self-help or reciprocity has been described as the symptom of an underdeveloped system.[9] It has also been severally and severely condemned by the Nigerian Courts as a situation capable of causing the breakdown of law and order. In *Eloichin Nig Ltd v. Mbadiwe,*[10] the Supreme Court, condemning the use of self-help, held Per Aniagolu JSC thus:

> The laws of all civilized nations have always frowned at self-help if for no other reason than that they engender breaches of peace…

Another alternative is a resort to the grievance remedial technique. A single chain of events can give rise to both a criminal offence and a civil wrong. In dealing with such cases, the aggrieved person can elect to pursue a criminal action or take out a civil claim or pursue both. For example, Bisi and Suleiman get involved in an argument and in the heat of the quarrel, Suleiman beats Bisi up. Bisi may decide to press charges against Suleiman for assault, in which case Suleiman may be convicted and sentenced, or she may bring an action in tort for battery, which may lead to an award of damages against Suleiman if she succeeds. Another approach may be private arrangement. An aggrieved party may opt to settle privately with the culprit.

Grievance-Remedial Technique

This is a civil law technique, which, according to Professor Summer, "defines remediable grievances, specifies remedies and provides for enforcement of remedial awards."[11] Here, the law creates rights, duties and remedies in the case that such rights are violated or when such duties are

---

[9] Op. Cit. Note 4

[10] (1986) 1 NWLR (Part 14) 47 See also *Military Governor of Lagos State & others v. Ojukwu* (1986) ANLR 233

[11] R. S. Summers, *The Technique Element in Law,* California Law Review 59 (1971), 733. Also reproduced in *Essays in Honour of Hans Kelsen* edited by the California Law Review with a preface by A. A. Ehrenzweig. Cited in Farrar & Dugdale (supra).

breached, as well as the means of enforcing such remedies. Unlike the penal technique which deals with public order, this technique deals with private wrong and exists purely in the realm of civil law. An example of this technique is in the law of torts. In our example of Bisi and Suleiman, the law protects Bisi from assault, and creates a duty on Suleiman and any other person not to violate that right. In the case of any violation, the law also provides for remedies in the form of damages and creates the court system by which Bisi can enforce such remedies.

This method is not limited to the law of torts but covers every area of civil law including contracts and labour relations, etc.

Alternatives

There are other alternatives to this technique. First is the penal technique. We have seen that a single action can constitute both a civil wrong and a crime. In the example of Bisi and Suleiman, Bisi can decide to pursue an action in tort against Suleiman or press criminal charges. Another alternative is private arrangement. Parties may decide to settle their grievances out of court via some form of private arrangement. For example, they could opt for insurance compensation where there is a motor accident, instead of going to court to claim damages. They could also use private arrangements like Alternative Dispute Resolution mechanisms (hereinafter referred to as ADR).

Private Arranging Techniques

Some aspects of social life are left entirely to the discretion and initiative of private citizens to decide for themselves, with the law only providing a framework within which such transactions are carried out. The law does not initially interfere with such areas of life. It does not put a duty on people to undertake such endeavours. Whether or not they want to do so is at their discretion, but once they decide to undertake such transactions, they are bound to apply the principles and procedures laid down by law for such endeavours, otherwise their actions will be invalid. Examples of such transactions include marriage, sale and purchase of land, making a will etc.

In the case of marriage, an individual cannot be legally compelled to get married. Whether or not he/she gets married is his/her choice. However where he/she decides to get married, he/she has the option of contracting his marriage under the Marriage Act, or under customary law or Islamic law. Where he/she decides to marry under the Marriage Act, he/she must ensure that he/she complies with the requirements of the law for that marriage to be validly contracted.[12] He/she cannot also enter into any other marriage with another person while the first one is subsisting. If he/she does he will be liable to imprisonment for five years.[13] Here we see how the law allows individuals the freedom to choose whether or not to marry and which form of marriage to contract, yet with the necessary legal framework to control such choices.

The same applies to making a will. A person is not duty bound to make a will. He/she can choose to make a will or refrain from making one. The law will not interfere with this choice; it gives the person that liberty. However, where a person decides to make a will, he/she must comply with the provisions of the law for his will to be valid. The will must be in writing, signed by the testator in the presence of at least two witnesses present at the same time, and the witnesses must attest and subscribe to the will in the presence of the testator.[14] Where a will fails to meet this requirement of the law, it is void and the testator's property will be shared as if he died intestate.

There are other areas of social life which are generally not within the discretion of private citizens, yet the law allows them some discretion to handle issues in these areas through their own private arrangement, with the law providing a basic legal framework within which such transactions are carried out, thereby providing amicable settlement of disputes amongst citizens. This is the core of the concept of ADR.

Nigerian law provides sufficient legal framework for ADR mechanisms in the settlement of disputes.[15] These mechanisms include arbitration, conciliation and mediation. Arbitration is a form of dispute resolution which involves a "formal" hearing of a dispute before a neutral third party called the arbitrator, under a relaxed atmosphere devoid of the pressures of the regular court system. Disputes are resolved without recourse to strict rules of evidence as is the case with a formal court setting.

The arbitrator (or arbitration panel, if there is more than one arbitrator) is usually an expert in the area of dispute before him. The decision of the arbitrator may or may not be binding on the parties.

---

[12] See Marriage Act CAP M2 Laws of Federation of Nigeria 2004.

[13] Section 47 Marriage Act.

[14] See Section 4 of the Wills Law of Lagos State CAP 194 Laws of Lagos State 1994 (this provision is similar to Section 9 of the Wills Act, 1837).

[15] Examples of such legal framework include Arbitration and Conciliation Act CAP A18, Laws of Federation of Nigeria 2004 and Section 17 Federal High Court Act.

Conciliation is a process in which a third party, called a conciliator goes between disputing parties with a bid to restore them to their pre-dispute status, in order to facilitate conflict resolution. It has also been described as a judge-initiated practice of guiding litigants (usually in a civil suit) to create an equitable, negotiated settlement instead of proceeding to trial.[16] In this regard, the parties are encouraged to reach an out-of-court settlement, which can then be made the judgment of court i.e. consent judgment. In *H.B. (Nig) Plc v. Lodigiami (Nig) Ltd*[17] Okoro JCA, re-echoing a well-honoured practice stated:

> … even where a matter has been filed in court, the parties are not precluded from exploring avenues for amicable settlement of their grievance out of court. Courts do encourage parties to settle their disagreement and thereafter inform the court of the settlement.

Mediation involves a neutral third party who assists disputing parties in reaching a resolution. He assists the parties in framing and clarifying issues, structuring negotiation, recognizing their own interests as well as the interests of the other party and developing options to enable the parties to work towards a mutually beneficial resolution. Unlike conciliators, mediators usually refrain from suggesting an outcome or solution.[18] When a case is before a court, the judge, with the consent of the parties, may encourage settlement of any matter before it by either:

a. arbitration
b. conciliation
c. mediator
d. any other lawfully recognized method of dispute resolution.[19]

Constitutive Technique

This technique of social control is such that the law constitutes a group of people into a single legal entity, with a legal name, legal rights, duties,

---

[16]*Training Manual on Alternative Dispute Resolution and Restorative Justice,*www.unodc.org/documents/corruption/publications_adr.pdf, p.17, accessed on 02/08/2012.
[17] (2010) 14 NWLR (Part 1213) 330.
[18] Op. Cit. note 16.
[19] See Order 17, High Court of Federal Capital Territory, Abuja Civil Procedure Rules, 2004. See also Order 25 High Court of Lagos State Civil Procedure Rules 2004.

liabilities, and protection for the purpose of effective legal control. The essence and distinctive characteristic of the constitution technique is the creation of separate legal personalities. In this way corporate bodies are created with perpetual succession and liabilities, distinct from their owners. Therefore, even if a member or all the members of a company dies or go bankrupt, the company will still continue to exist, because it has perpetual succession and its lifespan is different from that of its members. The law[20] provides that when a company is incorporated, the members of that company become a corporate body having the name contained in their Memorandum of Association, capable of exercising all the powers and functions of a legal person including the power to hold land. The company also has a perpetual succession and a common seal. If the company winds up, the members are only liable to contribute to its assets based on the liability that they take.

How does the constitutive technique ensure social control? First, the law sees incorporated bodies as different from their members. Therefore, if a company is indebted or bankrupt, creditors do not have to go after its members to recover their money since they are different from the company and are only responsible to the extent of their liability. The creditors can only go after the company's assets to recover their money. This insulates the members of that company from the company's liability. Secondly, investors want to be sure that their investments are secured. Therefore, if the law does not separate members of corporate bodies from such corporations, investments will not be secured and commercial transactions will be badly affected. For example, upon the death or bankruptcy of members of a company, investments will be lost if such individuals are not separate from the companies; as such investments would be tied to the lives of individual members. This could lead to numerous problems and chaos, particularly in the business world and in society more generally. The law therefore ensures that people are properly constituted into corporate entities for effective control.

Administrative Regulatory Technique

Under this technique the law puts in place regulatory measures to ensure compliance with standards. Regulatory bodies are set up and empowered to make rules prescribing proper standards of behaviour. Such rules are communicated in order to ensure compliance. Such regulatory

---

[20] See Section 37 of the Companies and Allied Matters Act CAP C20 Laws of the Federation of Nigeria 2004.

bodies are empowered to check the activities of persons responsible to them. They can also issue and withdraw licenses. They carry out periodic inspections and can take actions against anyone in violation of their rules. Examples of such regulatory bodies are the Vehicle Licensing Office (VIO), the National Agency for Food and Drug Administration and Control (NAFDAC), National Broadcasting Commission (NBC), Nigerian Communications Commission (NCC), Standard Organization of Nigeria (SON), etc. The Vehicle Licensing Office, for example, is empowered by law to issue licenses to vehicles that are considered roadworthy, carry out routine checks on vehicles and take action against anyone who drives a vehicle that does not meet the standard of roadworthiness. Another example is the National Broadcasting Commission. Anyone wishing to operate a radio or television station in Nigeria must first obtain a license from the Commission, which is the body empowered by law to license, monitor and regulate broadcasting in Nigeria. The National Agency for Food and Drug Administration and Control (NAFDAC) is established and empowered by law to regulate and control the importation, exportation, manufacture, advertisement, sale and use of food, drugs, cosmetics, medical services, bottled water and chemicals.

The difference between this method of social control and the penal technique is that while the penal technique prohibits certain kinds of behaviour, this technique only seeks to regulate proper conduct. This technique is also different from the grievance remedial technique in that it seeks to prevent a wrong from happening, while the grievance technique operates when a wrong has occurred.

The Fiscal Technique

All over the world, governments raise monies to finance their activities via taxes and other forms of levies. However, apart from being sources of revenue generation, taxes and levies are also used as instruments of social control. Governments usually achieve this by imposing some form of taxes and levies on certain kind of behaviours which they seek to discourage. The converse is also true. If governments want to encourage certain kinds of behaviours, they could exempt such behaviours from taxation or reduce the taxes imposed on them. For example, if a government wants to encourage people to invest in certain areas of society, it could grant tax holidays to those areas or reduce the taxes charged on certain businesses.

In Nigeria, taxes are imposed by the three tiers of government, i.e. federal, state, and local government, with each tier having its area clearly spelt out by the Taxes and Levies (Approved List for Collection) Act

1998.[21] Under the Act, taxes imposed by the federal government include companies' income tax, petroleum profit tax, value added tax and stamp duties on corporate entities. Taxes imposed by state governments include stamp duties for instruments executed by individuals and pool betting, lotteries, and casino taxes. Taxes imposed by local governments include liquor licenses, merriment and road closure fees etc. Governments (federal, state or local governments) can regulate the tax regime in their spheres of influence to encourage or discourage certain activities in those areas.

Governments also use the fiscal technique to curb certain anti-social behaviours by imposing fines on those behaviours. Examples of such fines include those imposed for incorrect packing and fines imposed by government agencies on vehicles that are not roadworthy.

Conferral of Social Benefit Technique

Under this method of social control, the law is not just seen as an instrument of prohibiting certain human behaviours, but as an instrument of promoting and enhancing social welfare. Funds generated from the fiscal technique are used to enhance the welfare of citizens.

If a government is to ensure peace and stability, it is obliged to provide certain basic amenities (or social benefits) for its citizens. It is believed that when such amenities are provided, there will be a reduction of the crime rate in a society. These benefits are usually provided for by statute. For example, the Education Tax (Amendment) Act[22] provides that an education tax, which shall be at the rate of 2 percent, shall be charged on the assessable profit of a company registered in Nigeria.[23] This tax, amongst other sources of revenues, enables the government to fund educational projects in Nigeria. Other benefits that can be conferred include healthcare and housing.

---

[21] CAP T2 Laws of Federation of Nigeria 2004.
[22] CAP E2 Laws of Federation of Nigeria 2004.
[23] Section 1(2), *ibid.*

CHAPTER FOUR

LEGAL REASONING AND APPROACH TO PROBLEMS

OYEKANMI IDODE ADEWOYE[1]

Introduction

This chapter will examine how lawyers reason in the legal profession and the methods of such legal reasoning. The chapter will briefly assess how lawyers apply legal reasoning to solve problems. It will also review the reasoning methods of lawyers and all those involved in formulation of policies, implementation and execution of law. The word 'legal' can mean anything connected with the making, execution and interpretation of law.

In the field of law, as in the other professions or calling, people are constantly coming up with ideas, reasoning, initiatives and arguments that will lead to a better society. Reasoning has to do with thinking logically, reasonably and sensibly or the presentation of facts or points logically, on issues relating to law. Problems are said to be challenges that arise from time to time which might or might not lead to conflicts but require solutions on how to improve the law and its use in solving individual, national and societal problems using law as an instrument for change.

The Language of the Law

This is the language in which the laws are expressed. It can also present a major obstacle to the easy application to facts. It is possible to express law in a specific language. This usually happens when the law does not want to leave anyone in doubt as to how the law should apply to the facts of a particular case. For example, Section 4(1) of the Constitution

[1] LL.M, Barrister-at-Law, Lecturer Faculty of Law, Benson Idahosa University, Benin City. Email: oadewoye@biu.edu.ng, oyeadewoye@yahoo.com.

of the Federal Republic of Nigeria, 1999[2] as amended vests the legislative powers on the National Assembly. It provides that:

> The legislative powers of the Federal Republic of Nigeria shall be vested in the National Assembly of the Federation which shall consist of a Senate and a House of Representative.

Section 4(2) of the Constitution goes on to provide that:

> The National Assembly shall have power to make laws for the peace, order and good government of the Federation or any second part thereof with respect of any matter included in the Exclusive Legislative list set out in part I of the Second Schedule to this Constitution.

It would be difficult however to express all statutory rules in this detailed way. The sheer volume of the resulting law would be unwieldy and somewhat lacking in coherence. In any case, it is often not possible to anticipate all possible eventualities and to draft laws specifically to meet them.[3] This has led to most statutory provisions being written at a higher level of generality. Thus law is usually expressed in general terms. This is because any law made will apply to a wide range of people in different circumstances and at different times. The law cannot possibly foresee all future situations that might arise for it to regulate or correct; hence, it is usually expressed in general language. For example, Section 383 of Criminal Code Act[4] provides that:

> (1) A person who fraudulently takes anything capable of being stolen, or fraudulently converts to his own use or to the use of any other person anything capable of being stolen, is said to steal that thing;
> (2) A person who takes or converts anything capable of being stolen is deemed to do so fraudulently if he does so with any of the following intents -
> (a) an intent permanently to deprive the owner of the thing of I;
> (b) an intent permanently to deprive any person who has any special property in the thing of such property;
> (c) an intent to use the thing as a pledge or security;
> (d)an intent to part with it on a condition as to its return which the person taking or converting it may be unable to perform;

[2] Constitution of the Federal Republic of Nigeria, 1999 as amended in 2011.
[3] J. H. Farrah and A. M. Dugdale, *Introduction to Legal Methods,* 3rd ed., (London: Sweet and Maxwell, 1990), pp.76-77.
[4] Criminal Code CAP C38 Laws of Federation of Nigeria, (2004).

(e) an intent to deal with it in such a manner that it cannot be returned in the condition in which it was at the time of taking or conversion; in the case of money, an intent to use it at the will of the person who takes or converts it, although he may intend afterwards to repay the amount to the owner, etc.

It is left to those applying the statute to determine how the general phrases of the above provisions apply to particular facts. The same characteristics of legal language can be seen in relation to case law sources. It is possible to regard the famous case of *Donoghue v. Stevenson*[5] as establishing that a manufacturer of ginger beer owes a duty not to allow snails to get into the product, that being the specific fact situation before the court.

According to Farrar,[6] "to express authority in this highly specific way would not be very helpful. It would make it difficult to provide future case law decisions. It would hinder the development of broader case law principles." Consequently, its authority has been viewed at a higher level of generality. It has been taken as establishing that a manufacturer of consumer goods owes a duty to anyone who suffers harm as a result of use of the goods so manufactured.

It might be difficult to determine the correct level of generality but it is clear that case law authorities should be viewed at some level of generality. Another characteristic of legal language is its use of abstract concepts. Lawyers use words to express law, enact laws, apply law and communicate generally in the legal profession. These are technical words which have their own meaning in law. Such words include:

- □ Contract
- □ Tort
- □ Sovereignty
- □ Legal Personality
- □ Rule of law
- □ Ownership
- □ Possession
- □ Separation of Powers
- □ Ministerial Responsibility
- □ Federation

---

[5] (1932) A. C. 562.

[6] J. H. Farrah and A.M. Dugdale, op. cit., note 3, 77.

Other remarkable features of legal language:

(a) Ordinarily, we use words in their ordinary literary meaning. Law on the other hand uses words in a technical, uncommon or specific sense. For instance, a lawyer arguing a case before a judge would usually say "It is submitted my lord that" instead of saying "the court should hold that" etc.
(b) Law uses Latin and French words and phrases such as *"res ipsa loguitur"*—the act speaks for itself; *"nemo dat guod non habet"*—you cannot pass a title you do not have; *"Caveat emptor"*—let the buyer beware; *"alibi"*—a plea of being somewhere else when a crime is committed; *"consensus ad idem"*—meeting of the minds, as in parties agreeing on a particular thing in contract; *"ex-parte"*—on the part of one side only; *"habeas corpus"*—a prerogative writ used to challenge the validity of a person's detention either in official custody or in private hands, etc.
(c) Law has its own slang or words with technical uncommon meaning such as 'hereinbefore', 'aforementioned' 'whereas', etc.
(d) Lawyers in court often use words with special meanings only known to them; for example: "My brief has not been perfected," which means "my professional fees have not all been paid or not even paid at all" or "I am speaking from the bar" which means that "I am speaking with integrity the truth as an officer of the court."

The use of these words can be traced to the received English law by Nigeria from Britain by virtue of colonization. It is suggested that as we move into modern times, much of this 'jargon' is gradually falling into disuse.

Methods of Legal Reasoning

One of the main functions of the judiciary is to interpret the laws made by the legislature and other laws derived from other sources like case law in settling disputes. Whether the laws are expressed in specific or general language, it is the duty of the lawyers and the judge to determine through a process of reasoning whether the law applies to particular facts. This therefore makes it necessary to study the various methods of reasoning usually adopted by lawyers.

Principles

Apart from first reading and understanding the law and its provisions, a major tool used by lawyers and judges is the use of established principles and rules. A legal principle can be said to be a legal proposition or truth which has been established and applied by the law courts over a period of time, and which forms the basis for the development of legal rules. For example, the principle of fair hearing as established in Section 36 of the Constitution[7] is founded on two main pillars, as follows:

(i) A person must not be condemned unheard *(audi alteram partem)* and
(ii) A person cannot be a judge in his own case *(nemo judex in causa sua).*

Some other well-established principles of law which serve as a guide to the process of legal reasoning are the rule of law, separation of powers, etc. On most occasions, any reasoning or argument which is contrary to time tested and approved principles of law is open to legal attack. Other tools used in legal reasoning include legal rhetoric, legal logic (deductive reasoning and inductive reasoning), common sense, experience, general knowledge, facts and persuasion.

Legal Rhetoric

Legal rhetoric can be said to be any legal argument, speech or writing meant to persuade another person, judge or court. Rhetoric on its own can be any speech or writing to persuade another person. For example, politicians when seeking votes make several promises to the electorate using persuasive words or rhetoric to persuade the people and win their votes. Whether such words or rhetoric are correct, honest or not is another matter entirely.

Plato, the Greek philosopher defined rhetoric as "the art of winning men's minds with words."[8] This makes it imperative for a serious minded law student or lawyer to continuously seek to improve his mastery of the English language and his communication skills, truth, knowledge of law, the facts of each matter, technique of persuasion, logic, common sense and

[7] Constitution of the Federal Republic of Nigeria 1999, CAP IV Laws of the Federation of Nigeria, 2004.
[8] Cited in A. O. Sanni, *Introduction to Nigerian Legal Methods* (Ile-Ife: Obafemi Awolowo University Press Ltd, 2006), 119.

experience.[9] Another notable Greek philosopher, Aristotle, classified rhetoric into two parts, forensic rhetoric and deliberative rhetoric. He was of the opinion that the pursuit of the latter was more worthy of a statesman. Lawyers more frequently employ forensic rhetoric, which is the art of using words to persuade a person to take one's opinion whether it is true or not.

On the other hand, judges more commonly use deliberative rhetoric as they seek to arrive at a rationalized decision that can stand the test of time and which is in the overall interest of the parties concerned and society more broadly. According to Odunsi, "although presentations are made in words, the principal rhetorical device used in law is the appeal to authority."[10] This, in other words, means citing or referring to existing laws (judicial or statutory) to back up or justify the position being canvassed.

In Nigeria and other common law jurisdictions, appeal to authority entails referring to judicial or statutory authorities which constitute what are known as primary sources of law. In some instances the opinions, writings, commentaries etc. of jurists and learned writers as well as judicial decisions of other jurisdictions can be referred to; however they have only persuasive effect. Opinions, writings, commentaries, among other things, constitute part of what is known as secondary sources of law.[11]

Finally one can say that rhetoric involves having a sound knowledge of law and legal principles. This is obtained through academic and professional training and sharpened through post-call practical experience obtained at the bar and in active practice.

Legal Logic

Logic can be said to be the study of the methods of correct and incorrect reasoning. Logic plays a prominent role in legal reasoning. We have deductive logic or syllogism and inductive logic.

---

[9] E. Malemi, *The Nigerian Legal Method*, (Lagos: Princeton Publishing Company, 2012), 363-365.

[10] B. Odunsi, "Legal Reasoning and Approach to Problems" in A. Sanni (ed.) *Introduction to Nigerian Legal Method*, 2nd ed., (Ile-Ife: Obafemi Awolowo University Press Limited, 2006), 120.

[11] *Ibid.*

Deductive Logic or Syllogism

This form of reasoning or logic usually assumes a major premise which may be true or false. Thereafter you have a minor premise from which a conclusion is reached (which also may be true or false). This process involves reasoning with general information and drawing specific conclusions from it.

For example:

All men must die	– Major premise
Elijah is a man	– Minor premise
Therefore Elijah must die	– Conclusion

When it comes to interpretation of statutory provisions, lawyers use this type of reasoning. The statute is the major premise; the lawyer identifies his case as falling within the statute and then deduces as the conclusion the way in which it applies to his client. Deductive logic is only applicable once a clear major premise has been established. It should be noted that there are certain limitations in using syllogism as a method of legal reasoning. For example, while the conclusion reached by using this form of legal reasoning is valid and reasonable, it may not be the truth.

Another limitation is that once a wrong premise is allowed to be established as 'true' then a wrong conclusion will be reached.

Inductive Logic

Inductive reasoning is reasoning from specific or particular facts and drawing general conclusions from it. According to Farrar,[12] for example:

> …if the source of the law is not a statute but case law (i.e. Judicial Precedent or court decision), no major premise is likely to be clear from just one case decision. Instead the lawyers will have to examine several cases to find a major premise which underlies them all. He will have to reason from a particular case decision to a general proposition. This form of reasoning is often referred to as inductive logic as opposed to deductive logic where the reasoning is from the general proposition to the particular conclusion in the case itself. Thus, a lawyer advising on the application of case law to a particular situation will employ, first, inductive reasoning to

[12] Op. cit. note 3, 79.

find a general preposition of law, and then deductive reasoning to determine how it applies to the facts.

Judicial officers also use deductive and inductive reasoning in deciding cases. In his book *Introduction to Legal Method*, Farrar[13] explained the process by which judicial officers use these forms of reasoning through citing the case of *Dorset Yacht Co v. The Home Office*,[14]per Lord Diplock. The question for determination in that case was whether Borstal Officers owed a duty of care to the public to prevent escape by those in their custody. The learned judge said that the court should proceed:

> …by seeking first to identify the relevant characteristics that are common to the kinds of conduct and relationships between the parties which are involved in this case for decision and the kinds of conduct and relationships which have been held in previous decisions of the courts to give rise to a duty of care.

The method adopted at this stage of the process is analytical and inductive. It starts with an analysis of the characteristics of the conduct and relationships involved in each of the decided cases. The analyst must know what he is looking for, and this involves his approaching his analysis with some general conception of conduct and relationships which ought to give rise to duty of care. This analysis leads to a preposition which can be stated in the form:

> In all the decisions that have been analyzed a duty of care has been held to exist wherever the conduct and relationship possessed each of the characteristics A, B, C, D etc, and has not so far been found to exist when any of these characteristics were absent. For the second stage, which is deductive and analytical, that preposition is converted to; 'In all cases where the conduct and relationship possess each of the characteristics, A, B, C, D, etc, a duty arises.' The conduct and relationship involved in the case for decision is then analysed to ascertain whether they possess each of the characteristics. If they do the conclusion follows that a duty of care arises in the case for decision.[15]

From the above extract, Lord Diplock adds one further element to the model of inductive and deductive reasoning: at the inductive stage the

---

[13] J. H. Farrah and A. M. Dugdale. *Introduction to Legal Methods,* 3rd ed., (London: Sweet and Maxwell, 1990), 80.
[14] (1970) AC 1004.
[15] Supra note 13, 80.

analyst must have some idea of what he is looking for. He must categorize the issue and decide which previous decisions are closely similar to the issue in question that can be used as a basis for inducing the relevant proposition of law. This form of reasoning is known as analogical reasoning and is not strictly logical as it is a looser form of reasoning which raises broader issues. Judges and legal advisers often use this form of reasoning to argue that previous decisions are or are not sufficiently similar to be relevant to the issue in question.

Legal Reasoning and Practical Reasoning

Another name for practical reasoning is common sense. Every normal rational human being has rational common sense or the ability to reason. Practical reasoning is not tied to deductive or inductive reasoning. Practical logic makes frequent use of analogy and is primarily concerned with weighing various considerations before arriving at a conclusion.

The study of logic, which is the application of formal rules in reasoning and reaching valid conclusions, only helps to sharpen the existing inherent common sense or the ability to reason.

Practical reasoning makes more use of what one may call "native sense" or "native faculties." Its conclusions more often than not are dependent on the prevailing value system of society, which may change with time. It relies more on practical experience. According to Oliver Wendell Holmes, "the life of law is not of logic but experience."[16]

Legal Reasoning and Justification

Any decision reached in a case (be it a judgement or ruling of any court for that matter) has to be justified by the judge in a reasoned judgement. The question now is how will a judge justify his decision? Definitely, the judge will not rely on logic alone to justify his decision, even though logic plays an important role in legal reasoning as logic alone is not law and law is not logic.

Therefore the judge will rely on many factors which include:

1. The admitted evidence (oral and documentary) presented by the parties in the case.
2. The case law or authorities applicable to the case.

---

[16] Cited in A. O. Sanni, *Introduction to Nigerian Legal Methods* (Ile-Ife: Obafemi Awolowo University Press Ltd, 2006), 128.

3. The sources of law.
4. The case cited as authorities and judicial precedents and arguments of counsels in the case.
5. The actual wording of the statute being considered and the interpretation to be accorded to it (e.g. whether to use the literal rule of interpretation, the Golden rule or the Mischief rule).
6. The extent to which a proposed decision will cohere with existing principles and authorities; the greater the inconsistency with the existing legal framework that will result from a proposed decision, the less likely it is to be adopted.
7. Whether the consequences of the decision for potential litigants and legal system will be acceptable in terms of justice or common sense.
8. Whether the decision is fair and just in the view of a reasonable man.
9. Whether the decision is in accordance with public policy.
10. Extra legal considerations, such as the school of thought to which the judge prefers to further base his decision on; for example, the realist theory of law, the utilitarian theory, the natural theory of law, the pure theory of law etc., as the case may be.

Conclusion

From the above one can see that to know which law applies to a particular situation can be as difficult as discovering the facts themselves. It is not always easy to predict how the courts will resolve hard cases where there is a choice as to how the law should apply to the facts. Although legal rhetoric and logic play an important role in the judicial adjudication of cases, in appropriate circumstances and when the interest of justice demand it, the judge can depart from them to ensure that justice is done in the case and technicalities set aside.

In the case of *Chinwendu v. Mbamali*[17] Justice Kayode Eso[18] stated thus: "Care should be taken by the court always not to sacrifice justice on the altar of technicalities. The time is no more when disputes are dealt with rather on technicalities and not on the merit."

---

[17] (1980) 3-4 SC 31 at 82.

[18] Justice of the Supreme Court (JSC) as he then was; now of blessed memory.

CHAPTER FIVE

LEGAL REASONING IN JUDICIAL PROCESSES

CHUKWUDUMEBI OKOYE[1]

Introduction

What is legal reasoning? Moreover, what does it mean to think like a lawyer? It is a myth to think of a conflict-free society because society comprises of complex individuals with complex idiosyncrasies; the possibilities of conflict cannot be over-emphasized. This situation therefore calls for an appropriate institutionalized process of settling disputes that must necessarily arise from the relationship between complex individuals.[2] This institutionalized process of settling disputes is known as the judiciary, which consists of both the bench and the bar.[3]

The judiciary is that branch of government invested with the judiciary power. Section 6 (1) of the 1999 Constitution (as amended 2011) states:

> The judicial powers of the Federation shall be vested in the courts to which this section relates, being courts established for the federation.

The system of courts in a country, including the body of judges and the bench, is that branch of government which is intended to interpret and apply the law.[4] In the process of interpreting and applying the law, lawyers and judges who are the judicial officers and co-worshippers in the temple of justice, engage in legal reasoning with a view to ensuring that justice is

---

[1] LL.B (Hons.) (Benin), LL.M (Benin), Lecturer, Faculty of Law, Benson Idahosa University, Benin City, Edo State. Email: cokoye@biu.edu.ng.

[2] E. Emmanuel, *Introduction to Nigerian Legal Method* (Ile-Ife: Obafemi Awolowo University Press Limited, 2006), 165.

[3] C. Oputa, "Hands off the Bar: the way out to the way forward," keynote address at the Plenary Conference of the Benches and Legal Practitioners of NBA, held at Jos, 26th – 27th August 1997.

[4] *Black's Law Dictionary*, 9th ed. (St. Paul, Minnesota: West Group, 2009).

done to all the parties before the court. Justice must not only be done, but must be seen to be done. Legal reasoning is the thinking process by which a lawyer argues and judges decide cases before them. It also involves the manner in which a lawyer in private practice answers a legal question, and regulates and formulates a legal argument in court. This chapter seeks to examine the main components of legal reasoning and its application in judicial process.

Legal Reasoning in Judicial Process

Although there is no precise dictionary definition of the phrase "legal reasoning in judicial process", from the synthesis of the definition of each relevant word[5] in the phrase, legal reasoning in judicial process may be literally defined as the process of careful thinking by a judicial officer in the course of resolving legal issues presented by parties to a legal action before his court for determination. According to Thomas Jefferson, "In a…nation, whose citizens are to be led by reason and persuasion, and not by force, the art of reasoning becomes of the first importance."[6] The judicial officer reasons on how to improve the law, better resolve disputes and improve the life of individuals, the nation and the world in general through the use of law.[7] The tools used for this purpose include the law and its provisions, rules and principles, general knowledge, facts, truth, language (spoken and written), persuasion, logic, common sense, experience and so forth.[8]

There are three main components of legal reasoning: reasoning by analogy, linguistic analysis and judicial discretion. Linguistic analysis deals with the meaning of words used by the legislature and judges as applied in *Shagari v. Awolowo;*[9]judicial discretion involves public policy and the personal view of judges about what the court's role is or what a

---

[5] The Longman Dictionary of Contemporary English, 6th Edition, defines the word "legal" as something "relating to law or falling within the province of law;" "reasoning" as "the process of thinking carefully about something in order to make a judgment; "judicial" is defined by the Black's Law Dictionary as "something relating to the law or court or judges of their decisions; "process" as the proceeding in any action or prosecution.

[6] Cited in the foreword to *Introduction to Logic* by I. M. Copi, et al, (Lagos: Pearson Educational Incorporation, 2005).

[7] E. Malemi, *The Nigerian Legal Method,* 1st ed. (Ikeja: Princeton Publishing Co., 2010), 353.

[8]*Ibid.*

[9] (1979) 6-9 SC. 51.

legal concept is;[10] while reasoning by analogy deals with the application of the doctrine of precedent.

The process of legal reasoning must be geared towards ensuring that justice is done, thus the preoccupation of legal reasoning in judicial process is the administration of justice.[11] The fact that legal reasoning in judicial process should be preoccupied with justice is emphasized in a number of cases, most notable of which is the *locus classicus* case of *R v. Sussex Justice, Ex parte McCarthy*[12], where Atkin L.J. stated that:

> Justice should not only be done but should manifestly and undoubtedly be seen to be done and next to the tribunal being in fact impartial is the importance of its appearing to be so.

The principle of justice in ordinary parlance means "fairness." Generally the human mind feels a natural disposition towards treating like cases alike (in the spirit of fairness). This tendency plays an important role in the functioning of the principles of justice which the courts observe.[13] Therefore in determining what is fair and ensuring this in judicial process, the doctrine of precedent which provides that courts should stand by the decision of its superior is very important. Therefore, in most legal systems there is a large apparatus of previously decided and recorded cases with the reasoning for those decisions systematically set out in the records of the courts.

Judicial process involves the determination of facts and law, the shift of facts and law, the determination of the *ratio decidendi*[14] of a previous case, distinguishing cases and the observance of the rules of precedence.

---

[10] *Roe v. Wade,* 410 U.S. 113, 93 S. Ct. 705, 35 L. E. d 2nd 147 (1973).

[11] Supra note 1.

[12] (1924) 1K.B. 259. See also *Olaseni v. Olaseni* (2010) 5 NWLR (pt. 1187) p. 253; *Niger-Benue Transport Co. Ltd v. Ogele Construction* (2010) 18 NWLR (pt. 1196) p. 258; *Yusuf v. State* (2011) 18 NWLR (pt. 1279) p.853; *Oladekoji v. Inspector General of Police* (2011) 16 NWLR (pt. 1273) p. 430.

[13] J. Farrar and A. Dugdale, *Introduction to Legal Method,* 3rd ed., (London: Sweet and Maxwell, 1990).

[14] The reason for the decision.

Sifting Facts and Law

Facts and Law Distinguished

Facts and law are different. While the law is found in statutes and courts decisions or even in textbooks, facts are to be found from the evidence, by hearing the witnesses and the expert's opinions.[15] The relationship between law and facts is that the law is applied to facts to produce legal decisions. However, situations arise where there is likely to be some uncertainty concerning the facts or the law or both in a case.[16] It may be that whilst certain facts are clear, others are a matter of inference; that whilst the basic principle of law is clear, its scope and application to the facts are not. At this juncture the line between questions of law and fact becomes blurred.

It is the duty of the court, when a case is brought before it, to determine the facts that led to the course of action and the relationship of those facts to the applicable law. In the *locus classicus* case of *Whitehouse v. Jordan*[17] the defendant, Jordan, a surgeon, upon an understanding, delivered a baby by caesarean section having failed to do so by "trial by forceps" i.e. per vaginal. After delivery, the baby was found to be suffering from irretrievable brain damage which the plaintiff averred was caused by the negligence of the defendant pulling too hard on the baby's head with the forceps. The court had to determine amongst others whether (1) the trial by forceps caused the brain damage; (2) whether legal duty was owed by Mr. Jordan and (3) whether his conduct was in breach of that duty.

The first and second issues were straightforward questions of fact (to be found from the evidence by hearing the witness and expect opinions) and law (legal duty to be found in the law of tort) respectively. The trial judge found it easy to conclude that the medical evidence showed that the damage was caused by the "trial by forceps." Thus the determination of the facts in issue—"the cause of brain damage of the baby"—was by evidence— "expert opinion." However, regarding the nature of duty owed by Mr. Jordan to the plaintiff, the court had to look upon previous cases or

---

[15] Section 175 and 68 respectively of the Evidence Act 2011 No. 18; John H. Farrar *et al,* supra note 13.

[16] *Ibid.*

[17] (1981) 1 W.L.R. 246 (H.L).

courts' decisions where she found the principle of law which states that a surgeon owes a duty to use reasonable care. [18]

However, with respect to the third issue of whether the conduct amounted to a breach of that duty, the court had to apply the standard of care expected of a reasonably competent member of his profession (medical profession). Recourse was had to evidence of the degree of force used upon the baby's head by Mr. Jordan. The courts heard the evidence of those present, and told of what they saw and in the case of Mrs. Whitehouse, what she felt. In inferring from the facts of the witnesses, the issues they were considering were neither purely factual nor purely legal in nature. They involved factual, legal and policy considerations[19] which interacted with each other, making the relationship between law and facts a complex one involving not just a sifting of facts and law but also applying the relevant law to the facts with policy issues under consideration.

In the event, the trial judge concluded that Mr. Jordan had used excessive force and was in breach of his duty. However the Appellate Courts, the Court of Appeal and the House of Lords both held that this was not the case and reversed the decision of the trial judge.

Sifting of Facts: Facts in issue and relevant facts

When faced with a lawsuit or a case in court, the lawyer and the judge are required to decipher from the entirety of the case, the existence of certain facts that have warranted the course of action or the institution of the lawsuit or case. Section 1 of the Evidence Act[20] provides that:

> Evidence may be given in any suit or proceeding of the existence or non-existence of every fact in issue and of such other acts as are hereafter declared to be relevant…

---

[18] To this extent, the court was able to sift the facts from the law and determine the relationship between the established facts of evidence and the principle of law.

[19] Policy considerations such as the surgeon's professional reputation being under attack; that if the court made findings of negligence on flimsy evidence or regarded failure to produce an expected result as strong evidence of negligence, doctors were likely to protect themselves by defensive medicine, adopting procedures which are not for the benefit of the patient but safeguards against the possibility of patients making claim for negligence. See J. Farrar, supra note 13.

[20] Evidence Act, 2011.

From the purport of the provisions above, a fact in issue or relevant fact is such that is so declared by the Evidence Act.[21] Therefore in Section 10, it is provided that in proceedings in which damages are claimed, any fact which will enable the court to determine the amount of damages which ought to be awarded is relevant. In addition, Section 11 of the Evidence Act provides that facts showing the existence of any state of mind such as intention, knowledge, good faith, negligence, rashness, ill-will or goodwill towards any particular person is relevant. In this same vein, Section 12 provides that where there is a question whether an act was accidental or intentional, or done with a particular knowledge or intention or to rebut any defence that may otherwise be open to the defendant, the fact that such act formed part of a series of similar occurrences, in each of which the person doing the act was concerned, is relevant. For example, Mr. Akpan sells his car to Mr. Obi for N100, 000 and Mr. Obi made a part payment of N50, 000 and promises to pay the balance five months later. If after five months Mr. Obi still has not paid, Mr. Akpan may decide to sue Mr. Obi in the law courts for the N50, 000 balance and also claim general damages to recover his expenses for pursuing the matter in court, along with interest on the N50, 000. The facts that must be deciphered from the case are as follows:

1. That Mr. Akpan sold his car to Mr. Obi for N100,000
2. That Mr. Obi agreed to buy the car and paid N50,000 as part payment
3. That Mr. Obi promised to pay the balance after five months
4. That Mr. Obi did not pay the balance after five months

A court is not expected to pronounce on every fact which is disclosed before it at the trial of a case. It is only the facts in issue between the parties and also facts which are relevant to the facts in issue that a court is bound to pronounce upon.[22] Therefore, parties to any proceedings are expected to prove the existence or non-existence of any fact in issue and facts relevant to a fact in issue[23]. In the above scenario, Mr. Akpan has to prove that Mr. Obi actually promised but failed to pay the N50, 000 balance after five months.

The principle of sifting of fact is based on a principle that whoever desires any court to give judgment on the existence of facts which he

[21] See Part 11 of the Evidence Act on relevant facts.
[22] T. Aguda, *The Law of Evidence* (London: Sweet and Maxwell, 2003), 7.
[23] Section 1 of the Evidence Act 2011.

asserts, must prove that those facts exist.[24] This is different from the obligation on a party to persuade the court either by preponderance of evidence or beyond reasonable doubt in order to have judgment given in his favour.[25] Proof of the existence of a fact or issue is called "evidential burden" and the principle depends on the nature of the case, depending on whether it is a civil or criminal case. For a proper understanding of this principle it is necessary at this juncture to classify cases brought before the court into two broad categories: civil and criminal cases respectively.

Proof of facts in court cases

In civil cases, whoever desires any court to give judgment on the existence of facts which he asserts must prove the existence of such "facts in issue," as defined by the Evidence Act. The burden of proof lies on the one who affirms (generally, but not always, the plaintiff), and not with one who denies *(Affirmanti Non Neganti Incumbit Probatio)*.[26] Applying this principle to the scenario given earlier, the duty lies on Mr. Akpan to prove the fact that he sold his car to Mr. Obi for N100, 000, who had made part payment of N50, 000 and had promised to pay the N50, 000 balance in five months but failed to do so. However, if Mr. Obi expressly or by implication admits the facts, Mr. Akpan is discharged of the burden of proving such facts; but if Mr. Obi denies making such a promise, then Mr. Akpan has the burden of proving that Mr. Obi made the promise but failed to fulfil it.

The burden of proof in civil action is not always on the plaintiff.[27] Sometimes it shifts to the defendant. For instance, if Mr. Obi had denied making a promise to pay the balance sum of N50, 000 in five months' time, and Mr. Akpan had produced a memorandum of payment signed by Mr. Obi, then the burden of proving the non-genuineness of the memorandum of payment and indeed that the promise was not made will shift to Mr. Obi.

---

[24] Section 121 of the Evidence Act 2011; A. O. Sanni, *Introduction to Nigerian Legal Method* (Ile-Ife: Obafemi Awolowo University Press Ltd, 1999), 82.

[25] Usually referred to as "burden of proof" in Section 131-133 of the Evidence Act.

[26] Section 131 of the Evidence Act 2011. Even where the defendant denies the facts stated in the statement of claim, the burden of proving those facts denied still resides in the plaintiff.

[27] Section 133 (2) of the Evidence Act 2011, No. 18; *G & T Investment Ltd v. Witt & Bush Ltd* (2011) 8 NWLR (pt. 1250), 500 S.C.

Proof of fact in criminal cases

In criminal cases, the general rule[28] is that the burden of proving the facts rests solely on the Prosecutor. That burden, unlike in civil cases, does not shift to the accused.[29] However, there are exceptions to the above general rule. Situations exist where the burden of proving facts in a criminal case will shift to the accused. They are:

1. Where the accused raises a defence of exemption or qualification from the provision of law creating the offence with which he is charged;[30]
2. Where the onus of proving certain facts is specifically imposed on the accused by statute;[31]
3. Where special facts are within the knowledge of the accused;[32]
4. Where the accused raises the defence of intoxication or insanity.[33]

The Determination of the Law Applicable To the Relevant Fact Proved Before the Court

There are different sources of law in the Nigerian legal system. These are generally categorized as statute[34] and case laws respectively. Case laws are legal pronouncements by judges on principles of law and they serve as a guide to judges in determining subsequent cases with similar facts and influence the judgment of the court in subsequent cases. Where the facts have been proven before the court, the next line of action is to determine the applicable law to the proven facts. Some of these laws are found in decided cases and are binding on subsequent courts, depending on the

---

[28] Section 139 Evidence Act 2011.

[29] Section 33 (5) of the 1999 Constitution; Section 137 (2) of the Evidence Act 2011, No. 18; *State v. Oladotun* (2011) 10 NWLR (pt. 1256) p. 572; *Abiodun v. FRN* (2009) 7 NWLR (pt. 1141) 489; *George v. FRN* (2011) 10 NWLR (pt. 1254) p. 67.

[30] Section 141 of the Evidence Act 2011.

[31] *Ibid.*

[32] Section 140 of the Evidence Act 2011; *Alibi-Rasaki v. State* (2011) 16 NWLR (pt. 1273), 251.

[33] Section 138(2) (c), *ibid*; *Igabete v. State* (2006) 6 NWLR (pt. 975) 100; *Abiodun v. FRN* (2009) 7 NWLR (pt. 1141) p. 509.

[34] Statute is a law enacted by a piece of legislature and is usually in written form or code. A law is usually made by Parliament, a delegated authority, or other law maker.

status of the court in hierarchy. Therefore courts are duty bound to follow the decisions of earlier courts where the facts are found to be similar; this is known as the doctrine of *stare decisis* or precedents. In accessing the case law applicable to the established facts, the courts are mindful of certain features of the decided case. They are the *ratio decidendi* and the *obiter dictum*.

Ratio Decidendi

Literally, *ratio decidendi* means the reason for the decision. The *ratio decidendi* of a case consists of the rule of law applied in the determination of a case. It is the reason or principle for the judgment and the point of law which determines the ruling or judgment in a case.[35] The *ratio decidendi* is often made up of the material facts and the principle of law. It is the part of the case that has authority and which in appropriate instances is binding as judicial precedent.[36]

It is noteworthy that the *ratio decidendi* of a case may be wide or narrow. It is wide when the principle of law stated is wider than the material facts. In such instances the principle of law is considered in a later case as an *obiter dictum* to the extent of its deviation from the material facts. Conversely, the principle of law is too narrow in relation to the material facts thereby restricting the application of the principle; it is the duty of the court in a later similar case to state the principle of law in its proper form.[37] There are instances where a court bases its decision in a case on more than one legal principle, thus having more than one *ratio decidendi*. The case becomes an authority in respect of all such areas of law.[38]

The Determination of the *Ratio Decidendi* of a Case

In determining the *ratio decidendi* of a case, the courts usually consider any one or more of the following factors:[39]

1. The reason for the decision as stated by the judge;

---

[35] G. Williams, *Learning the Law* (London: Stevens & Sons, 1982), 67; *Aseimo v. Abraham* (1994) 8 NWLR (Pt.361), p. 91 CA.
[36] *Buhari v. Obasanjo & Ors*. (2005) 2 NWLR (pt. 910) 321.
[37] A. Obilade, *The Nigerian Legal System* (Ibadan: Spectrum Law Publishing, 2000).
[38] *Ibid.*
[39] *Ibid.*

2. The principle of law stated by the judge as that on which the decision was based;
3. The actual decision in relation to the material facts;
4. The interpretation of the case in any later case determined before the instant case.

Obiter Dictum

The word "obiter" is a Latin word meaning "by the way" or "in passing." *Obiter dictum* is the statement of law, made by the way in the judgment which is not relevant to the issues before the court.[40] It is what is said by a judge in the course of his judgment. They include explanation, analysis, illustration, sayings by the way, chance remark, opinion, analogy, suggestions, observation and example.[41]

> The court summarized the term "obiter dictum" in the following words: "Pronouncement of the court on the issue joined that can and does embody the resolution of the court. Any observation or comment by the court which though made in pronouncing the resolution is not necessarily involved in the resolution or essential to it.[42]

Generally, an *obiter dictum* is not binding as a rule of law or judicial precedent. It is however a persuasive opinion and is usually respected depending on the reputation or evidence of the judge or the hierarchy of the court that stated the opinion or analysis of the circumstances of its pronouncement.[43] The persuasive effect of an *obiter dictum* is determined by the following factors:[44]

1. The level of the court within the judicial system that the obiter was made.
2. The eruditeness of the judge who made it.
3. The circumstance of its pronouncement.

---

[40] *AIC v. NNPC* (2005) 1 NWLR (PT. 937) Pg. 573; E. Emmanuel, *Introduction to Nigerian Legal Method* (Ile-Ife: Obafemi Awolowo University Press Ltd, 2006), 185.

[41] E. Malemi, *The Nigerian Legal System*, 3rd ed., (Ikeja: Princeton Publishing Co; 2009), 3; NWLR (Pt. 643), 63, 80.

[42] *Chief Loveday Ebee v. John Onyege* (2000) 2 NWLR (pt.643), 63, 80.

[43] *Ibid.*

[44] A. Obilade, supra note 37.

Although an *obiter dictum* does not have a binding effect on subsequent cases, it is a useful analogy or explanation which throws light on the case.

Per Incuriam

"Incuriam" literally means "carelessness" or "through want of care." A case is decided *per incuriam* where the case is decided without the normal care of considering and applying existing judicial precedents.[45] It is noted that the basis of regarding a decision as being reached *per incuriam* is where a relevant statute or rule, which would have had effect on the decision, was not brought to the attention of the earlier court and the earlier court's judge failed to address his mind to such statute or rule of law.[46]

Distinguishing Cases

To distinguish means to "differentiate." Distinguishing cases involves differentiating one case from another based on the material facts of the cases. The decision of a court in a case is not a binding precedent for any court in any subsequent case if the cases are different from each other in terms of material facts.[47] Distinguishing cases involves more than identifying factual differences or the dissatisfactory or restrictive nature of the legal principle[48] it establishes; it also involves using it as a justification for departing from the ruling in the earlier case.

---

[45] E. Malemi, supra note 41, 180.

[46] Emmanuel, supra note 2.

[47] *Buhari v. Obasanjo & Ors* (2005) 2 NWLR (Pt. 910), p. 321; *Amori v. Iyanda* (2008) 3 NWLR (Pt. 1074), p. 261. According to Obilade, it is often not as difficult for a court to avoid following a previous decision if it finds that the material facts are different from those of the instant case because it is within the province of the court in the instant case to interpret a previous decision. See Obilade, supra note 37.

[48] Glanville William considered distinguishing of cases from two broad headings: restrictive and non-restrictive. Non-restrictive distinguishing of cases occurs where the court accepts the expressed *ratio decidendi* of the earlier case and does not seek to curtail it, but finds that the case before it does not fall within it because of some material differences of facts. Restrictive distinguishing of cases cuts down the *ratio decidendi* of the earlier case by treating as material some facts which the earlier court regards as immaterial.

As Malemi,[49] rightly puts it, distinguishing a case is not the overruling of the earlier case, but a mere expression of the inapplicability of the earlier case, because it is dissatisfactory, because of the restrictive nature of the legal principle it establishes, or because the facts of the two cases are not similar, etc.

Methods of Legal Reasoning

The main methods of reasoning include:

1. Deductive reasoning, deductive logic, or syllogism; and
2. Inductive reasoning or inductive logic.

Deductive and Inductive Reasoning[50]

Deductive and inductive reasoning involves analytical reasoning or the ability to know what one is looking for, the features, similarities and dissimilarities before one can reach a conclusion.[51] Deductive reasoning is reasoning in which a reasonable or valid conclusion is naturally reached from two existing premises.[52] It involves reasoning or arguing from a general proposition to make a specific proposition and conclusion, or judgment. Inductive reasoning on the other hand is reasoning with one specific fact or piece of information and drawing general principles, conclusions or judgments from it.[53] Unlike deductive reasoning (reasoning from general proposition to specific proposition), inductive reasoning involves reasoning from a specific proposition and drawing a general conclusion from it. For instance, a lawyer who is arguing his client's case may say that the facts of the case are similar to the facts of several cases which were decided in a particular manner in the past and therefore his client's case should be similarly decided.

---

[49] E. Malemi, supra note 41.
[50] The word "deductive" is derived from the root word "deduct," which means to draw a conclusion or reach a judgment about something from the facts, evidence or information available. Thus, where the facts, evidence or information is dishonest the conclusion that will be reached logically will be wrong, false, untrue, misleading and unreliable. The word "inductive" comes from the root word "induct" which means to add or admit a particular person to a general body of his kind or admit a thing to a general body of its kind.
[51] E. Malemi, supra note 41, 372.
[52] *Ibid*, 367.
[53] *Ibid*.

In doing so he applies the IRAC rule. IRAC is the acronym of "Issues" "Rule of Law" "Application of the rule of law to the instant case" and "Conclusion" (usually drawn from the issues raised, rule of law and the application of the rule of law.) Applying the IRAC rule in the case of *Ryland v. Fletcher*:[54]

- I: the major issue raised is whether the defendant is liable for damage caused to the plaintiff as a result of the escape of noxious fumes from his factory.
- *R:* The rule of common law is that a person who brings a non-natural user into his premises is liable for the consequences of its escape.
- *A:* Applying the above rule of law to the issue is to determine whether the noxious fume constitutes a "non-natural user."
- *C:* Conclusion is drawn from the inference of the propositions in "I," "R" and "A" above.

In a subsequent case based on similar facts as that of *Ryland v. Fletcher*, which has been applied in a plethora of other cases,[55] a lawyer will usually argue that the same general principles applied in Ryland's case and other cases (a body of cases) be applicable to his and therefore it should be induced or added to this body of cases by deciding it likewise. Put succinctly, where the facts of a specific case are similar to a body of earlier decided cases, the court in the instant case should follow the judicial precedence or apply the doctrine of *stare decisis* and decide the case accordingly.[56]

The Doctrine of Judicial Precedent/*Stare Decisis*

"*Stare decisis*" literally means to stand by decided matters or to follow previous decisions. The doctrine states that lower courts are bound by the previous decisions and judgments of higher courts until they are seen to have been overruled.[57] Such decisions and judgments to all intents and purposes cannot be jettisoned.[58] This doctrine, known as the doctrine of judicial precedents and its principles, is based on hierarchy of courts.

---

[54] (1866) LRL Ex 265; affd (1868) LR 3 HL 330.

[55] For example in *NEPA v. Alli* (1992) 8 NWLR (pt. 259) p. 276; *NEPA v. Akpata* (1991) 2 NWLR (Pt. 175) P. 536.

[56] E. Malemi, supra note 41, 370.

[57] *Dalhatu v. Turaki* (2003) 15 NWLR (pt.1843) p. 310.

[58] *Chedi v. A.G Federation* (2008) NWLR (Pt. 1067) 168; *Odugbo v. Abu* (2001) 14 NWLR (Pt. 732) 45; *Ritz & Co v.Techno Ltd* (1999) 4 NWLR (Pt 598); *Fayemi*

What serves as binding precedent for lower courts is the *ratio decidendi* of the decision of the higher court and not the obiter dicta.[59] In *A.I.C. Ltd v. Nigerian National Petroleum Corporation*[60], the court in elaborating on the meaning of *ratio decidendi* stated thus:

> The *ratio decidendi* of a case represents the reasoning or principle or grounds upon which a case is decided while obiter dicta reflects, inter alia, the opinions of the judge which do not embody the resolution of the court. In other words, the expressions of a court in a judgment must be taken in reference to the facts of the case, which the court is deciding, the issues calling for decision and answers to those issues. In effect, the manner in which the court chooses to argue the case is not all important. Rather it is the principle that court is deciding.

Therefore, it is trite law that a decision of a court of competent jurisdiction not withstanding that it is probably null and void, unattractive or unsupportable, remains good law, and uncompromisingly binding until set aside by a court of competent jurisdiction.[61] The case of *General Sani Abacha and Ors v. Chief Gani Fawehimi,*[62] per Achebe J.S.C, stated this position succinctly as follows:

> By the time honoured doctrine of precedent as it operates in Nigeria and all common law countries controls the decision on a given issue of law handed down by the Apex court which for us in Nigeria is the Supreme Court, is not only superior but binds all subordinate courts including all courts exercising appellate jurisdiction. It is the law that the decision of a court of competent jurisdiction, no matter that it seems probably dull and void unattractive or unsupportable, remains good law and uncompromisingly binding until set aside by a superior court of competent jurisdiction.[63]

The force of authority of a particular decision on other courts depends on the hierarchy of court even when the decision is given *per incuriam.*[64] Justice Ubaezoni J.C.A. noted that:

---

v. Oni (2009) 7 NWLR (part 1140); *Dalhatu v. Turaki*; (2003) 15 NWLR (Pt. 1843) 310; *Rechitt & Colman Ltd v. Congoni Co. Ltd* (2001).

[59] *Buhari v. Obasanjo & Ors* (2005) 2 NWLR (pt. 910), 321.

[60] (2005) NWLR (Pt. 937) p. 572.

[61] *General Sani Abacha and Ors v. Chief Gani Fawehimi* (2000) NWLR (part 4), p. 533.

[62] (2000) NWLR (Part 4), p. 533.

[63] See also *Babatunde & Anor v. Olatunji & Anor* (2000) NWLR (Pt. 648), p. 557; *Ezeokafor v. Ezeilo* (1999) NWLR (Part 619) P.369.

[64] *Ndili v. J.M. Akinsumade & Anor* (2000) NWLR (Part 5), p. 750 at p. 786.

> It will be an act of judicial impertinence for a lower court to refuse to follow the decisions of higher courts because the lower court thinks that the decision of the higher court is wrong or given *per incuriam*. The principle by which the a lower court follows the decision of a higher court, whether the decision of the higher court is right or wrong is the principle of *stare decisis*. That is the binding force of precedent. It makes for clarity and certainty in our judicial decisions... it is wrong for the lower court... to refuse to follow the decision of the court of appeal... even if the decision of the higher court is given *per incuriam*, a lower court is bound to follow it.[65]

If any decision is found to be given *per incuriam*, the honour and privilege belong to the superior court to correct it, although it is not totally out of place if a lower court draws the attention of the higher court to it so that it may reconsider its position in its future decision.[66] In the light of the foregoing, it is manifestly clear that it does not lie within the competence of a lower court to say that the decision of a superior court was arrived at *per incuriam.*

At this juncture, it is important to note that a case shall only be binding precedent where the facts in the case are on all fours with a subsequent case under consideration.[67] The authority of a decision of any court, no matter its status in the hierarchy of courts, cannot extend to an issue not decided by the court. To be binding, the decision must be based on an issue raised in the proceeding before the court.[68] In *Amori v. Iyanda,*[69] the court held that a decision is only authority for the facts and law in which it was decided. When the facts can be distinguished, the lower court need not 'willy-nilly' apply the decision of the superior court on law, which does not support the facts before it.[70]

Hierarchy of Courts

There are two broad categories of courts in Nigeria: the superior courts of record and the inferior courts. Section 6(5) (a-f) of the 1999

[65] *Ibid.*

[66] After drawing the attention of the High Court to the earlier decision given *per incuriam*, the lower court is still bound to follow that decision.

[67] *Aduku v. FRN* (2009) 1 NWLR (Pt 1146) 377.

[68] *Action Congress v. Jang* (2009) 4 NWLR (Pt. 1132) 485.

[69] (2008) 3 NWLR (Pt. 1074) 261.

[70] *INEC v. Hashidu* (2009) 4 NWLR (Part1130) p. 78; *Yusuf v. Obasanjo* (2003), 16 NWLR. (Pt. 847) p. 544; *PDP v. Haruna* (2004) 16 NWLR (Pt. 904) p. 597.

Constitution (as amended 2011) enumerated the superior courts of record to include the following, in order of superiority:

(a) The Supreme Court of Nigeria[71]
(b) The Court of Appeal[72]
(c) The Federal High Court[73]
(d) The National Industrial Court
(e) The State High Court[74]
(f) A Sharia Court of Appeal of a State[75]
(g) A Customary Court of Appeal of a State[76]

Inferior courts of record include

(a) Magistrate Courts
(b) Customary Courts
(c) Area Courts
(d) Alkali Court
(e) Juvenile Courts

This chapter will attempt an examination of the most popular superior courts of record to substantiate the doctrine of precedents.

Supreme Court

The Supreme Court is the highest court in Nigeria.[77] All courts in Nigeria are bound by the decision of this court.[78] In *Obi v. INEC,*[79] the court reiterated the fact that all courts in Nigeria are bound by the decision of the Supreme Court of Nigeria. This follows the doctrine of *stare decisis* which is fully entrenched in the Nigerian jurisprudence to ensure certainty

---

[71] Established under Section 230 (1) of 1999 Constitution of the Federal Republic of Nigeria (as amended 2011).
[72] Established under Section 237 of the 1999 Constitution (as amended 2011).
[73] Established under Section 247 of the 1999 constitution (as amended 2011).
[74] Established under Section 270 of the 1999 constitution (as amended 2011).
[75] Established under Section 275 (1) 0f the 1999 constitution (as amended 2011).
[76] Established under Section 280 of the 1999 Constitution (as amended 2011).
[77] Section 235 of the 1999 Constitution (as amended 2011).
[78] *Obi-Odu v. Duke* (2008) 10 NWLR (pt.932) 120; *Concord Press (Nig) Ltd v. Olutola* (1999) 9 NWLR (pt. 620) 578; *Comptroller of Nigerian Prison v. Adekanye* (1999) 10 NWLR (pt 623) 400.
[79] (2007) 11 NWLR (pt 1046) 565.

of the law. It is a well-settled principle of judicial policy which must be strictly adhered to by all lower courts. However, as stated earlier, the lower courts can only follow the principle of law upon which a particular case is decided; such a principle is called the *ratio decidendi*.

The Supreme Court is not bound by its own decisions, thus it may or may not follow its own previous decisions;[80] it may even overrule itself.[81] In *Oshoboja v. Amida,*[82] the court gave circumstances where the Supreme Court usually departs from its previous decisions. These are as follows:

1. If the previous decision is proved wrong;
2. If the previous decision is given *per incuriam*;
3. If the previous decision is proved to be perpetuating injustice;[83]
4. If the previous decision is proved to be impeding the proper development of the law;
5. If the previous decision is inconsistent with the provisions of the constitution; or
6. Capable of fettering the exercise of judicial discretion of a court.[84]

Court of Appeal

Next to the Supreme Court in order of superiority is the Court of Appeal. The Court of Appeal is bound at all times by the decision of the Supreme Court[85] whether or not it is persuaded by its reasoning. The Court of Appeal, unlike the Supreme Court, is bound by its previous decisions.[86]

However, there are exceptions to this rule:

(a) Where there are two conflicting decisions of the Court of Appeal, it is entitled to decide which one to follow;[87]

---

[80] See *Yakugbe v. C.O.P* (1992) 4 NWLR (pt 234) p.152; *Utih v. Onoyivwe* (1991) 1 NWLR (pt.116) p.166.

[81] See *Afro-Continental Nig. Ltd v. Ayantuyi* (1991) 3 NWLR (pt178) p. 211.

[82] (2009) 18 NWLR (pt. 1172) 194.

[83] See *Owie v. Ighiwi* (2005) 5 NWLR (pt. 917) 814.

[84] See *Alhaji Karimu Adisa v. Emmanuel Oyinwola* (2000) 10 NWLR (pt. 674) p. 116.

[85] See *Pharmatek Industrial Projects Ltd v. Trade Bank* (Nig) Plc (2009) 13 NWLR (Part 1159) 596.

[86] *Ibid*; *INEC v. Action Congress* (2009) 2 NWLR (pt. 1126), 546.

[87] See *Hill Station Hotel Ltd v. Adeji* (1996) 4 NWLR (Pt 442) p. 294.

(b) Where a Court of Appeal's decision, though not expressly overruled, cannot stand with a decision of the Supreme Court. In this instance, the Court of Appeal will refuse to follow it;[88] or
(c) Where the Court of Appeal is satisfied that its own decision was given *per incuriam*, it is not bond to follow it.
(d) It is not bound to follow the *obiter dictum* of any of its justices.[89]

It must be reiterated that the court is only bound by the decision of a superior court if in the particular case, the facts on which a decision of a superior court is made are same with that of the instant case.[90] Thus if they are different from the set of facts of a case before a Lower Court, the lower court shall not be bound by the decision of the superior court.[91]

The Federal High Court

The decision of the Federal High Court binds all magistrate and district courts in Nigeria. The Federal High Court is in turn bound by the judgment or precedent of the Court of Appeal and the Supreme Court. The Federal High Court is of equal powers with the State High Courts, though it is given exclusive jurisdiction in certain matters.[92]

The State High Court

The High Court of a State, Federal High Court and the High Court of the Federal Capital are of co-ordinate jurisdiction. The decision of a High Court of a State is only persuasive precedent for the High Court of another state.[93] The decision of the State High Courts constitutes a binding precedent to magistrate and district courts within and outside the state.

Courts of Concurrent or Co-Ordinate Jurisdiction

The Federal High Courts and the State High Courts are equal in hierarchy. So too are the judicial divisions of the Courts of Appeal (in each state of the federation) all of equal status. They are known as courts of co-

---

[88] *Imo Concord Hotel v. Anya* (1999) 4 NWLR (Pt. 234) p. 210.
[89] *Chief Loveday Ebere & Ors v. John Onyenge* (2000) 2 NWLR (pt 643) p. 63 at p. 80.
[90] *Buhari v. Obasanjo* (2005) 2 NWLR (Pt 910) p. 321.
[91] *Ibid.*
[92] Section 251 of the 1999 Constitution (as amended 2011).
[93] *Barclays Bank v. Hassan* (1961) NNLR. 293.

ordinate jurisdiction. That is, they are courts of equal powers and none is strictly bound by another's decision. However in practice, each division does pay attention to the rulings (decision) of the other and the decision of each division has a strong persuasive influence on the other.[94] In *Uwazurike v. A.G. Federation*, the court held that courts of similar or concurrent jurisdiction are not bound to follow the decision of each other. In that case, the Federal High Court, Owerri and the trial court which is the Federal High Court, Abuja were held to be courts of concurrent jurisdiction and thus the trial court was not bound by the order of the Federal High Court Owerri.[95]

Conflicting Judgment of Courts of Co-ordinate Jurisdiction

In *Ansa v. Registered Trustees of the Presbyterian church of Nigeria & Anor,*[96] the Court held that where there are conflicting judgments of courts of equal or co-ordinate jurisdiction over a subject matter in dispute, the rule is that the decision that is later in time operates as precedent.[97] The Supreme Court held in the case of *Mackson Ikeni and Anor v. Chief William Akuma Efamo*[98]that:

> The law is well settled in Nigeria that where there are two or more conflicting judgments, it is the interest in time that constitutes *res judicata.*

Conclusion

Legal reasoning in judicial process involves all factors that influence the judge's judgment. The end process of legal reasoning is that justice is seen to be done. Therefore in the determination of a particular case, it is the duty of the court to determine and sift the facts and the law; determine the burden of proof of such cases whether civil or criminal; determine when the burden of proof shifts between the parties; and apply the relevant case law to the established facts. The doctrine of precedent ensures uniform application of relevant legal principle. There are several factors

---

[94] *Uwazurike v. A. G Federation* (2008) 10 NWLR (pt. 1096) 452; *Olutola v. University of Ilorin* (2005) NWLR (pt. 905), 416.

[95] *Ibid.*

[96] (2008) 1 NWLR (Pt. 1069).

[97] *Mkpedem v. Udo* (2000) 9 NWLR (pt. 673) P. 631; *Nwangwu v. Ukachukwu* (2000) 6 NWLR (pt 662) p. 674; *Alao v. V.C. Unilorin* (2008) 1 NWLR (pt 1069), p. 425.

[98] (2001)14 NWLR (pt.734) p. 539 at 546.

that influence the reasoning process in court. They include amongst others, personal interest of the judge, socio-cultural background of the judge, job satisfaction, and self-discipline of the judge and the ability of the judge to defend at all costs the independence of the judiciary.[99] However, it is the duty of the court to ensure that justice is done.

[99] See J. Farrar and A. Dugdale, supra note 13.

CHAPTER SIX

LEGAL REASONING IN LEGISLATION

JESUOROBO EMMANUAL IDUGBOE[1]

Introduction

In this chapter, we shall examine the various components of legal reasoning in legislation. These include the passage of bills into law, the policy behind legislative enactments, legislative drafting, and the use of semantics, logic, judicial precedents and analogy in legislation. Legislation generally is the end product of the process of law making in a constitutional democracy. Thus, the term "legislation" can be used interchangeably with the terms "statute," "enactment," "law" and "Acts of Parliament."[2] The law making power of the legislature is exercised through the passage of bills. A bill proposes either a change in the existing law or makes a new legislative proposal.

Introducing a bill in the legislature is a simple procedure which however sets off a complex and variable chain of events that may or may not result in final passage. It is easier to defeat legislation than to pass it, and the route a bill must travel before it wins final approval allows many opportunities for its opponents to defeat or delay it. Dingell[3] of the United States House of Representatives aptly described the uncertainty of the legislative process in the following words; "Some bills have so little support that they are ignored and left to die in committee. Bills that are non-controversial are expedited through the legislature. There are also major bills that generate so much debate that they occupy the major

---

[1] LL.B (Hons) Ife, LL.M. Jos, B.L., Senior Lecturer and Sub- Dean, Faculty of Law, Benson Idahosa University, Benin City. Nigeria. E-Mail: jidugboe@biu.edu.ng; ijesuorobo@yahoo.com.

[2] E. Azinge and V. Madu, *Fundamentals of Legislative Drafting* (Abuja: NIALS Press, 2012), 50.

[3] Dingell, Washington Post, June 26, 1983, p. A14.

portion of the time of the legislature." Many jurisdictions have their own peculiar forms of legislating.

A lot depends on the composition of legislative organs. Legislative assemblies under the parliamentary system of government differ to a reasonable extent from legislative bodies under the presidential system of government. In Nigeria for instance, the constitution prescribes that the Senate and the House of Representatives shall be responsible for making laws, for peace, order and good government of the Federation.[4] Section 4(1) states that:

> The legislative powers of the Federal Republic of Nigeria shall be vested in the National Assembly of the Federation which shall consist of a Senate and a House of Representatives.[5]

For the purpose of this discourse bills are classified into ordinary and appropriation bills. Legislative power extends to the powers conferred on the President of the Federal Republic of Nigeria to assent to ordinary bills and appropriation bills passed by both chambers of the National Assembly. The President shall within thirty days signify that he assents or that he withholds assent to a bill presented to him for assent.[6] However, where the President withholds his assent to an ordinary bill and the bill is again passed by each house of the National Assembly by a two-thirds majority, the bill shall become law and the assent of the President shall not be required.[7] If the President withholds his assent to an appropriation bill for thirty days, the bill shall become law if a joint session of both houses by two-thirds majority passes the bill; the assent of the President, in such a situation, shall no longer be required.[8] Bills can come from a variety of sources. They can be initiated by the executive branch, by a member of the legislature, by a standing or special committee of the legislative house, by a special interest group (like trade unions, ethnic associations, student unions and women associations), or by a private citizen. However, the major responsibility of initiating bills in the chamber of the legislative house lies on the part of the members of the house. Although the law making process is equally attractive to government departments, institutions and persons outside the legislature, the point must be made that the right to introduce bills is the exclusive constitutional preserve of

[4] Section 4(2) of the 1999 Constitution of Nigeria (as amended in 2011).
[5] Section 4(1) of the 1999 Constitution of Nigeria (as amended in 2011).
[6] Section 58(4) of the 1999 Constitution of Nigeria (as amended in 2011).
[7] Section 58(5) of the 1999 Constitution of Nigeria (as amended in 2011).
[8] Section 59(4) of the 1999 Constitution of Nigeria (as amended in 2011).

the members of the legislature. Thus even when the President or a Governor recommends a bill to the National Assembly or State House of Assembly, it must be sponsored by a member of the legislative house.

Thus, it is correct to posit that Parliament, for legislation making purposes, is composed of the President, Senate and House of Representatives.[9] In the United Kingdom, parliament is composed of the Sovereign (otherwise referred to as the Crown of the Realm), the House of Lords and the House of Commons. As is the case in Nigeria, parliaments in other jurisdictions exercise power over money bills and other legislative matters.[10] It should be added also that the legislative arm of local government councils also make bye-laws with the assent of the executive chairperson of the council.

Origination of Legislation in the National Assembly

Either arm of the National Assembly (the Senate or the House of Representatives) can originate a bill which however shall not become law unless it has been passed and assented to by the President. The normal flow of the legislative process in the National Assembly is that a bill is introduced in one house, passed by the required majority of that house,[11] and sent to the other house which shall also pass it by the required majority (after agreement has been reached by both houses concerning any amendments to be made). Thereafter the bill is presented to the President for his assent which shall be given within thirty days of the presentation of the bill. Where the President withholds or fails to give his assent within the prescribed period of thirty days and the bill is again passed by each house by a two third majority vote, the bill becomes law, even without the President's assent.[12] This procedure concerns only ordinary or non-monetary bills.

The procedure in a money bill is slightly different from the above, due to the special importance of such bills. What is meant by a money bill is "an appropriation bill or a supplementary appropriation bill,[13] including any other bill for the payment, issue or withdrawal from the Consolidated Revenue Fund or any other public fund of the Federation of any money charged thereon or any alteration in the amount of such a payment, issue

[9] At state level, it is the Governor and the House of Assembly.

[10] See Sections 58 and 59 of the Constitution (as amended in 2011).

[11] Section 56(2) 1999 Constitution (as amended in 2011).

[12] Section 58 1999 Constitution (as amended in 2011).

[13] E. Malemi, *The Nigerian Legal Method* (Lagos: Princeton Educational Press, 2010), 492.

or withdrawal; and a bill for the imposition of or increase in any tax, duty or fee or any reduction, withdrawal or cancellation thereof."[14]

Where a money bill is passed by one arm of the National Assembly but is not passed by the other house within two months from the commencement of a financial year, the Senate President shall within fourteen days thereafter convene a meeting of the Joint Financial Committee to enable the two houses to reach an agreement on the content of the bill. Where no agreement is reached by the two houses at the meeting of the joint finance committee, the bill shall be presented to a joint session of the National Assembly and if it is passed at this meeting it shall be presented to the President for his assent. A money bill, passed at a joint session of the National Assembly but vetoed by the President, that is not assented to by the President within thirty days after its presentation, must be returned to the Joint Session of the National Assembly and passed by a two third majority of the members present.[15] When this happens, presidential assent is no longer necessary. It is worthy of note that the National Assembly has the exclusive jurisdiction to legislate on matters on the exclusive legislative list and the concurrent legislative list. A State House of Assembly has the jurisdiction to legislate on the concurrent list and any matter not listed in either the exclusive or concurrent list i.e. residual list. The legislative arms of local government councils make bye-laws on matters relating to their constitutional functions. Any Act of the National Assembly that is inconsistent with the provisions of the Constitution will be declared null and void by the Supreme Court.[16] Similarly any law made by a State House of Assembly that is inconsistent with the provisions of an Act of the National Assembly or the provisions of the Constitution will be declared null and void to the extent of its inconsistency by the court.[17] A bye-law suffers the same fate if it is inconsistent with the provisions of the Constitution, or an Act of the National Assembly or a law of a State House of Assembly.

---

[14] This Committee is established pursuant to Section 62(3) of the 1999 Constitution (as amended in 2011).

[15] See generally Section 59(2), (3) and (4) of the 1999 Constitution (as amended in 2011).

[16] *A.G. Bendel State v. A.G. of the Federation and 22 Others* (1982) All NLR P.85; *National Assembly v. President* (2003) 9 NWLR (Part 824) p.104; *A.G. Ondo State v. A.G. of the Federation* (2002) 9 NWLR (Pt 772) p.722.

[17] *Akwule and Others v. The Queen* (1963) N.N.L.R. 105; *Gallagher v. Lynn* (1937) A.C. 863; *Chiroma Giremade v. Bornu Native Authority* (1961) All NLR p.469.

Companion Bills

It may sometimes become necessary for a major piece of legislation to be introduced in both houses of the National Assembly in the form of companion (identical) bills, primarily to speed up the legislative process by encouraging both chambers to consider them simultaneously.

Nature of a Bill

A bill will generally take the form described below but not all the parts are essential to every bill. A bill has a short title which is normally the name by which the eventual Act will be known and cited. Usually the name chosen is one that makes for easy identification and indexing. A bill also has a long title which sets out in brief terms the purposes of the bill or provides a short description of the scope of the bill. A bill may have a preamble which is a comparatively rare incorporation that states the reasons why the enactment proposed is desirable. Preceding the clauses of a bill is the enacting formula which summaries the legislative authority of the enacting legislature. In most cases a bill contains a commencement provision (the day from which it takes effect). A definition or interpretation clause sets out the meaning of certain words in the context of the bill. The substantive provisions of a bill are contained in clauses numbered consecutively. Clauses may be divided into sub-clauses, sub-clauses into paragraphs and paragraphs into sub-paragraphs. Large bills are divided into parts. When a bill has become an Act, that is after it has received executive assent, clauses are referred to as sections. Schedules are used to avoid cluttering the bill with details or materials that would destroy the readability of the clauses. Some bills also have attached to them explanatory memoranda that summarise the provisions of the bill. The name or names of member(s) who introduced or presented a bill are usually contained on the back cover of the bill. Bills are drafted by specially trained lawyers working in the legislative house, commonly referred to as legislative counsel.[18]

Legislative Process

Although some differences do exist from legislature to legislature as regards the due process which a bill must go through to become an Act,

[18] K. N. Nwosu, *Law and Practice of the Legislature in Nigeria* (Lagos: Nayee Ltd., 2003), 208.

there are quite a lot of similarities in practice and procedure.[19] The general sequence of stages or steps through which a bill passes on its way to becoming a law will be enumerated presently.

Presentation and First Reading

The rules of the legislative house provide for the manner of presentation of bills, usually by a member giving notice of motion for leave to present the bill to the Clerk of the House or, in some legislatures, to the Rules and Business Committee of the House.[20] The bill is then given a number, printed and copies sent to every member. Executive bills are usually sent to the presiding officer of the chamber. Every bill receives three readings. On presentation of a bill the short title only is read by the Clerk and the bill is then deemed to have been read the first time. This stage is therefore purely formal and no questions are asked, neither is any debate entertained.[21]

Second Reading

Debates concerning the principle and purpose of the bill commence here. Since the whole principle of the bill is in issue at this stage, debate does not normally extend to matters which can be discussed at the committee stage.[22] However, it is the practice of most legislatures to permit reference to amendments proposed to be moved at the committee stage. Debate at this stage is not strictly limited to the contents of the bill.

Committee Stage

The use of committees in the legislative process is one of the major dynamics of modern legislative practice. Over the years, there has been a tremendous growth in the volume of legislative business, which frequently has to do with a number of complex and technical issues requiring specialized knowledge. The committee system therefore evolved in the legislature as a response to the need for division of labour and efficiency in the conduct of legislative business. Particular issues are assigned to a

---

[19] *Ibid.*
[20] *Ibid.*
[21] *Ibid.*
[22] T. E. May, *Erskine May's Treatise on the Law, Privileges, Proceedings and Usage of Parliament*, 21st ed., (London: Butterworths, 1989), 440.

small segment of the members of the legislature called a committee (who are usually knowledgeable in that area) to handle and report to the house in its plenary session.[23] Due to their dominant role in the policy-making process, committees have come to be described as the "little legislature."[24]

Virtually all legislatures have adopted the committee system. Provisions are made in the 1999 Constitution for the appointment of committees in both the Federal and State legislatures but it is left for each legislative house to fix the number of members of a committee, their terms of reference and quorum. A legislative house may delegate any of its functions to any of its committees.[25]

However, although it can make recommendations to the house, a committee lacks the power to decide whether or not a bill should be passed into law; that decision is for the entire house to make. The constitutional provisions concerning the use of committees are the same in the federal and state legislatures; the only difference is that the Senate and the House of Representatives are given the additional responsibility to appoint a Joint Finance Committee, consisting of an equal number of persons appointed by each house, and may appoint any other joint committee (as they may consider necessary).

After the reading of a bill for a second time, it is committed to a Standing Committee. Occasionally the bill may be referred to a Committee of the whole House. The latter is often the case, for instance with bills of constitutional importance and budget proposals. Occasionally a bill will go to Select, Special or Ad-hoc Committee. Committees have the power to call witnesses.

Report Stage

A committee to which a bill is referred is expected to present a formal report to the house upon conclusion of the committee's proceedings. On receipt of the report, the house considers the bill as amended; it may also make further amendments. A bill amended by the committee is reprinted as amended, and distributed to members before being considered by the house.[26]

---

[23] *R v. Secretary of State, Hillingdon LBC* (1986) 1WLR p.192; *Griffin v. Donnelly* (1881) 6 QBD p.307.

[24] *See* J. A. Akintola *Law Practice and Procedure of Legislature* (Lagos: Learned Publications Ltd, 1999), 109.

[25] E. Malemi, supra note 13, 162.

[26] *Ibid.*

Third Reading

When the House receives the Committee's report on a bill, the bill is ordered to be read the third time, either immediately or on a future date as the Rules and Business Committee may appoint. At the third reading, a bill is reviewed in its final form and amendments may be made for the correction of error or oversight. However, no amendment of a material character can be proposed at this stage. Debates are generally short as the house's main duty at this stage is to decide whether to pass the bill into law or reject it.[27]

In parliamentary parlance, a bill finally approved and passed by a State House of Assembly at its third reading is called a law, subject to the assent of the State Governor. A clean copy of the bill in its final form is certified by the speaker and the Clerk of the House before it is sent to the Governor for his assent. However, a bill passed in one chamber of the National Assembly is passed to the other chamber where it goes through similar stages of procedure as in the first subject to the assent of the President.

The unicameral nature of the State House of Assembly has simplified the mode of exercising legislative power in the state. Here there is no distinction between ordinary and money bills. A bill passed by a simple majority in a State House of Assembly is presented to the State Governor for his assent within thirty days. Where the Governor withholds or fails to give his assent within the prescribed period and the bill is again passed by a two-third majority of members of the house, it becomes law irrespective of the Governor's withheld assent.[28]

Policy Consideration

Policy considerations refer to the plan of action of the government of the day as evidenced by the political manifesto of the ruling party, the programmes or agenda of the President and the ever-unfolding collective decisions of the Federal Executive Council, which is the highest policy-making organ of government. While some policies are internalized as conventions and guidelines for running of government, others are further processed for statutory enactment.[29]

---

[27] *Ibid.*

[28] *House of Assembly Bendel State v. A.G. Bendel State* (1984) 5 NCLR p.161.

[29] E. Azinge and V. Madu, supra note 2, 51.

Classification of Policy Thrust

The policy thrust of government can be classified along the following lines: Media Policy, Economic Policy, Political Policy, Education Policy, Foreign Policy, Security Policy, Employment Policy, Environmental Policy, Anti-Graft Policy, etc. These are policies that can find expression in legislative processing.[30]

Policies of Executive Bills

Executive bills are draft proposals which are prepared by the executive arm of the government and sent to the National Assembly or State Assembly as the case may be. Most executive bills are public bills as they always promote the public interest. More significantly however, executive bills strive to address issues of serious national importance. In this regard, the scope extends to security, health, political and criminal matters.[31]

Policies of Private Bills

Private legislation is legislation of a special kind for conferring particular powers or benefits on any person or body of persons including individuals, local authorities, statutory companies or private corporations. Private bills or private members bills are bills other than executive bills presented by members of the National Assembly or a State House of Assembly sponsored by individuals, agencies or pressure groups, non-governmental organizations, independently, or through the support of members of the National Assembly or State House of Assembly. All private bills have objectives and policy thrust. In some jurisdictions, the proceedings for private bills are peculiar and distinct from other bills; in Nigeria, there appears to be no remarkable difference. What is relevant however is that private bills are geared towards engendering social harmony, economic prosperity and political stability.[32]

Public Hearing as Policy Shaping Methodology

Public hearings give an opportunity to the general public to participate in debates on executive or private bills. This is independent of memoranda

[30] E. Azinge and V. Madu, supra note 2, 52.
[31] E. Azinge and V. Madu, supra note 2, 54.
[32] *Ibid*, p. 55.

submitted by stakeholders. During public hearings, arguments are advanced on both sides of the divide and areas of discord are streamlined.

Amendment and Repeal

This can come about as a result of policy formulation. Policy is therefore critical for all types of bills. That a particular law should be amended because portions of it no longer serve the need of the moment is a product of policy formulation. So also is the idea that a particular law or statute has outlived its usefulness. That a punishment clause should be made stiffer than it is, is also a product of policy formulation. Thus for purposes of amendment and repeal of a law, policy issues are critical ingredients for consideration by all stakeholders.

Policy and Legislative Drafting

It is ultimately the responsibility of a legislative draftsman to translate policy into law and ensure that the intention of parliament is captured as accurately as possible. As V.C.R.A.C. Crabbe[33] succinctly put it, "Parliamentary counsel thus has a vital role to play in the conception and birth of an Act of Parliament. They have a duty to express legislative policy in a language free from ambiguity. Transforming government policy into law is the prime function of parliamentary counsel."

Drafting Legislation

It begins with communication. What does it means to communicate? Communication is: "a process by which information is exchanged between individuals through a common system of symbols, signs or behaviour."[34] It follows that effective communication would mean the most efficient use of the 'common system of symbols, signs or behaviour' in disseminating information.

Language has been observed as a medium of communication. Macmillan Dictionary[35] describes language as "the method of human

---

[33] V.C.R.A.C. Crabbe, *Legislative Drafting*, Volume 1, (London: Cavendish Publishing Limited, 1998), 19.

[34] Merriam Webster's Dictionary, Available at http://www.merriam-webster.com.dictionary/communication. Accessed on 18/08/2012.

[35] Available at http://www.macmillandictionary.com/dictionary/british/language? Accessed on 19/08/2012.

communication using spoken or written words." Language has also been identified as 'a system of vocal or linguistic symbols used in a particular society as a means of communication.[36] The interface between language and its expression results in communication. Language is much more, however; it "expresses human thought and human endeavour; it reflects our very way of life. Every aspect of our lives is affected by language. We communicate with each other and conduct our daily affairs by the means of language. Language, especially written language, has a magnet of its own. Whether the language is emotive, informative or prescription, its influence is great."[37]

The final terminology requiring definition is 'legislative drafting.' What does it mean? A literal meaning would be to legislate by drafting but the term means much more than that. Crabbe[38] sees legislative drafting as "involving the attempted solution of problems faced by governments, and by society as a whole." He explains further that "it is also a form of communication. It lays down our rights and our obligations, our power, our privileges and our duties. In this it tells us what to do and what not to do. It is a command to others. It is part of the language of a people. It will be understood as language of that jurisdiction. In that respect, an Act of Parliament should be drafted in accordance with principles that govern language as a means of communication in that particular jurisdiction."

The Nature of Legislative Drafting

No discussion of the nature of legislative drafting can be undertaken with any realistic hope of thoroughness within the limited space in this chapter. What is aimed for instead is providing a cursory insight illuminating the peculiarities of communication through this medium. A good preamble to understanding the nature of legislative drafting would be to say a little about 'legislation.' Nutting and Dickerson see legislation simply as 'laws enacted by legislatures rather than developed by courts.'[39] To Crabbe, 'legislation is the framework by which governments achieve their purposes.'[40] Legislation as a source of law is of great importance to a

---

[36] G.C. Thornton, *Legislative Drafting,* 4th ed., (London: Butterworth, 1996), p. 47-48.
[37] V.C.R.A.C. Crabbe, *Legislative Drafting*, (London: Cavendish Publishing Ltd, 1998), 21.
[38] *Ibid.*
[39] C. B. Nutting and R. Dickerson (ed.), *Cases and Materials on Legislation,* 5th ed. (St. Paul, Minnesota: West Publishing Co., 1978), 369.
[40] V.A.C.R.A.C Crabbe, supra note 37.

society respecting the rule of law; the conduct of society and its well-being is regulated by law, but more importantly, legislation transforms government policies into binding rules of conduct for society.[41]

Legislative drafting aims at capturing the purpose of government in a written form. It breathes life into conceived policies of government. So important is the role played by the legislative draftsman in this regard that

Crabbe[42] warns that "legislative drafting is a difficult task. It is an extremely onerous, exacting and highly-skilled task. What is clearly conceived in the mind may not be easily expressed with clarity and precision in words." He warns further that "it is not a task for children, amateurs and dabblers."[43]

> It is a highly technical discipline, the most vigorous form of writing outside of mathematics. Few lawyers have the special combination of skills, aptitude and temperament necessary for a competent draftsman.... It becomes the burden of the legislative draftsman to "perform an extremely difficult task. There is much that is beyond their control. There are many pressures on them. The nature of the task requires them to think of the past, the present and the future. The conduct of society in the past, the present and particular problems of society have to be taken into account. The resulting law is prospective in character by laying down rules of conduct for the guidance of society. The legislative draftsman has to think of the problems involved from as many different angles as possible – the simple as well as the complex. It is not a question of changing a few ideas around. They have to think of the legal practitioners who will try to read the law – even if in bad faith – to suit a particular case and who will take advantage of a loophole.[44]

---

[41] N.K. Nampoothiry, "The Role of Parliamentary Counsel in Legislative Drafting" (2010) 36 (1) Commonwealth Law Bulletin http:/web.ebscohost.com/ehost/pdfviewer/pdfviewer?vid=7*hid=13&sid=1b6c9533-b28f-a2ac-c348e9/28880%40sessionmgr15, accessed on 20/08/2012.

[42] V.A.C.R.A.C Crabbe, "*The Ethics of Legislative Drafting*" (2010) 36 (1) Commonwealth Law Bulletin, http:/web.ebscohost.com/ehost/pdfviewer/pdfviewer?vid=7*hid=13&sid=1b6c9533-b28f-a2ac-c348e9/28880%40sessionmgr15. Accessed on 20/08/2012.

[43] *Ibid*: The warning comes actually from Reed Dickson: *Legislative Drafting* (Boston: Little, Brown and Co; 1954) p.3, who is quoted by Crabbe in the above context.

[44] V.C.R.A.C. Crabbe, "The Role of Parliamentary Counsel in Legislative Drafting" (2000) (Paper written following a UNITAR Sub-Regional Workshop on Legislative Drafting for African Lawyers), http:www2. unitary.org/dfm/ Resource Center/Document Series/Document11/Doc Series 11.pdf, accessed on 18/08/2012.

Legislative drafting aims to communicate the meaning of legislation without infusing it with the emotions or political persuasions of the draftsman. Thus, legislation speaks in a seeming 'monotone' aiming for a consistency devoid of the excitement of 'soft-selling journalism' or the figures of speech of a work of literature. 'In order to maintain consistency of language and uniformity of form the draftsman adopts a method of presentation which enables lawyers, judges, legislators and the common man to understand the law without doubt and without ambiguity.'[45]

Thornton[46] identifies three categories of persons to whom the communication of legislation is relevant: the members of the law-making authority;[47] the members of society who are concerned with or affected by the law[48] and the members of the judiciary.[49]He is of the view however that the style which is appropriate to any particular enactment will to some considerable extent depend on the identity of those people in the group to whom the law should be communicated.[50] He argues further that 'although there are some laws such as road traffic laws, which are applicable to the conduct of all the persons who make up a society, most laws have narrower application and regulate those who practise a particular task.[51]

---

[45] N.K. Nampoothiry, supra note 41.

[46] *Ibid.*

[47] According to Thornton, this group, in theory at least, may be said to transmit the communication.

[48] http:/web.ebscohost.com/ehost/pdfviewer/pdfviewer?vid=7*hid=13&sid=1b6c9533-b28f-a2ac-c348e9/28880%40sessionmgr15, accessed on 20/08/2012.

[49] According to Thornton, this group may also be said to receive the communication. It is concerned to construe it definitively, although the construction of a particular court may be subject to reversal by a higher court.

[50] G.C. Thornton supra note 36, 45; Thorton's view on the group of individuals who are interested in the communication of a legislative document appears to be shared by Nampoothiry, who has identified lawyers, judges, legislators and the common man as the persons who should understand the law without doubt and without ambiguity. Each of these groups of individuals can conveniently be pigeon-holed into the three groupings by Thornton; lawyers and judges would belong in the category Thornton has identified as "members of the judiciary'; legislators would belong in the group Thornton identifies as 'members of the law making authority' while Nampoothiry's common man would belong to the group Thornton identifies as 'members of the society who are concerned with or affected by the law'.

[51] G.C. Thornton, supra note 36.

Utilisation of Words

A legislative draftsman must develop a mastery of words and their usage. Words have a power of their own. Words in their proper order are critical to the communication of meaning in legislative drafting. There is so much to be said about the need to develop more than a passing interest in the principles governing the use of words. 'Understanding that the connection of language and reality is only through the mental image which makes it easier to accept and remember the axiomatic but absolutely fundamental principle that words have no "proper" meaning and no "absolute" meaning.'[52] In *Carter v. Bradbeer*[53] Lord Diplock pointed out: "…words mean whatever they are said to mean by a majority of the members of the appellate committee dealing with the case, even though a minority may think otherwise."

> The starting point to understanding words, their meaning and usages in the construction of the architecture of language is to go back to the basics and this would involve making a hard study of the parts of speech of the English language or whatever language of communication the draftsman is interested in. Lesson from the basics can provide useful insights to the various attitudes the word form can assume. It will also help the draftsman learn how to avoid ambiguity[54] in the various usages of the word-form. In some cases however, ambiguity is inevitable. For instance, the word "bank" could mean a financial institution; it could also be taken to mean the bank of a river. In such cases of word capable of more than one meaning, the draftsman should know how to take it as his responsibility to narrow down the meaning of the word to fit the purpose of the legislation through the aid of a definition clause.
>
> Another useful lesson to be learnt by a draftsman is the use of punctuation marks in construction of sentences. This may appear to be stating the obvious. There is however a dire need for a reiteration of the importance of punctuation marks. An improper punctuation mark can alter completely the meaning of a statute. Its absence can make a potentially wonderful legislative draft completely meaningless. The purpose of

---

[52] G.C. Thornton supra note 36.

[53] (1975) 1 W.L.R. 1204 at 1205.

[54] Thornton writes that: "Ambiguity is of two kinds. The first may be termed grammatical or syntactical ambiguity and results from combining words which are unequivocal taken separately in such a way that the meaning of the words together is equivocal… The second kind of ambiguity arises from the word itself and not from its use with other words. This may happen when more than one thought or reference…is signified by one symbol. (G.C. Thornton, supra note 36, 15).

punctuation is to assist the reader to comprehend more quickly the intended meaning by providing signposts to sentence structure.[55]

Semantics

Semantics or the choice of language means making a decision as to the style of writing. The choice to be made is between the traditional legal writing approach and the plain English approach. The draftsman does not have the luxury to engage in any debates but must make a choice as to how best to make the proposed legislation communicate to the intended users. Some useful insights can be distilled from the following:

(i) Before beginning the draft, the draftsman must ensure he thoroughly understands the intentions of the sponsors of the legislation as well as the policy behind the proposed law.[56]
(ii) The draftsman should then build a mental picture of the end users of the legislation. In this connection, Thornton's categorization of persons who are interested in the content of legislations[57] comes in handy. By having his end users in mind, the draftsman would be properly guided as to his choice of language: a draftsman preparing legislation to regulate the practice of law for instance would know that he is writing for a purely legal audience. This knowledge would help him determine how best to communicate the policy in the legislation in a manner that can be easily understood by lawyers.
(iii) At the writing stage, the draftsman should call to his aid the lesson he has learnt about words and their usage in the construction of sentences. Words with double meanings should be identified whenever they are used and given a narrow meaning to suit the meaning intended by the draftsman in the legislation
(iv) Punctuations should be properly deployed to aid comprehension by readers. The rules of punctuation are well established and should be diligently followed by the draftsman.
(v) Clarity and precision are equally desirable goals. A draftsman must try to strike a balance to ensure that his work attains both goals.
(vi) As with any form of writing, peer review or any form of review by another pair of eyes can prove very useful in minimizing unnecessary errors. A draftsman must learn to submit his work to this process and be humble enough to listen to criticisms when they come. There is a general consensus among scholars that criticisms are not a sign of lack of effective

[55] G.C. Thornton, supra note 36, 33 and 48.
[56] A little more will be said on this issue in the next paragraph.
[57] G.C. Thornton, supra note 36, 49.

communication skills in legislative drafting rather, they strengthen the quality of work that result thereby.

Understanding the policy behind legislation

A legislative draftsman must fully understand the policy being promoted by a proposed legislation before he begins work on it. A failure to do so would contribute to ineffectiveness in achieving the ends of communication. His work begins from when the idea is first conceived to the point when a legislative draftsman is brought into the picture. Nutting and Dickerson write that:

> The draftsman's problems begin with the substantive ideas that he is called on to express, ideas that in more cases than not are imperfectly formed when he first makes contact with them. Briefly, the draftsman's job is to help his client do legislatively exactly what the client wants to do in fact and to help him do it in a way that will work as smoothly as possible… an architect doesn't design a house for a client until he knows exactly what his client is trying to accomplish. Similarly, the legal draftsman must be brought into the picture long before he picks up his pencil, and he must find out as much as possible about what his client's particular problem is and then help the client bring about the desired result.[58]

There is a lot of wisdom in the above view. The draftsman must succeed in immersing himself in the mind of the sponsors of a proposed piece of legislation, in order to envision what exactly they seek to achieve. There is also an additional responsibility placed on the draftsman to consider and advise on the merits of the legislation in the general corpus of legislation in that legal system. However, no matter his level of involvement in matters of policy makers, Crabbe has warned that draftsmen must realize their limitations[59] and direct themselves accordingly.

The skills of a legislative draftsman require facility in the use of language, a critical, enquiring, imaginative, and systematic mind, as well as orderliness in the formulation of thought and the ability to pay meticulous attention to detail. A draftsman must also have an analytical and original mind capable of conceiving distinctly the general purpose of a statute and its subordinate provision in a language perfectly adequate and not ambiguous. The ability to write short simple sentences devoid of ambiguous and distracting repetitions is a pre-requisite, as well as a style

---

[58] V.A.C.R.A.C. Crabbe, supra note 44

[59] *Ibid.*

that is both concise and simple, leaving a minimum of opportunity for individual differences of opinion.[60]

These qualities for legislative drafting are not hard to come by. Yet few people are willing to undertake the arduous and highly skilled tasks that legislative drafting imposes. It demands the ability to work with colleagues and those skilled in other disciplines. It requires the ability to pay heed to criticism, and graciously accept it whether it is offered in bad or good faith. Common sense is a prerequisite, and a sense of honour is desirable. So also is the awareness of the cultural, economic, political and social factors that created the problem that will have to be dealt with and it is hoped solved by legislation.[61]

Legal Reasoning

In legal writing, it is not enough for an argument to "make sense" or "get the point across." A legal argument must exhibit "pristine logic."In order to exhibit "pristine logic," a legal argument should adhere to the form of the logical syllogism.

A syllogism consists of a major premise, a minor premise, and a conclusion. A major premise usually states a general rule. In legal arguments, this is generally a statement of law. A minor premise makes a factual assertion about a particular person or thing or a group of persons or things. In legal arguments, this is usually a statement of fact. A conclusion connects the particular statement in the minor premise with the general one in the major premise, and tells us how the general rule applies to the facts at hand. In legal arguments, this process is called applying the law to the facts.[62]

> Example: A member of the Senate or House of Representatives will be liable for recall if (1) if there is presented to the Chairman of the Independent Electoral Commission (INEC) a petition in that behalf signed by one-half of the persons registered to vote in that member's constituency alleging their loss of confidence in that member and (2) the petition is thereafter in a referendum within 90 days of the date of receipt of the petition approved by a simple majority of the votes of the persons registered to vote in that member's constituency. (Major premise, states a rule of law) The votes cast in support of the petition for recall of a Senator

[60] *Ibid.*

[61] *Ibid.*

[62] A. Malec, "Studies in Logic, Grammar and Rhetoric" (University of Bialystok; 2001), 17-24 malec@hum.uwb.edu.pl. Accessed on 23/08/2012.

is less than a simple majority of the number of registered voters in the constituency. (Minor premise; makes a statement of fact) Therefore the Senator cannot be recalled. (Conclusion, correctly applies the law to the facts).[63]

In order for a syllogism to be valid, it must be logically impossible for its premises to be true and its conclusion to be false. In other words, a syllogism is valid if, given the truth of its premises, the conclusion "follows" logically such that it, too, must be true. Note that an argument is not valid simply because its premises and conclusion are all true. Consider this example:

Example: "All cats are mammals. Some mammals are excellent swimmers. Therefore, some cats are excellent swimmers."

Explanation: Each of these statements is true. Cats are indeed mammals. Some mammals (e.g. whales and dolphins) are excellent swimmers. And, as it happens, some cats (e.g. tigers and jaguars) are also excellent swimmers. But this argument is not valid. The fact that cats are mammals and that some mammals are excellent swimmers does not prove anything about the swimming ability of cats. Based on the information given in the premises, it is logically possible that no cat in the history of the world has ever stepped foot in water. Because it is logically possible for the premises to be true and the conclusion to be false, this argument is not logically valid.

The example above is a fallacious argument. Learning how to spot and avoid such logical fallacies can enormously strengthen your legal writing and advocacy by helping you adhere to the "pristine logic" of correct syllogistic reasoning.[64]

However useful syllogistic logic may be in testing the validity of conclusions drawn from given premises, it is inadequate as a method of reasoning in certain aspects of law, where the premises are not given but must be created. Legal rules, viewed as major premises, are always subject to qualification in the light of particular circumstances.[65] It is a rule of Nigerian, English and American law, for example, that a person who intentionally strikes another is civilly liable for battery, but such a rule is subject, in legal practice, to infinite modification in the light of possible defence (for example, self-defence, defence of property, parental privilege, immunity from suit, lack of jurisdiction, insufficiency of evidence, etc.). In

---

[63] Section 69 of the 1999 Constitution of Nigeria (as amended in 2011).

[64] *Ibid.*

[65] *Ibid.*

addition, life continually presents new situations to which no existing rule is applicable; we simply do not know the legal limits of freedom of speech, for example, since the social context in which words are spoken is continually changing. Thus legal rules are continually being made and remade.

Also the "minor premises"—the facts of particular cases or the terms of particular legal problems—are not simply "there" but must be perceived and characterized, and this, too, requires interpretation and evaluation. Indeed, the legal facts of a case are not raw data but rather those facts that have been selected and classified in terms of legal categories.[66]

Finally, the conclusion, that is, the application of the rule to the particular case or problem, since it is a responsible decision directly affecting particular people in particular situations, is never mathematically inevitable but always contingent upon the exercise of judgment. In the telling words of Immanuel Kant, "there is no rule for applying a rule"; that is, there are no rules that can tell us in advance, with certainty, how a particular judge (legislator, administrator, etc.) ought to resolve a concrete case or problem that is before him—and this would be true even though we were able to say in advance what rules are relevant to such a resolution. Once a legal conclusion is reached, it may often be stated in syllogistic form; but in the process of reaching it, the determination of the major and minor premises may have come last.[67]

To say that legal reasoning cannot be reduced to the classical rules of formal logic is not, however, to deny that it has logical qualities. It is characteristic of legal reasoning that it strives toward consistency both of legal rules and of legal judgments; such a striving for consistency is implicit in the belief that law should apply equally to all who are subject to it and that like cases should be decided in a like manner. Even the judgments of the ancient Greek oracles were believed to reflect a hidden consistency.

Judicial Precedent Analogy

Judicial precedent or the doctrine of *stare decisis* presupposes that there is a hierarchy of courts in a judicial system and that the decisions of the higher courts bind the lower ones. However, it is the *ratio decidendi* (i.e. the principles on which the cases were decided) of these decisions that actually bind the lower courts who are expected to follow them in deciding

---

[66] *Ibid*

[67] *Ibid.*

similar cases.[68] This is consistent with the characteristics of legal reasoning which strives towards continuity in time; it looks to the authority of the past, embodied in previously declared rules and decisions, and it attempts to regulate social relations in such a way as to preserve stability.

The most pervasive form of legal logic is that of analogy, in the broad sense of the comparison and contrast of similar and dissimilar examples. Analogical reasoning is implicit in the striving for consistency; the striving for continuity (that is, historical consistency) also involves analogical reasoning, the analogies being found in past experience; similarly, the dialectical quality of legal reasoning involves comparison and contrast between the examples put forward by the opposing sides. (It should be noted that the term "analogy" also has a technical legal meaning, signifying the extension of a legal category to a situation which is "similar to" but not "the same as" those situations which the category "logically" includes; in contrast, we use the term "analogy" here more broadly and include under it the process by which it is determined that one situation is "the same as" another).[69]

In a legal system such as that of Nigeria, England or the United States, which stresses the authority of past judicial decisions (precedents), analogical reasoning in adjudication characteristically takes the form of (*a*) comparison of the fact situation before the court with the fact situations of previously decided cases in order to find a previously decided case whose fact situation is comparable; (*b*) extraction from the previously decided comparable case of the principle upon which that case was decided; and (*c*) application of that principle to the case at hand. It is generally recognized that each of these three steps is dependent upon the other two.

Conclusion

It is important that the National Assembly and the State Houses of Assembly in Nigeria should note the scope and limit of their legislative powers and legislate within the confines of such powers so that their legislation is not declared invalid by the Supreme Court.

What appears incontrovertible is the fact that bills are anchored on policy considerations. It is therefore the duty of draftsmen and women to strive to grasp the intention of policy makers. It must however be noted that "policy makers" are a chain of people involved in the formulation of

---

[68] E. Malemi, supra note 13, 29.
[69] *Ibid.*

policies for the enactment of laws. The most crucial place to determine the policy behind any law is the legislative history or legislative reports of parliament. Therein lies the intention of parliament and all arguments for enacting any law. Therein lies the policy of the law.

An effective communication skill for a legislative draftsman is crucial. The demand of drafting legislation in such a manner as would be comprehensible to the intended users of the legislation makes it imperative that the draftsman communicates the meaning intended by policy makers in exactly the way they have been conceived.

In developing effective communication skills, the draftsman must understand the nature of legislation. They chronicle the policies of government on the way society should be governed. In view of this singular distinction, the language of legislation must aim for precision and clarity and avoid repetition. There must also be consistency in the use of language. The certainty of construction makes the law predictable and devoid of ambiguity.

An essential component of language is the 'word.' In the past, words were regarded as the smallest significant units of speech. That is no longer the prevailing view. Words however continue to be central to the language of law. Their proper deployment in sentences contributes to effective communication. Used improperly or without clarification in cases where they are capable of double meanings opens the resulting legislative draft to ambiguity and the possibility of being invalidated for vagueness. The best approach is to strive for precision and clarity.

Developing effective communication skills in legislative drafting is a continuing engagement for the legislative draftsman. It calls upon the draftsman to return to the basics and update his knowledge on language structure and the proper construction of sentences. It requires a consistency of purpose and a dogged determination to succeed. It requires receptiveness to criticisms from others. It requires a proper understanding of the policies behind proposed legislation, a commitment to capture the essential principles of that policy and a restraint from usurping the role of policymakers. These attributes combined are what makes a legislative draftsman effective in communication.

CHAPTER SEVEN

SOURCES OF LAW IN NIGERIA

JOSEPHINE OMI OBASOHAN[1]

Introduction

The word "source" generally means the origin or beginning of something. Sources of law therefore refer to authoritative rules and principles of law from judicial review. It also includes opinions and statements of jurist or legal scholars on legal issues, mostly recorded in textbooks, journals etc. In addition, Legislation, conventions, treaties and the customary law are also major sources of law. This chapter will examine the various areas from which our legal system can be sourced and how it has helped in enriching our laws.

Sources of law can be divided into two main categories, namely:

- ❖ Primary sources
- ❖ Secondary sources

Primary sources comprise of:

- ➢ English law (consisting of the received English law as well the extended English law).
- ➢ Nigerian legislation.
- ➢ Subsidiary Enactment; Nigerian case laws or judicial precedents
- ➢ Customary law (rules) including Islamic law where applicable.[2]
- ➢ International law.

---

[1] LL.M (DELSU), LL.B (Hons) EDSU, B.L., MPA (DELSU) Lecturer in Law, Benson Idahosa University, Benin City, Edo State, Nigeria. Email: jobasohan@biu.edu.ng.

[2] A. O. Sanni, *Introduction to Nigerian Legal Method* (Ile-Ife: Obafemi Awolowo University Press Limited, 2006), 245.

Secondary sources comprise of:

- Law reports.
- Textbooks.
- Legal periodicals.
- Law digest.
- Legal dictionaries.
- Newspapers, etc.

In addition, these sources could be classified into statutory and judicial materials, which are as follows:

a. Statutory Materials

1. The Constitution.
2. Nigerian legislation.
3. English law:
   (a) English statutes applied directly to Nigeria before Independence
   (b) Received English law (British laws received into Nigeria by local legislation:
      i. The common law.
      ii. The doctrines of equity.
      iii. Statutes of general application in force in England on the first day of January, 1900.
      iv. Statutes.
4. Customary law.
5. Islamic law.
6. International law.

b. Judicial materials

i. Judicial precedents
ii. Case law

Sources of Nigerian Law

The Oxford Dictionary defines the word "source" to mean a place, person or thing from which something originates.[3] The expression "sources of Nigerian law" is capable of bearing several meanings, depending on the context in which it is used. It could mean either the starting point of Nigerian law or the places from which the law can be gotten,[4] and also the origin from which a rule derives its validity.[5]

It must be pointed out here that only the primary sources can have binding force on a court of law in Nigeria; the mentioned secondary sources can merely serve for persuasive purposes and are usually relied upon where no primary source is available.[6]

The various sources are:

(I) The formal source of law or the legal source of law which includes:

- Constitution
- Statutory enactments
- Judicial precedents
- Local statutes (customs)

The formal source of law can also be regarded as the very foundation of the entire legal order.[7]

(II) The historical source of law includes:

- Local customs
- Moral and religious beliefs
- Business practices
- Human experience
- Consciences or reasoning
- Social economic and environmental factors
- Writing and opinions of jurists

---

[3] S. Hawker, Oxford English Dictionary 3rd ed., (New York: Oxford University Press, 2006), 668.

[4] J. O. Asein, *Introduction to Nigerian Legal System*, 2nd ed., (Lagos: Abab Press Ltd, 2005), 22.

[5] N.O. Osita, *Modern Nigerian Legal System,* (Enugu: CIDJAP Publishers; 2002), 40.

[6] A. O. Sanni, supra note 2, 125.

[7] *Ibid.*

(III) The literary source (material source) of law includes:

- Statute books,
- Law reports
- Textbooks
- Law digest
- Periodicals
- Encyclopaedias etc.

The Constitution

The Constitution of the Federal Republic of Nigeria is superior to all other laws of the land and regulates the judicial, executive and legislative organs.[8] The States and the Federation have legislative powers in accordance with the provisions of the Constitution. They became a Federal State after many years of existence as a unitary country, having been ruled by Great Britain for a century as her dependent territory, thereby influencing the sources of her laws.[9]

The Constitution under a military regime—one characteristic feature of all past military administrations in Nigeria—is the arrogation of ultimate power to themselves. Unlike civilian governments which, as elected representatives of their constituencies, derive their legislative authority from the Constitution (as the supreme law of the land), military regimes, in fact, subdue the Constitution.[10]

Nigerian Legislation

Nigerian legislation is a potent and formidable source of Nigerian law. It forms the most substantial portion of the *corpus juris* of Nigeria. It is the most precise and exact source of Nigerian law.[11] Nigerian legislation consists of statutes and subsidiary legislation. Statutes are laws enacted by the legislature, being the law-making arm of government, while subsidiary legislation is law enacted in the exercise of powers given by a statute.[12] They consist of rules, orders, regulations, bye-laws and other instruments

---

[8] *Constitution of the Federal Republic of Nigeria*, 1999 as amended in 2011, Section 1. See also *I.N.E.C v. Musa* (2003) 10 W.R.N 1.

[9] N. Tobi, *Sources of Nigerian Law,* (Lagos: MIJ Professional Publisher Limited, 1996), 59.

[10] J. O. Asein, supra note 4, 36.

[11] E. Malemi, *The Nigerian Legal System*, (Lagos: Princeton Publishing Company, 2009), 39.

[12] *Ibid*.

made under the authority of statutes.[13] The laws made by the National Assembly are Acts, while those made by the State Houses of Assembly are known as Laws. In a military regime, the laws made by the Armed Forces Ruling council or the ARC are known as decrees, while those made by the State Administrators are known as edicts.

Nigerian statutes consist of Ordinances, Acts, Laws, Decrees and Edicts. A piece of legislation or statute is a law enacted by a legislature, and it is usually in a written form or code. Though common law and equity remain important parts of Nigerian law, before and since independence, legislation or statutory enactment have been on the increase in power and coverage.[14]

Ordinances

Ordinances are the laws that were enacted by the colonial leaders for the entire region of Nigeria. An example of an ordinance is the Co-operative Society Ordinance of 1935.

Acts of Parliament

Acts are enactments by the National Assembly and are applicable in the whole Federation; examples of such include the Electoral Act 2006, Independent Corrupt Practice Act 2000, etc. They are assented to by the President.

Laws

Laws are enactments made by the State Houses of Assembly. They are only applicable to the State wherein they are made. These laws are signed by the Governor.

Decrees

Decrees are laws promulgated by the military, applicable throughout the country. Since the first military coup in 1966, successive military leaders have administered the country by decrees usually promulgated by the Ruling Army Council. However, this is no longer the case, since we are apparently under a democratically elected government.

---

[13] *Ibid*, p. 36.
[14] *Ibid*, p. 36.

Edicts

These are laws promulgated by the Military Administrator or Governor as the case may be for the administration of a particular State.

Rules

These are laws that guide certain categories of person, such as Civil Service Rules.

Bye-Laws

Bye-laws are laws enacted by the local government councils.

English Law

The received English law as a source of Nigerian law consists of common law, doctrines of equity, statutes and subsidiary legislation which has been introduced into Nigerian law by Nigerian legislation. They are applied by the courts in the administration of justice.

English Statutes applied directly to Nigeria before Independence

The British government came into Nigeria, bringing with them their laws which were referred to as English law. A number of reasons could be adduced for the introduction of English laws into Nigeria. Firstly, since the British government colonized Nigeria, the introduction of English law was a relic or by-product of colonialism.[15] Aside from the general influence of external values in the formulation of its laws, Nigeria has had a body of English laws imposed on it by its erstwhile colonial masters.[16] Secondly, English law could be seen to counter the inadequacy of customary law in coping with the growing commercial life of the new colony and the dynamics of colonial life.[17] This is coupled with the fact that customary law was treated as a question of fact that has to be proven to the satisfaction of the court before it was applied. Finally, the arrogance inherent in the colonial system viewed English law as the best form of law

---

[15] N. Tobi, (Supra note 9), 59.
[16] J. O. Asien, Supra note 4, 101.
[17] *Ibid.*

that could ensure the best form of justice, while most customary law was condemned as barbaric and crude.

Received English Law (British statutes received into Nigerian by Local Legislation).

A large number of English statutes have been pronounced by the courts to be of general application and as such are in force within jurisdiction.[18]

Examples are:

a) Fraudulent Conveyances Acts 1571.
b) Conveyancing Act 1881.
c) Settled Land Acts 1882 (as Amended).
d) Land Transfer Acts 1897.
e) Partition Acts 1868 and 1876.
f) Statutes of Frauds 1677.
g) Limitation Acts (Real Property Limitation Acts 1833 as amended in 1874).
h) Wills Acts 1837.
i) Infants Relief Acts 1874.
j) Fatal Accident Acts 1846 and 1864.
k) Sales of Goods Acts 1893.
l) Trustee Acts 1888.

This recognizes that not all statutes which qualify as statutes of general application in England can be exported to Nigeria. However, such English statutes can be applicable only when subject to relevant local enactment. In contrast to the position expressed above where there is no law in Nigeria applicable on a subject matter but such law exists in England, the applicable law on such subject matter would be the English law subject to its qualification as statute of general application[19]. It is doubtful if statute which does not answer to the description of statute of general application will have any bearing on filling up the lacuna described above.

---

[18] C. O. Okonkwo, *Introduction to Nigerian Law*, (London: Sweet and Maxwell, 1980), 1; see the case of *Chief Young Dede v. African Association* (1910)1 NLR 130.

[19] A. O. Obilade, *The Nigerian Legal System,* (Lagos: Spectrum Law Publishing, 1979), 69-79.

Statutes and Specified Matters

A statute is a formal written enactment of a legislative authority that governs a state, city or country. Statutes are considered as primary authority and sometimes referred to as legislation because they are established by the legislative enactment.

Ideally all statutes must be in harmony with the fundamental law of the land; in this case, the constitution. Furthermore, before a statute becomes a law, in some countries it must first be agreed upon by the highest executives.

Common Law

Section 45(1) of the Interpretation Act[20] which provides that "the Common Law of England and the Doctrines of Equity shall be in force" made it possible for these laws to become functional within jurisdiction. The common law evolved from the old common law courts, and from general and local customs prevailing in England. This law was originally known as *commune ley* in French law.

The term "common law" is used in several senses but as a division of Nigerian law, it means the law developed by the old common law courts of England, namely, the King's Bench, Queen's Bench, the Court of Common Pleas and the Court of Exchequer.[21] The common law of England evolved and originated from the basic and general customs of England. It seems that the word, 'law' acquired the appellation 'common' because its application cut across the entire populace, distinct from the different local customs.[22] The common law, with its inadequate writ system and technicalities, was anything but satisfactory and most litigants went away disappointed and without obtaining redress. While contending with the unavailability of remedies or suitable writs, litigants also had difficulties enforcing judgements against powerful and influential defendants.[23] As a result of the rigidity of the common law, hardship was occasioned (where laws or rules are applied strictly without room for flexibility) and led to injustice. This further hastened the development of equity by the Court of Chancery. Ultimately, resident law of England has always professed to be a complete system. That is to say, it has always had an answer to every case brought before it, even if the answer was only that

---

[20] 1964.

[21] A. O. Obilade, supra note19, 10.

[22] C.K. Allen, *Law in the Making*, 3rd ed., (Oxford: Clarendon Press, 1964), 542.

[23] J. O. Asien, supra note 4, 104.

no course of action existed in the circumstances.[24] It follows therefore that common law forms the residual law but on other matters customary law fulfils that role (e.g. in a chieftaincy dispute).

The Doctrines of Equity

Equity is the set of legal principles that supplement strict rules of law where their application would ordinarily operate hardship. Equity is commonly said to "mitigate" the rigours of common law. This allows the court to use its discretion by applying justice in accordance with natural law. These courts were presided over by the clergy.[25] The court came to be known as a court of conscience and this flexible form of justice was called equity. Equity stands for fair play and justice. Examples of these principles are injunction, trust, rescission, specific performance etc., which are practiced in our courts.

The following maxims reflect the general juridical philosophy of the court of equity:

1. Equity acts *in personam*.[26]
2. Equity will not suffer a wrong to be without a remedy.[27]
3. Equity follows the law.[28]
4. Equity looks to the intent rather than the form.[29]
5. Equity sees that as done that ought to be done.[30]
6. Equity imputes intent to fulfil an obligation.[31]
7. Equitable remedies are discretionary.[32]
8. Delay defeats equity.[33]
9. He who comes into equity must come with clean hands.[34]
10. He who comes to equity must do equity.[35]

---

[24] A. E. W. Park, *The Sources of Nigerian Law,* (London: Sweet and Maxwell, 1963), 19.
[25] Ekerete Utioh, http://articlevoice.blogspot.com, accessed on 18/08/2012.
[26] *B.J. Export & Chem.CO. Ltd v. Kadunna Refining & Petro-Chem. Co. Ltd* (2003) FWLR (pt 165) 445.
[27] *Alaka v. Alaka* (1904) 1N.L.R 55.
[28] *Archibong v. Duke* (1926) 4 N.L.R 92.
[29] *George v. Fajore* (1939) 15 N.L.R.1.
[30] *Savage v. Sarrough* (1937)13N.L.R. 141.
[31] *Ojule v. Okoya*(1968) 2All N.L.R 342.
[32] *Ibeziako v. Abutu* (1954) 3 E.N.L.R 24.
[33] *Oil field Supply Centre Ltd v. Johnson* (1987) 2 N.W.L.R 625.
[34] *Brown v. Adebanjo* (1986) 1 N.W.L.R 383.

11. Where there are equal equities, the law will prevail.[36]
12. Where there are equal equities, the first in time prevails.[37]
13. Equity, like nature does nothing in vain.
14. Equality is equity.[38]

Statutes of general application in force in England on the first day of January, 1900

These are laws enacted and applicable in England before 1900 and implied to have been enacted in Nigeria. Examples of such are the Sale of Goods Act 1893, Infant Relief Act 1874, and Statutes of Fraud 1677.

Customary Law

The word "customary" means according to or relating to custom or usage; it means founded on or growing out of, or dependent on a custom.[39] This is the basic meaning it conveys in law. Taking this definition further, customary law generally means a law relating to the custom or usage of a given community. Customary law emerges from the traditional usage or practice of a people in a given community, which, by common adoption and acquiescence on their part, and by long and unvarying habit has acquired, to some extent, an element of compulsion and force of law with reference to the community.[40]

Customary law consists of unwritten customs accepted by members of a community as binding among them. It is "a mirror of accepted usage" and flexible because its rules change from time to time, thus reflecting social change and economic conditions. Putin a more simplistic form, the customs, rules and traditions which govern the relationship of members of a community are regarded as the customary laws of the people.[41] Thus it would be proper to say that customary law means the acceptable usage of the rules and customs of people indigenous to some part of Africa which govern their day to day activities.

---

[35] *Ibidapo v. Lufthansa Airlines* (1997) 4 N.W.L.R (pt 498)124.

[36] *Martins v. Malade* (1930) 9 N.L.R. 53.

[37] *John Holt (Nig) Ltd v. Halt African Workers Union of Nigeria & Cameroon* (1963) 1 All N.L.R 397.

[38] *Taiwo v. Lawani* (1961) All N.L.R 703.

[39] A. B. Garner, *Black's Law Dictionary* 9th ed. (St. Paul, Minnesota: West Group, 2009).

[40] *Ibid*, p. 25.

[41] N. Tobi, supra note 9, 103.

In *Owoniyin v. Omotosho,*[42]the plaintiff alleged that his ancestor was the first to settle on the land in dispute; that the defendant's ancestor came later and farmed with the permission of the plaintiff's ancestor; that in recent years the two families agreed jointly to apportion parts of the land to newcomers; that when one Onitabo encroached on the land in 1946, the defendant, with the consent of the plaintiff, sued and ejected him, but afterwards began to behave as if the land was his; and the plaintiff claimed in a declaration that the land belonged to both families according to native law and customs. The defendant alleged that his ancestors founded the land, and the plaintiff's ancestors came later to settle with him; that the defendants' family allocated land to tenants without reference to the plaintiff's family, and the defendants sued Onitabo without reference to the plaintiff; and that after ejecting Onitabo, he started to allocate land to people and the plaintiff began to interfere.

The judge held that on the evidence of the plaintiff, the land belonged to both families, but was reluctant to accept that an original owner and settler made a stranger a joint owner. The court also held that native law and custom is a mirror of accepted usage.

In *Ojisua v. Aivebelehin,*[43] the appellants claimed against the respondent the sum of N2, 000.00 for general damage caused by trespass on the land situated at Umuegua farmland, Ososo. The matter was initially heard by the district Customary Court of Ososo and judgment was delivered on the 6th October 1994. Dissatisfied, the appellants appealed to the Customary Court of Appeal, which also gave judgment against the appellants on the issue of jurisdiction raised by them. The appellants appealed to the Court of Appeal. The court held that customary law is a law relating to the customs and traditions of a people, and affects the cultures and ethos of the people. The element of law in the custom is important; though it is not common law and is not a law enacted by any competent legislature in Nigeria, it is enforceable and binding within Nigeria as between parties.

Having been able to put the definition in place, we are now able to briefly discuss the characteristics of customary law, which are as follows:

(a) It must be in existence;
(b) It must be custom as well as law;
(c) It must be acceptable;
(d) It is largely unwritten and related to its unwritten nature is its flexibility; and

---

[42] (1961)1 All NLR 304.
[43] (2001) 11 NWLR Pt. 723, p. 44.

(e) It should be universally applicable within the area of acceptability.

Customary laws are recognised as binding in the day-to-day dealings of the local communities to which they belong. However, they are subject to validation as such by the relevant statutes. The method adopted in this country is to make each rule of customary law that is to be applied subject to formal endorsement by the court.[44] The element of law in a custom is however important because it is that which in reality carries sanction in the event of breach. In *Meribe v. Egwu*,[45] the Supreme Court held that a customary law which permits the marriage of a woman by another woman is repugnant to natural justice, equity and good conscience by virtue of Section 18 (3) of the Evidence Act.[46]

The rules of customary law are subject to the test of validity as prescribed by statute. Customary laws are enforced by any court of law in Nigeria after the test of validity has been passed.

Repugnant to natural justice, equity and good conscience

The courts have never clearly explained the meaning of the repugnancy clause. However, the decisions and opinions expressed by them in some of the cases that have come before them points to the conclusion that any rule of customary law which is considered to be unjust, unfair or unconscionable, fails the repugnancy test and is therefore invalid and unenforceable.[47] In *Solomon v. Gbabo*,[48] the court struck out a custom that attempted to restrict the freedom of divorce action by married women. The Okrika custom that allows a husband to divorce his wife at will but does not allow the wife to be set free unless the husband agrees or consents to her divorce, was held to be repugnant to natural justice, equity and good conscience.

---

[44] J. O. Asien, (Supra note 4), 119.

[45] (1979)3 S.C.23; *Olagbemiro v. Ajagungbade* 111(1990) 3 NWLR (Pt.136) p. 37.

[46] 2011.

[47] A. J. Beredugo, *Nigerian Legal System: an Introductory Text*, 3rd ed. (Lagos: Malthouse *Press* Limited, 2009), 63.

[48] (1974) UILR (Pt. 111) 396; *Edet v. Essien* (1932) 11 N.L.R. 47; *Mariyama v. Sadiku Ejo* (1961) N.R.N.L.R 81.

Incompatible either directly or by implication with any law for the time being in force

A rule of customary law on a subject matter is incompatible with a local statute or subsidiary legislation if the local enactment is manifestly intended to govern the subject matter to the exclusion of customary law.[49]For an example of this, see the case of *Aoko v. Fagbemi,*[50]where the accused was convicted of adultery in a customary court; on appeal to the high court, the conviction was quashed because it violated the applicant's constitutional rights in as much as she had not violated any written law, and as such, the native laws and customs for which she was convicted were incompatible with the express provision of the Nigerian Constitution, which states that no person shall be convicted of a criminal offence unless that offence is defined and penalty therefore is prescribed in written law.

In *Rotibi v. Savage,*[51]the court had to determine whether the parties intended English law to govern their transaction. In view of the facts, the learned judge Waddington, J noted that "the giving and taking of promissory note is very strong evidence that the parties intended their transaction to be governed exclusively by English law …"

Contrary to Public Policy

The term public policy is not defined under the Evidence Act. However, it could rightly be argued that if a particular custom is repugnant to natural justice, equity and good conscience, or incompatible with any local enactment, then such a customary law is equally against public policy.[52] In *Cole v. Akinyele*[53] the Supreme Court held invalid a particular custom on the ground that it was contrary to public policy.

Islamic Law

Islamic law, as the name implies, gets its name from Islam, the religion and way of life of Muslims.[54] Islamic law is therefore the law of Islam. Being a divine law makes it not subject to change. It is too important,

---

[49] *Ibid.*

[50] (1961)1 All N.L.R. 400; *Adesubokan v. Yinusa* (1971) N.W.L.R.71.

[51] (1944) 17 NLR 77; *Agidigbi v. Agidigbi* (1992) 2 NWLR pt 221 p. 98; *Pawodu v. Danmole* (1958) 3 FSC 46.

[52] *Ibid.*

[53] (1960) 5 F.S.C. 84.

[54] N. Tobi, supra note 9, 135.

unable to be removed or changed, thereby making it constant. It is known to have been received from Almighty Allah and must be obeyed by the Islamic sect. Its religion is however based on the Qur'an and not the Bible.[55] This was further illustrated in the case of *Wan v. Ibrahim.*[56]The respondent in this case sought for and on behalf of one Ibrahim Wndil at the Upper Area Court the inheritance of the estate of one late M. Sirake. The Upper Area Court entered judgment against the respondent.

The court of appeal quashed the decision of the Sharia Court of Appeal, which affirmed the decision of the Upper Area Court and made an order that the Sharia Court of Appeal retry the case by a different panel. The Sharia Court of Appeal reversed the decision of the Upper Area Court. On appeal to the High Court, the High Court transferred the appeal to the Sharia Court of Appeal, which allowed the appeal. The appellant further appealed to the Court of Appeal. The court held that the original and primary source of Islamic law is the Holy Koran, by virtue of the provision of Chapter 49, verse six, of the Holy Koran, which states that no judge shall give judgment on any issue brought before him without conducting proper investigation.

International Law

The law that regulates legal relations among sovereign nations is known as international law. International law is the consensual rules developed from the customs, practices and treaties which sovereign nations apply in regulating their relationship.[57]

Starke,[58] defines international law as:

> that body of law which is composed for its greater part of the principles and rules of conduct which the States feel themselves bound to observe, and, therefore, do commonly observe in their relations with each other, and includes also the rules of law relating to the functioning of international institutions or organizations, their relations with each other, and their relations with States and individuals...

It therefore becomes a source of Nigerian law, especially when it is domesticated in Nigerian law as required by Section 12 (1) of the 1999 Constitution of Nigeria, as amended 2011. It states; "No treaty between

[55] *Ibid.*
[56] (1997) 9 NWLR pt. 519 p. 160.
[57] A. Obilade, supra note 19, 64.
[58] A.J Beredugo, supra note 47, 4.

the Federation and other country shall have the force of law except to the extent to which any such treaty has been enacted into law by the National Assembly."

Thus international law is a source of Nigerian law, just as it is a source of law in many countries.[59] International law is subdivided into public international law and private international law. Public international law is the aspect of international law that deals generally with the legal relationship between independent state and international organizations, while private international law refers to the body of rules which regulate the rights of individuals residing in foreign countries.[60]

Judicial Precedents

Precedent is one of the sources of law. It is also the principles of law upon which a judicial decision is based. This entails judgments passed by some learned jurist. Where there is no law on a particular point which arises in changing conditions, the judge depends on their own sense of right and wrong. The decision of a court of superior jurisdiction binds a court of subordinate jurisdiction. These decisions become an authority or guide for subsequent cases of a similar nature. Judicial precedents are a direct consequence of common law practice.[61] It gives room for orderliness in our legal system and practice.

Case Law

Case law refers to that body of principles and rules of law which, over the years, have been formulated or pronounced upon by the courts as governing specific legal situations.[62] These are decisions of the courts or judgments used in law reporting. These decided cases are reduced to an arrangement called law reports. Case law can be defined as an existing valid judgment of a superior court of law which is regarded as a binding authority for deciding a different case with the same or a similar set of facts.[63] They serve as a reference for lawyers and the general public. There are law reports from Nigeria and outside the country. They include:

---

[59] E. Malemi, *The Nigerian Legal Method*, (Lagos: Princeton Publishing Co, 2010), 189.
[60] *Ibid.*
[61] Ekeretie Utioh. http.//articlevoice.blogspot.com, accessed on 09/08/2012.
[62] J. O. Asien, (supra note 9), 73.
[63] A. J. Beredugo, supra note 47, 35.

1 Chancery Report
2 All England Law Report
3 Kings Bench
4 Queen's Bench
5 West Africa Court of Appeal
6 All Nigerian Law Report
7 Supreme Court Quarterly Report
8 Supreme Court Cases
9 Nigeria Weekly Law Report
10 Federation Law Reports etc.

CHAPTER EIGHT

SECONDARY SOURCES OF LAW

CHUKWUEMEKA CELESTINE OKORO ESQ[1]

Introduction

'Sources of law' basically refers to the origin or background from which rules which regulate human conduct emanate or from which they derive binding force or validity. Every legal system owes its existence and validity to certain factors of law which trigger off the overall development of law. These factors are the sources of law. A learned author, T. O. Dada, once stated that "a mastery of the sources of law of a given society also enhances an understanding of the historical factors that have influenced the evolution of the laws to such a direction as it had taken."[2]

The phrase, 'sources of law' has been described as a three-dimensional legal phenomenon[3] which can be subjected to three distinct meanings, namely: ultimate origin of a legal system, materials containing the rules of law and the historical background of a legal system. These sources can be grouped into two broad categories, namely (i) primary sources and (ii) secondary sources. In this chapter, we will be dealing with the secondary sources.

---

[1] LL.M (Benin), LL.B (UNN), BL., Dip (ECS) LORCA, Lecturer, Department of Private and Property Law, Benson Idahosa University, Benin City; E-mail: cokoro@biu.edu.ng.

[2] T. O. Dada, *General Principles of Law*, 2nd ed., (Lagos: T.O. Dada & Co., 1998), 50.

[3] M. M. Gidado & S. S. Shikyil, *The Legal Province of Legal Method*, (Jos: Mono Expressions Ltd, 2010), 159.

Secondary Sources of Law

Secondary sources are publications which describe, comment on, or analyse the law (as opposed to primary sources which contain the actual text of the law). In other words, these sources are not the law and as such cannot be binding precedent. The courts, in consequence, do not have to follow them, though occasionally certain types of secondary sources of law can be used as persuasive authority. According to the American Library of Congress,[4] secondary sources of law offer an analysis, commentary or a restatement of primary law. They are used to locate and explain primary sources of law. These sources may influence a legal decision but they do not have the controlling or binding authority like the primary sources of law.

Examples of secondary sources include:

1. Legal encyclopaedias;
2. Periodical/articles/journals;
3. Treatises;
4. Restatements;
5. Loose leafs;
6. Legal dictionaries

Legal Encyclopaedias

Legal encyclopaedias are generally known to provide a general overview of the law on a variety of topics. They are a good introductory source if one (a researcher) knows little to nothing about an area of the law. Encyclopaedias can be general in nature or cover a specific jurisdiction.[5] Each legal encyclopaedia has many volumes, and has a subject index near the end of the set of volumes. To find encyclopaedia articles by subject, look up words related to your subject matter of research in the subject index. You will then be directed to a topic and section number. Find the volume of the encyclopaedias that includes the topic to which you are referred, and then look for a specific number within that topic.

---

[4] http:/www.loc.gov/law/help (accessed July 2012).

[5] There are legal encyclopaedias that discuss American law in general, including federal law and the most common types of state law. These are called national legal encyclopaedias. The two most popular ones are American jurisprudence and *corpus Juries speculum* which give general overviews of laws in a majority of U.S. states.

Periodicals/Articles/Journals

Periodicals and law review articles can be useful in obtaining an overview of an area of the law. They are helpful in finding references to primary and secondary authority (sources of law) as well as developing ideas for analyzing a question of first impression or resolving a conflict of law.

Unlike the encyclopaedias which are not usually updated regularly, periodicals, journals and articles provide more current information on a wide range of law subjects.

Treatises

Treatises provide in-depth treatment of a single subject such as contracts or constitutional law. They are often written by influential legal scholars and are well respected. There are usually treatises in every major area of the law. For instance, many are on Westlaw & Lexis.[6]

Restatements

Restatements of the law summarise in a concise manner the common law rules on a subject. They are basically what the majority of renowned authors say. Restatements are available in print and on Westlaw & Lexis and have been published in agency, conflict of laws, contract law, etc.

Loose Leafs

Conventionally, a loose leaf service is published in a binder and limited to a specific topic. Loose leafs contain a wealth of information including cases, analysis of administrative decisions and legal news. Legal practitioners usually resort to loose leafs because they are so specialized and can be used to monitor a specific area of law.

Legal Dictionaries

Legal dictionaries provide definitions of words in their legal sense or use. These publications provide a short definition for foreign and Latin

---

[6] One good example of Treatises is E. Allan Farnsworth, *Farnsworth on Contracts,* 3rd ed., (New York: Aspen publishers, 2004). Another example is *The New Wigmore*: *A Treatise on Evidence*, (New York: Aspen Law & Business, 2002).

legal words and phrases, refer to cases and other legal sources for authority and may give examples of the use of these words in various situations. Legal dictionaries also include tables which define legal abbreviations and acronyms. A leading example of a legal dictionary is Black's Law Dictionary.[7]

Importance of Secondary Sources of Law

It is generally accepted that secondary sources of law lack binding authority in contra-distinction to the primary sources which provide veritable binding influence and authority. Nevertheless, they remain useful in the following contexts:

1. Explanation of the law

Secondary sources often attempt to define and explain the nature of the law relevant to a queried subject, for instance, legal dictionaries and treatises. In most cases, they are used to obtain a background or overall understanding of a specific area of the law if one is unfamiliar with an area of law. Legal encyclopaedias, treatises and periodicals are useful for these purposes.

2. Contextualization

The secondary sources of law provide a broader analysis of the law by presenting an extended and organized overview of a legal topic.[8] Secondary sources more often than not are used to locate primary authority (the law) on a question under research. In other words, they offer a useful guide in statutory and case law research.[9]

3. Persuasive Authority

Secondary sources of law occasionally provide strong persuasive authority in the judicial resolution of legal issues and as such exert considerable influence upon the development of the law.

---

[7] A. B. Garner (ed.) *Black's Law Dictionary*, 9th ed., (St. Paul, Minnesota: West Group, 2009).

[8] Andrew Plumb-Larrick, *The Many Values of Secondary Sources*, 11th October, 2011, The Judge Ben C. Green Law Library (www.lawlibrary.case.edu).

[9] A good example in this regard is the American Law Reports (ALR) and Digests.

They can also be relied upon by the court when reaching a decision if necessary, when there is no primary authority governing a legal question. Examples include law reviews, treatises and restatements.

Conclusion

The importance of a study of the sources of law for a particular legal system cannot be over-emphasized. An average researcher on any law subject can scarcely make meaningful headway without an understanding of the root base or the substructure upon which all other superstructures of law are based, the substructure being the sources of law. Furthermore, a good grasp of the formal sources of law will no doubt facilitate a clear conception of the processes by which law derives its validity.

CHAPTER NINE

USE OF SOURCE MATERIALS

THERESA UZOAMAKA AKPOGHOME[1]

Introduction

This chapter deals with the use of source materials in legal writing or research. This topic is very important because a research effort will be frustrated except if one is able to locate the sources one needs in a library. Knowing how to navigate a library or access data online will make research efforts easier. In order to help the growing number of students and staff in this area, this chapter has been divided into eight sections. Section one deals with the concept of legal research, and its aim and objectives. Section two deals with the law library and the law librarian, while section three deals with the types of materials to be found in the law library. The fourth section will deal with the arrangement of library materials using various classification schemes, particularly the Moys Classification Scheme, as well as the use of the library catalogue. The fifth section will treat legal opinion, and how to read and understand it. The sixth section will discuss note taking and analysis; the seventh section will discuss the use of authorities in legal argument, and the eighth and final section will focus on legal writing. For a better understanding of the use of source materials in legal research, it is necessary to first understand the concept of research.

---

[1] PhD (UNIJOS), LL.M (Benin), LL.B (Calabar), Senior Lecturer, Faculty of Law, Benson Idahosa University, Benin City, Edo State, Nigeria. Email: takpoghome@biu.edu.ng, teremajor@yahoo.com, teremajor@gmail.com.

What is Research?

Research in common parlance refers to a search for knowledge. It can also be defined as a scientific and systematic search for pertinent and very important information on a specific topic. Research is an art of scientific investigation. It is "a careful study of a subject especially in order to discover new facts or information about it."[2] Some people have considered research to be a movement, from the known to the unknown. It is actually a voyage of discovery. Research is an academic activity and as such the term should be used in a technical sense. It is thus, an original contribution to the existing stock of knowledge making for its advancement. In fact, the search for knowledge through objective and systematic methods of finding a solution to a problem is research.

Legal Research

Legal research is the process of identifying and retrieving information necessary to support legal decision making. In a broad sense, legal research includes each step of a course of action that begins with an analysis of the facts of a problem and concludes with the application and communication of the results of the investigation.[3] Thus, legal research is the careful and detailed study of facts and law in order to achieve a desired legal result, for instance, to find applicable laws, principles, rules, case law, facts, arguments, ideas, the writings of other jurists or persons or to discover useful information that will help to achieve a desired legal point or purpose.[4] The processes of legal research vary according to the country and the legal system involved. However, a legal researcher must find primary sources of law in a given jurisdiction;[5] there is also the need to find secondary sources[6] of law for background information about a legal topic, and finally search for non-legal sources for investigation or supporting information. Legal research is performed by anyone with a need for legal information and these include lawyers, law students, judges,

---

[2] *The Oxford Advanced Learner's Dictionary of Current English*, 7th ed., (Oxford: Oxford University Press, 2005), 1242.

[3] J. J. Myron and M. M. Roy, *Fundamentals of Legal Research*, 8th ed., (Foundation Press, 2002), 1.

[4] E. Malemi. *The Nigerian Legal Method*, (Lagos: Princeton Publishing Co., 2010), 592.

[5] These include cases, statutes and regulations.

[6] The secondary sources include law reviews, legal dictionaries, legal treatises and legal encyclopaedias.

law librarians and legal assistants. The sources of legal information range from printed materials like books to free legal online sites such as findlaw.com, lawyers.com, lawteachers.com, LexisNexis, West Law and Bloomberg Law, Legapadia, and Compulaw.

Law libraries around the world provide research services to help their users find the legal information they need in law schools, law firms and other research environments. Many law libraries and institutions provide free access to legal information on the web, either individually or through collective action through resource sharing.

Aim and Objectives of Research

The aim of research is to find out the truth which is hidden and has not been discovered. The objective of research is to discover answers to questions through the application of scientific procedure. Although every research exercise has its specific purpose, the objectives are as follows:

(a) To gain familiarity with a phenomenon or to achieve new insight into it;
(b) To portray accurately the characteristics of a particular individual, situation or a group;
(c) To determine the frequency with which something occurs or with which it is associated with something else;
(d) To test a hypothesis of a causal relationship between variables;
(e) To find applicable law/statutes, case law or judicial precedents;
(f) To discover the works, writings, opinions or propositions of other jurists in the same or other jurisdiction;
(g) To identify the existing gaps and make a case for reforms;
(h) To help in the development of legal skills and capacity of legal professionals;
(i) To have enough legal materials in preparing a case in order to persuade the court;
(j) To meet the needs of clients and other challenges in the legal profession like the passing of examinations and interviews.

The Law Library

A law library is a library designed to assist law students, law lecturers, lawyers and judges and their law clerks and anyone else who finds it necessary to correctly determine the state of the law. Most universities with a law faculty have law libraries; at least one section of the university library will be devoted to law. Law libraries are also found in the courts and judge's chambers. The law libraries in the universities are attached to the faculty of law where they exist as a separate entity. The establishment of a law library is a prerequisite for the accreditation of any law faculty.

A conscientious law student will spend a lot of his/her time in the law library because a good lawyer is one who knows where to look for the law. For students to master the use of a law library there is the need for a guided tour organized by a member of staff or the law librarian. Presently in most universities, the law library is made up of the physical library of books and other materials and the E-library with internet access. Apart from having access to the internet, there are E-law materials that are very useful to students and they include Compulaw, Legalpadia, LexisNexis, etc. This software contains information in all areas of law with decided cases, statutes, journal publications, law maxims, law dictionaries and so forth.

The 21st century law student must avail himself of these opportunities if he is to make an impact in the field of law.

The Law Librarian

The law librarian is the person in charge of the law library. He is responsible for the day-to-day running of the law library and is directly responsible to the university librarian. To be a law librarian, one is expected to have both a qualification in the field of Library and Information Science, and also be a qualified lawyer, having been admitted to the Bar. Without these requisite qualifications, one cannot aspire to the position of a law librarian. It is an academic position in the university and the law librarian is expected to publish and obtain higher degrees in the fields of law and librarianship to remain relevant.

Apart from being in charge of the library, the librarian must also ensure that:

(a) There are relevant books, journals and law reports in the library;
(b) That all books, journals and other materials are properly catalogued, classified and arranged in the library;
(c) He/she is always available to offer information or advice on the use of the library;
(d) He/she must train his/her staff to be able to assist the users in locating relevant information in the library;
(e) He/she must ensure that the materials in the library are safeguarded against fire, flood and other hazards;

(f) He/she must ensure that the library is in a position to offer support services to its clients. For instance, the library should be able to offer photocopying, downloading of materials from the e-library, interlibrary lending, and bindery services;
(g) The law librarian should also coordinate the library officers and assistants under him to ensure that they carry out their responsibilities effectively.

Types of Book in a Law Library

There are several kinds of books and information materials in the law library. These materials are stocked to help broaden the scope of the students and help them become independent in their thinking and their general disposition towards issues that they will encounter as lawyers.

These information sources in the law library include:

(a) Textbooks;
(b) Law reports;
(c) Statute books;
(d) Reference books;
(e) Periodicals and journals;
(f) Newspapers and magazines.

(a) Textbooks

Textbooks in the law library may relate to any legal subject or related fields. They may be written by foreign or local authors. In Benson Idahosa University law library, books on all areas of law are stocked, e.g. Jurisprudence, Company Law, Labour Law, International Law, Intellectual Property Law, Land Law, Equity and Trust, Law of Evidence, Criminal Law, Commercial Transaction, Law of Torts, Environmental Law, International Humanitarian Law, Human Rights Law, Family Law, Nigerian Legal System, Law of Contract, Constitutional Law, Information Communication and Technology (ICT) Law, Legal Methods, etc. These textbooks are carefully arranged for easy access by students and other library users.

(b) Law Reports

Law reports contain the decision of the courts, including the Supreme Court, Court of Appeal and the High Courts. These reports are published in volumes and at such intervals as the publishers may determine, i.e. weekly, monthly, quarterly, etc.

We have the Nigerian law reports and foreign law reports. The Nigerian law reports include:

Supreme Court Report	- SC
Supreme Court of Nigerian Judgment	- SCNJ
All Nigerian Law Report	- All NLR
Nigerian Weekly Law Report	- NWLR
Federation Weekly Law Report	- FWLR
Weekly Law Report of Nigeria	- WLRN

The foreign reports include:

All England Law Report	- All ER
Kings Bench Reports	- KB
Queens Bench Reports	- QB
Weekly Law Reports	- WLR
Probate Reports	- P
Chancery Reports	- CH
English Reports	- ER
Common Wealth Law Reports	- CLR Commonwealth
All India Reports	- AIR India
Ghana Law Reports	- GLR Ghana
Dominion Law Reports	- DLR Canada

Journals and Periodical

Journals

Law journals are published by law faculties, bodies or persons all over the world. A law journal may be local or foreign. Nigerian law journals include the BIU Law Journal, UNIBEN Law Journal, Kogi State University Law Journal, University of Maiduguri Law Journal, Igbinedion University Law Journal, Delta State University Law Journal, UNIJOS Law Journal, Lagos State University Law Journal, Ambrose Alli University

Law Journal, University of Calabar Law Journal, Akungba Law Journal, Nassarawa State University Law Journal, University of Ife Law Journal, University of Ibadan Law Journal, etc.

Foreign law journals are also published by law faculties of universities, public and private organisations, and institutes across the world. These journals are numerous and include: American Journal of International Law, International Review of the Red Cross, Harvard Law Review, Yale Law Journal, Washington Law Review, African Yearbook on International Humanitarian Law, Washington University Journal of Law and Policy, Harvard Journal of Human Rights, African Security Review, International Law and Politics, Fordham International Law Journal, Stanford Journal of International Law, European Journal of International Law, Journal of Refugee Studies, Temple International and Comparative Law Journal, International Comparative Law Quarterly, Yale Law Journal, Journal of International Criminal Justice, Annual Survey of International Law and Comparative Law, and the Yale Journal of International Law.

The good thing about these international journals is that most of them can be accessed online at no cost to the student.

Reference Books

Reference books are those books containing facts and information on various subjects. They include dictionaries, encyclopaedias, brochures, catalogues, directories, lists of statutes, etc. Reference books may be local or foreign and they include:

Blacks Law Dictionary
Index to Nigerian Weekly Law Reports
Osborn's Concise Law Dictionary
Dictionary of Law
Halsbury's Laws of England
Encyclopaedia of the Laws of England, etc.

Statutes

Statutes are usually published in volumes as statute books. They are made up of the laws made by the States and National Assemblies and can be on any subject matter. They include the Laws of Federation of Nigeria both past and present, of all the 36 States of Nigeria e.g. The Laws of Edo State of Nigeria. Currently there is the Laws of Federation of Nigeria, 2004, and some of these have also been amended in 2007 and 2011.

Foreign statutes are also included here and may be found in the law library, for example Statutes of the Realm, which cover the period 1235 to 1713.

Newspapers and Magazines

Several newspapers and magazines are found in the library. They may be foreign or local. These are provided for information and relaxation.

Arrangement of Library Materials

In all libraries—public, private, academic or special—books are arranged in order on a shelf, section or room according to their subject, and this is achieved through a process known as cataloguing and classification. The basic tools used are the Anglo-American Cataloguing Rules II (AACR II), the Library of Congress Classification Scheme (LC), and the Dewey Decimal Classification Scheme (DDC). In the Benson Idahosa University Library, the Library of Congress (LC) is used, while the Law Library uses the Elizabeth Moys Classification Scheme.[7]

Library of Congress (LC)

The Library of Congress is the largest library in the United States of America. The classification scheme applies in the Library of Congress. It is the commonest system of classifying books in academic libraries worldwide. The scheme uses a combination of alphabets and figures to classify books. The classification begins with a letter followed by figures. Each book is classified and assigned a call number, which is the identification number with which the book can be traced on the shelf.

21 out of the 26 letters of the alphabet are used to represent broad subject areas and they are:

A - General
B - Philosophy
C - History (General)
D - History (Old World)
E - American History (General)
F - American History (Local & Latin American)

---

[7] *Moys Classification and Thesaurus for Legal Materials*, 4th ed., (Munchen: K.G. Saur Verlag GmbH, 2001), 1-552.

G - Geography
H - Social Sciences
J - Political Science
K - Law
L - Education
M - Music
N - Fine Arts
P - Language and Literature
Q - Science
R - Medicine
S - Agriculture
T - Technology
U - Military Science
V - Naval Science
Z - Bibliography

Books on the various subject areas are classified and arranged in a section, and using a combination of alphabets and figures, the sub-areas are identified and properly located. These numbers cannot be the same in all the academic libraries. The numbers are determined by the volumes of books available in a particular library. Examples of call numbers or identification numbers using the Library of Congress Classification Scheme include the following:

K61.M3 - Land Law by R.H. Maudsley.
K30.W9 - Administrative Law by H.W.R. Wade.
K24. S2 - Law of Torts by J.W Salmond.[8]

Here the letter K represents Law, 61 is an identity of the subtopic which is land law and the number 3 is a further identification of the book.[9]

Moys Classification and Thesaurus for Legal Materials

Like we noted earlier, the law library uses a specialized classification scheme known as Moys Classification Scheme. It is specifically designed for the classification of law materials. It makes use of a combination of two alphabets and numbers. The broad areas are as follows:

---

[8] E. Malemi, supra note 4, p. 604.
[9] *Ibid.*

K - Journals and Reference books
KA - Jurisprudence
KB - General and Comparative Law
KC - International Law
KD - Religious Legal Systems
KE - Ancient and Medieval Law
KF - Common Law, Primary Materials, British Isles
KG - Common Law, Primary Materials, America
KH - Common Law, Primary Materials, Australasia
KL - Common Law, treatises, general
KM - Common Law, treatises, public law
KN - Common Law, treatises, private law
KP - Preferred Jurisdiction
KR - Africa
KS - Latin America
KT - Asia and Pacific
KV - European
KW - European Community Law
KZ - Non Legal Subjects
Appendix 1 - Criminology
Appendix 2 - Civil Procedure Rules Terminology.

Example: KM 300; 346.4 Administrative Law by William Wade and Christopher Forsyth.

KM 31; 346.1 Constitutional and Administrative law by Hilaire Barneth.

KR 1467. 133 Law of Banking and Negotiable Instruments by K.I. Igweike.

Dewey Decimal Classification Scheme (DDC)

This scheme is mostly used in school libraries. The scheme makes use of the numbers 000-999. The difference between the Dewey Decimal Classification Scheme and the Library of Congress is that Dewey is used in school libraries and special libraries while Library of Congress is used by academic libraries. Dewey uses numbers while Library of Congress combines alphabets with numbers.

The subject areas covered by Dewey include:

000 -	009	:	General Books
100 -	199	:	Philosophy and Psychology
200 -	299	:	Religion
300 -	399	:	Social Sciences
400 -	499	:	Languages
500 -	599	:	Pure Sciences
600 -	699	:	Applied Sciences and Technology
700 -	799	:	Recreation and the Arts
800 -	899	:	Literature
900 -	999	:	Geography, History and Related Subjects.

Arrangement of Books in a Law Library

In a law library, books are arranged in a different section of the library according to their subject area, sub topic or group. For instance, all the books on Jurisprudence must be together; the same applies to company law and other subject areas. Statutes, textbooks, law reports and journals are all in different sections of the law library and the shelves are labelled for easy access. For law reports, the local and foreign reports are separated and arranged on different shelves. The foreign reports are arranged according to their countries of origin and their type.

To find a law report, the student must have the full details of a decided case. For instance:

Mojekwuv. Mojekwu (1997)7 NWLR (Pt. 512) p.283.CA,
Agidigbi v. Agidigbi (1992) 2 NWLR (Pt. 221) p.98 SC,
R v. Chima (1944) 10 WACA 223.

How to Identify a Book Using the Library Catalogue

When a reader walks into the library, he is not expected to go to the shelves to look for books. This is due to the fact that he may not be able to locate the materials he is looking for because the materials have been systematically arranged.

The first step is to consult the librarian or any of the library staff who will direct him accordingly or assist him in locating the material he needs. Usually, books are arranged either by using the author's surname, the title of the book, the subject area or in any other way the library deems fit. For instance, the library may arrange the books using the name of the publisher, place of publication, date of publication or the serial number.

This is where the library catalogue becomes essential. The library catalogue is a list of all the books and information available in a given library. The catalogue may be in the form of a book catalogue, or a card catalogue made up of cards measuring 3 x 5 inches arranged alphabetically in a wooden cabinet called the catalogue cabinet. Presently, most libraries do not have catalogue cabinets anymore because cataloguing is done online using the Online Public Access Catalogue (OPAC).

Information in catalogue cards are arranged using either the name of the author, title of the book or the subject matter of the book. The author(s) name which would be the surname is the major entry with respect to any book. This will be followed by the title of the book, the edition, publisher, year of publication, subject matter, number of pages, the serial number, and the measurements of the book. Using the author(s) name is very important because it is one of the quickest ways of identifying or locating a material in the library catalogue.

The library catalogue has several uses:

(a) The catalogue holds the information about the library stock;
(b) It saves the time of the library user because it makes searching easy;
(c) It helps the library and the users know the books that have been borrowed or the particular location of the library materials.

The catalogue cabinet is usually located at the entrance of the library, in the librarian's office or table or any other convenient location in the library.

Citation of Cases and Reports

Law reports are very important and constitute an essential tool for law students and practitioners. Decided cases from courts of records are contained in the law reports. These cases are referred to in addressing issues. It is this decision of higher courts that are referred to as judicial precedents. Judicial decisions from higher courts like the Supreme Court and Court of Appeal are binding on the lower courts such as the High Courts, whether Federal or State. The decision of the Supreme Court is also binding on the Court of Appeal but where there are two conflicting decisions of the Supreme Courts, the Lower Courts will be at liberty to choose, but this liberty will cease once the Supreme Court overrules itself.

It is essential that a student read the reported facts of a case if he/she is to understand the reason behind a decision. In reading the facts and the proceedings in a particular case, the student will discover that the court would have considered several principles of law in arriving at a decision and these principles are what the student will rely on in answering his examination questions or tackling any legal issue in the future.

Before one can locate a law report to read a particular case, the person must first and foremost get the citation of the case correctly. Once the citations are correct, locating the law report and identifying the particular case will be an easy task. This would include knowing the name of the parties in a particular case, the title of the law report, the part where the report is in parts, the year and sometimes the court that decided the case.

For instance:

Incorrect: *Mojekwu v. Mojekwu* NWLR p. 283
Correct: *Mojekwu v. Mojekwu* (1997) 7 NWLR (Pt. 512) p. 283, CA.

Opinions

In law, an opinion is usually a written explanation by a judge or group of judges that accompanies an order or ruling in a case, laying out the rationale and legal principles for the ruling. When two people disagree and that disagreement leads to a lawsuit, the lawsuit will sometimes end with a ruling by a judge in favour of one side. The judge will explain the ruling in a written document referred to as an "opinion." The opinion explains what the case is about, discusses the relevant legal principles, and then applies the law to the facts to reach a ruling in favour of one side and against the other.[10] Modern judicial opinions reflect hundreds of years of history and practice. They usually follow a simple and predictable formula. To understand an opinion one must learn the parts. They include:

a. The Caption

The first part of the case is the title of the case; for example, *Akpoghome v. Oshiobugie.* The title tells you the last names of the parties involved in the lawsuit. The names will indicate the party that is suing and the person being sued. These two sides are often referred to as the "parties" or the "litigants" in the case. In criminal matters, the cases are

---

[10] O. S. Kerr, "How to Read A Legal Opinion" *The Green Bag (GB),* Vol.11, No. 1, (2007): 51.

brought by State prosecutors. At the High Court the parties will read *The State v. Aideyan* or *The Attorney General of The Federation v. Jones.*

b. The Case Citation

Below the case name, one will find some letters and numbers. These letters and numbers are the legal citation for the case. A citation tells the researcher the name of the court that decided the case, the law report in which the opinion was published, and the year in which the Court decided the case. For example: *Agididgbi v. Agidigbi* (1992) 2 NWLR (Pt.221) p. 98 SC. In this case, the parties are *Agidigbi and Agidigbi*, the case was decided by the Supreme Court in 1992 and it was reported in the Nigerian Weekly Law Report, volume 2, part 221 at page 98.

c. The Author of the Opinion

Another important piece of information is the name of the judge who wrote the opinion. Sometimes an opinion will use the Latin phrase *"per incuriam"* instead of a judge's name. *Per incuriam* means "by the Court." It signals that the opinion reflects a common view among all the judges rather than the writing of a specific judge.

d. Facts of the Case

The first part of the body of the opinion presents the facts of the case; that is, what happened. The facts might be that Clinton pulled out a gun and shot Vincent, or that Vincent stole a handset belonging to Victory, or that Bobby had carried out a job for Jude and Jude has refused to pay. It is important to note that there are no particular rules for what facts a judge must include in the fact section of an opinion. Sometimes the recorded facts are long and sometimes they are short. Sometimes they are very clear and accurate, while at other times, the facts may appear vague or incomplete. The facts of the case will also cover the "procedural history" of the case. This history will explain how the dispute worked its way through the legal system to the court that is issuing the opinion. It will include the various motions, hearings and trials that took place after the case was initially filed.

e. The Law of the Case

After the presentation of the facts in the opinion, the law will be discussed. Most opinions present the law in two stages. The first stage discusses the general principles of law that are relevant to cases such as the one the court is deciding. This section may also explore the history of particular field of law or include a decision of past cases known as "precedents" that are related to the case the court is deciding. This part of the opinion gives the reader a background to help understand the context and significance of the court's decision. The second stage of the legal section applies the general legal principles to the particular facts of the dispute. This part is in many ways the heart of the opinion, since it goes to the bottom line of the reason the court is ruling for one side and against the other.

f. Concurring and/or Dissenting Opinions

Most of the opinions read by law students are "majority" opinions. When a group of judges get together to decide a case, they vote on which side should win and also try to agree on a legal rationale to explain why that side has won. A majority opinion is an opinion joined by the majority of judges on that court. Although most decisions are unanimous, some are not. Some judges may disagree and will write a separate opinion offering a different approach. This is called a "dissenting opinion" but where the judges agree it is known as a "concurring opinion." These opinions come after the majority opinion has been presented.

A "concurring opinion" explains a vote in favour of the winning side but based on a different legal rationale, while a "dissenting opinion" explains a vote in favour of the losing side. To conclude this section, it is needful to summarise the essentials in reading a case:

- know the facts,
- know the specific legal arguments made by the parties,
- know the disposition of the court,
- understand the reasoning of the majority opinion,
- understand the significance of the majority opinion and finally,
- understand any concurring and/or dissenting opinions.

Finally, these are two major reasons why we use the case method and they are:

1. The legal system we inherited from England is largely judge-focused. The judges have made the laws what they are through their written opinions. To understand that law, we need to study the actual decisions that the judges have written. Again, we need to learn to look at law the way that judges look at law and this is known as the historical reason.[11]
2. The second reason is that it teaches an essential skill for practicing lawyers. Lawyers represent clients, and clients will want to know how the law applies to them. To advise a client, a lawyer needs to understand exactly how an abstract rule of law will apply to the very specific situations a client might encounter. This is more difficult than one might think, in part because a legal rule that sounds definite and clear in the abstract may prove murky in application. For example, if one was at a public path and saw a sign that says "No vehicles in the park," that plainly forbids a car, but what about bicycles, wheelchairs, toy cars, aeroplanes or ambulances? Are these vehicles for the purpose of the rule or not? As a result good lawyers need a vivid imagination; they need to imagine how rules might apply, where they might be unclear, and where they might lead to unexpected outcomes. The case method and the frequent use of hypothetical's will help train the brain to think this way. Learning the law in light of concrete situations will help deal with particular facts to be encountered as a practicing lawyer.[12]

Note-Taking and Analysis

Note-taking is an essential part of the training for lawyers. This is due to the fact that no matter how much material one can retain just by memory, note-taking will be one of the most important skills to develop as one makes his/her way through law school. Good notes will help a student keep up during class discussions and will also become crucial when the time comes to outline and study for final examinations.[13] Listed here are some tips a law student should note.[14]

---

[11] *Ibid*, p. 62.
[12] *Ibid*, pp. 62-63.
[13] Michelle, Fabio "10 Do's and Don'ts for Note Taking in Law School," http://www.lawschool.about.com/od/survivinglawschool/a/notetaking.htm. Accessed on 27/07/2012.
[14] *Ibid*.

1. Choose a method of note-taking and stick with it. There are now lots of options for law school note-taking, from software programmes to the good old paper and pen method. Try some out early in the semester, but decide quickly which one is the best learning style and then keep going with it.
2. Consider preparing notes before class. Whether one does the classic case brief or something more free-flowing by using computer software or hand-written notes, always use a different colour or entirely different pages to separate class notes from personal notes. As the semester wears on the two should increasingly be converging; if not, one is probably not picking up important concepts and what your lecturers want you to focus on.
3. Write down important concepts, rules of law and lines of reasoning. These things may be difficult to pinpoint at first, but one gets better at this as one's study years go on.
4. Take note of recurring themes in your lecturer's lectures. Does he/she bring public policy into every discussion? Does he/she painstakingly parse words of statutes? When these themes are found, pay special attention and take particularly copious notes as to how the lecturer's reasoning is flowing: this way one knows what questions to prepare for both in lectures and examinations.
5. Review notes after class to make sure the recorded things are understood; if something is unclear either conceptually or factually, now is the time to clear it up either with classmates in a study group or with the lecturer.
6. Do not write down everything the lecturer says verbatim. This holds especially true if using a laptop. It can be tempting to transcribe lectures if one has the typing ability but one will be losing valuable time which one should have employed engaging with the material and group discussions. This after all is where learning takes place, not simply from memorizing and regurgitating rules and laws.
7. Don't write down what fellow law students say. Yes, they may be smart and some may even be right, but unless the lecturer puts his/her explicit seal of approval on a student's contribution to the discussion, it is most likely not worth a spot in one's notes. The tests will not be based on the opinions of a fellow student so there is no sense in recording them for posterity.
8. Do not waste time writing down the facts of the case. All the facts needed to discuss a case will be in the case book. If particular facts are important, highlight, underline, or circle them in the textbook with a note in the margin to remind yourself of their importance.

9. Do not be afraid to go back through several days of notes at the same time to try to make connections and fill the gaps. This review process will help at the time with class discussions and later when outlining and studying for exams.
10. Do not forgo taking notes because the notes can be gotten from a classmate. Everyone processes information differently so one is always going to be the best person to record notes for future study sessions. It is great to compare notes, but one's own notes should always be the primary source of studying. This is why commercial outlines and those prepared by previous law students are not always the most helpful either. Throughout the semester, the lecturer gives a map of what the exam will be like throughout the course; it is one's job to record it and study it.

Use of Authorities in Legal Argument

It is no secret to observe that lawyers have their own unique discipline and approach to the resolution of legal problems. Not surprisingly there are laws about determining the law. One of the most important of these laws is the law of precedent or *stare decisis.*[15]

The Doctrine of *Stare Decisis*

The operation of the doctrine of *stare decisis* is best explained by reference to the English translation of the Latin phrase *"stare decisis"* which means "to stand by decided matters." The phrase "*stare decisis*" is itself an abbreviation of the Latin phrase "*stare decisis et non quieta movere"* which translates as "to stand by decision and not to disturb settled matters."[16]

Under this doctrine, the decision of a higher court within the same jurisdiction acts as binding authority on a lower court within that jurisdiction. The decision of a court of another jurisdiction only acts as persuasive authority. For instance, the decision of the Supreme Court of Nigeria is binding on all the other courts in Nigeria but the decision of the Supreme Court of the United States of America will only have a persuasive effect on Nigerian courts.

[15] P. M. Perell, "Stare decisis and techniques of legal reasoning and legal argument" (1987) http://www.legalreasoning.org. Accessed on 27/07/2012.
[16] G. L. Gall, *The Canadian Legal System*, 2nd ed. (Toronto: Carswell Legal Publications, 1983), 220.

It is important to note that the degree of persuasiveness is dependent upon various factors:[17]

(a.) The nature of the other jurisdiction;
(b.) The level of the court which decided the precedent case in that other jurisdiction;
(c.) The date of the precedent case, on the assumption that the more recent the case, the more reliable it will be as authority for a given proposition, although this is not necessarily so;
(d.) The judge's reputation may affect the degree of persuasiveness of the authority.

In learning the law, *stare decisis* is described in practical terms thus:

> What the doctrine of precedent declares is that cases must be decided the same way when their material facts are the same. Obviously it does not require that all the facts should be the same. We know that in the flux of life all the facts of a case will never recur, but the legally material fact may recur and it is with these that the doctrine is concerned.[18]

It simply means that where the facts are relatively the same, the judgment is likely to be the same, but where there is an emergence of a new fact, the cases will be distinguished and a different decision will be reached by the court. Adherence to precedents must therefore be the rule rather than the exception if litigants are to have faith in the even-handed administration of justice in the courts.[19]

In *Sweney v. The Department of Highways*[20], Middleton J.A stated:

> But, in my view, liberty to decide each case as you think right, without regard to principles laid down in previous similar cases, would only result in completely uncertain law in which no citizen would know his rights or liabilities until he knew before what Judge his case would come and could guess what view that judge would take on a consideration of the matter, without any regard to previous decisions.[21]

---

[17] *Ibid.*

[18] G. Williams, *Learning the Law*, 9th ed., (1973), pp 67-68. See also S. M. Waddams, *Introduction to the Study of Law,* 2nd ed., (Toronto: Carswell, 1983), 102- 118.

[19] B. N. Cardozo, *The Nature of Judicial Process* (New Haven: Yale University Press, 1921), 9-50.

[20] (1933) O.W.N 783 (CA).

[21] *Ibid*, pp. 783- 4.

That the doctrine of *stare decisis* is related to justice and fairness may be appreciated considering the observation of American philosopher William K. Frankena as to what constitutes injustice. He opined that:

> The paradigm case of injustice is that in which there are two similar individuals in similar circumstances and one of them is treated better or worse than the other. In this case, the cry of injustice rightly goes up against the responsible agent or group; and unless that agent or group can establish that there is some relevant dissimilarity after all between the individuals concerned and their circumstances, he or they will be guilty as charged.[22]

The critics of the doctrine accept it as the general rule but chafe under it when the staleness of old law leads to unfairness and injustice. For instance, Lord Denning, the former Master of the Rolls argued thus:

> If lawyers hold to their precedents too closely, forgetful of the fundamental principles of truth and justice which they should serve, they may find the whole edifice come tumbling down about them. Just as the scientist seeks for truth, so the lawyer should seek for justice, just as the scientist takes his instances and from them builds up his general propositions, so the lawyer should take his precedents and from them build his general principles. Just as the prepositions of the scientist fail to be modified when shown not to fit all instances, or even discarded when shown in error, so the principles of the law should be modified when found to be unsuited to the times or discarded when found to work injustices.[23]

There is considerable literature about whether the doctrine of *stare decisis* is a good or bad one,[24] but the doctrine is usually justified by arguments which focus on the desirability of stability and certainty in the law and also notions of justice and fairness.

Stare Decisis and the Hierarchy of Court

In Nigeria, the Supreme Court is the highest court of the land, followed by the Court of Appeal and the High Courts, either Federal or State. The Federal and the State High Court have concurrent or co-ordinate jurisdiction but in respect of subjects listed in Section 251 of the Nigerian

---

[22] W. K. Frankena, *Ethics*. 2nd ed., (Englewood Cliffs: Prentice-Hall Inc, 1973), 49.
[23] The Rt. Hon. Lord Denning, *The Discipline of Law* (London: Butterworths, 1979), 292.
[24] *Ibid*, pp. 285 – 314.

Constitution as amended the Federal High Court exercise exclusive jurisdiction. These are the courts of record. Therefore, on issues of *stare decisis*:

- The Supreme Court is not bound to follow its own prior decision, especially where there is a new decision on the matter which has properly reconciled the competing interests involved;
- The Court of Appeal is bound by the decision of the Supreme Court but where there is a conflicting decision of the Supreme Court on a particular subject matter, the Court of Appeal will be at liberty to choose either of the decisions;
- The Court of Appeal is not bound to follow the decision of the appellate court of another jurisdiction;
- The Court of Appeal will generally be bound by its own prior decision unless the liberty of the subject is involved or unless the prior decision was given *per incuriam;*[25]
- All the High Courts, including the Federal High Court, are bound by the decision of the Court of Appeal;
- The decisions of coordinate courts are not binding; however they are highly persuasive.[26]

Legal Argument When There is a Precedent

Thus, noting the court ranking of the judge before whom the lawyer will be appearing and guided by the doctrine of *stare decisis*, the lawyer will then prepare his or her argument. Usually the best position for the lawyer occurs when there is a precedent case supporting his or her client's case. The lawyer will then argue that the court is either bound, or that the court if not bound ought to be persuaded by the precedent case to find in the clients favour. In his/her research, the lawyer will therefore look for cases with results which support the client's position and will prepare to argue that the *ratio decidendi* of those precedent cases cover the facts of the case at hand. Please note that skill is necessary to analyse and organize the material facts of both the precedent case and the case at hand.

The techniques that are available are a consequence of accepting and then manipulating the doctrine of *stare decisis*. The techniques structure

---

[25] That is, if the decision was given inadvertently without consideration of an applicable authority or statutory provisions.

[26] This is because of the concept of judicial comity, which is the respect one court holds for the decision of another.

and direct the lawyer's reasoning and argument. The following are generally recognized:

1. The lawyer can argue that the precedent case does not stand for the legal proposition for which it has been cited. In other words, the lawyer articulates the *ratio decidendi* of the case differently.
2. The lawyer can argue that while the precedent case does articulate the legal proposition for which it has been cited, nevertheless the proposition was *obiter dicta* (things said by the way).[27]
3. The lawyer can argue that while the precedent case does stand for the legal proposition for which it has been cited, the case has been effectively overruled by a decision of a higher court or by the introduction of a new law/statute.
4. The lawyer can argue that while a precedent case does stand for the legal proposition for which it has been cited, the case at hand is different; that is, the cases are factually distinguishable.
5. Where the case being relied upon has a built-in public policy factor, the lawyer who wishes to distinguish the case may argue that public policy has changed, and while the legal principle of the precedent case is still good law, it is distinguishable because of the change of circumstances. See *Nordenfelt v. Maxim Nordenfelt Cums and Ammunition Co.*,[28] an important case with respect to the principle that contracts in restraint of trade may be voidable on grounds of public policy.
6. The lawyer can argue that while the precedent case does stand for the legal proposition for which it has been cited, there is another precedent of equal weight which stands for the opposite proposition. The lawyer then goes on to argue that it is that other case which the court should follow.[29]

---

[27] Subject to an exception for considered pronouncements of the law by appellate courts, comments by the judge which are not part of the *ratio decidendi* are *obiter dicta* and are theoretically not binding in a subsequent case.

[28] (1894) A.C 535.

[29] This type of argument is related to but ultimately different from the "*per incuriam* argument" because it does not necessarily challenge either decisions as having been given *per incuriam*. The rule is rather that the court may decide which one of the conflicting decisions to follow.

Legal Argument When There Is No Binding Precedent

1. Where a lawyer cannot find a binding precedent he/she may rely on a non-binding precedent from another jurisdiction. While not obliged to do so, the court may be impressed with or persuaded by the reasoning and may be prepared to adopt the rule established by the foreign case.
2. Where no binding precedent exists, the lawyer may form a legal argument from first principles. This approach identifies legal principles from decided cases and argues that while the factual circumstances of the cases may appear different, analytically they are the same. This type of approach may be used with respect to the issues of liability. See the case of *Hedly Byrne & Co Ltd v. Heller*[30] and *Wertheim v. Chicoutimi Pulp Co*[31] on issues of damages.
3. Where a lawyer cannot find a precedent, he/she can go beyond first principles and instead develop an argument that the decided cases have evolved to a general principle which covers the immediate case. This is a very sophisticated and creative type of argument which lawyers and judges take particular pride in. This type of argument was identified in the majority judgment of Lord Atkin in *Donoghue v. Stevenson.*[32]

In that case there were two strong dissenting judgements of Lord Buckmaster and Lord Tomlin and their legal argument was that the plaintiff's claim did not come within the reach of the established authorities but represented a new type of claim. Lord Atkin's response was that while the decided cases might each examine a particular type of liability, there must be a common rationale. His Lordship stated: "At present I content myself with pointing out that in English law there must be and is some general conception of relations giving rise to a duty of care or which the particular case found in the books are but instances."[33] Lord Atkin then went on to complete his famous speech which is the foundation of the modern law of negligence.

---

[30] (1963) 2 All ER 575.
[31] (1911) A.C 301 (PC).
[32] (1932) A.C 562 (HL).
[33] *Ibid*, p. 580.

Legal Writing

The written word is one of the most important tools of the legal profession. Words are used to advocate, inform, persuade and instruct. Although mastering legal writing skills takes time and practice, superior writing skills are essential to success. One's legal writing skills can be improved through the following tips:[34]

a. Remember Your Audience

Every written word should be tailored to the need of the reader. Documents that embody the same research and message may vary greatly in content and tone based on the document's intended audience. For instance, a brief submitted to the court must advocate and persuade, while a memorandum to a client must analyse the issues, report the state of the law and recommend an appropriate course of action. Always keep the audience in mind when crafting any piece of writing.

b. Organize Your Writing

Organization is the key to successful legal writing. Create a road map for your writing by using visual clues to guide the reader. Introduce your subject in an introductory paragraph, use transitional phrases such as "moreover", "furthermore", "however", "in addition", etc. between each paragraph, introduce each paragraph with a topic sentence and use heading and sub headings to break up blocks of texts. Limit each paragraph to one topic and sum up your message with a concluding sentence or paragraph. Organizational structure guides the reader through your text and promotes readability.

c. Ditch The Legalese

Legalese—specialized legal phrases and jargon—can make a piece of writing abstract, stilted and archaic. Examples of legalese include words such as aforementioned, herewith, heretofore and wherein. Disregard unnecessary legalese and other jargon in favour of the clear and simple. To avoid legalese and promote clarity, try reading your sentence to a

---

[34] S. Kane, "Seven Ways to Improve Your Legal Writing Skills," in http://www.files.legalwriting/legal-writing-skills-About.comGuide. Accessed on 24/07/2012.

colleague or substituting abstract words with simple, concrete terms. For instance, instead of “I am in receipt of your correspondence,” “I received your letter” is clearer and more succinct.

d. Be Concise

Every word you write should contribute to your message. Omit extraneous words, shorten complex sentences, eliminate redundancies and keep it simple:

For example: Incorrect – “Due to the fact that he defendant has not attempted to pay back the money owed to our client in the amount of ₦5,000, it has become absolutely essential that we take appropriate legal action in order to obtain payment of the aforesaid amount.”

A more concise version reads: “Since the defendant has not paid ₦5,000 owed to our client; we will file a lawsuit seeking reimbursement.”

The latter sentence conveys the same information is 18 words versus 44. Omitting unnecessary words helps clarify the meaning of the sentence and adds impact.

e. Use Action Words

Action words make your legal prose more powerful, dynamic and vivid. Add punch to your writing with verbs that bring your prose to life.

Examples:	Weak	-	The defendant was not truthful
	Better	-	The defendant lied
	Weak	-	The witness quickly came into the court room
	Better	-	The witness bolted into the courtroom
	Weak	-	The judge was very angry
	Better	-	The judge was enraged

f. Avoid Passive Voice

Passive voice disguises responsibility for an act by eliminating the subject of the verb. Active voice, on the other hand, tells the reader who is doing the acting and clarifies your message. For example, instead of “the filing deadline was missed; say “Claimant’s counsel missed the filing deadline.” Instead of “a crime was committed,” say “the defendant committed the crime.”

g. Edit Ruthlessly

Edit your writing ruthlessly, omitting unnecessary words and rewriting for clarity. Careful proof reading is particularly important in legal writing. Spelling, punctuation or grammatical errors in a document submitted to the court, opposing council or a client can undermine your credibility as a legal professional.

Conclusion

This chapter examined the concept of legal research, the law library, its arrangement and its importance in the field of legal research. It also examined the types of materials that can be found in the law library and how to access them for effective legal research. The importance of legal research was highlighted. The chapter also considered legal opinions, citation of cases and reports and their importance to a law student.

Note-taking and analysis which is the foundation of legal training were examined and key points for effective note-taking were discussed. Use of authorities in legal argument was also a part of this chapter. The principles of *stare decisis* in legal argument were exhaustively discussed. It was also noted that there may be circumstances where there is no precedent, and suggestions were made on what the lawyer should do in this scenario.

Finally, the chapter considered the issue of legal writing and noted key points that a student must learn and practice. It is our considered view that the information contained here will help the students through their school years and in practice.

CHAPTER TEN

LEGAL RESEARCH WRITING IN NIGERIA

OKECHUKWU TIMOTHY UMAHI[1]

This chapter will focus on legal research writing and documentation in Nigeria. It is a practical exercise towards redirecting, re-educating and re-informing students, researchers, lecturers and professionals in Nigeria on the basic tenets of writing long essays, proposals, theses, dissertations and articles. The basic principle of legal research writing and documentation needs to follow the acronym of *"WWHWWW,"* (*known as the "what, why, how, where, who, when"*) as a guide for students, markers and readers of any legal research writing. This chapter acknowledges that most students, researchers, lecturers and professionals understand this principle, but their research outcome or final documentation does not apply the principle. This may be the result of either a lack of proper understanding of the principle or practice or the late entry of lawyers and law lecturers into modern research methods.

The chapter is divided into five sections. The first section will introduce the chapter; the second section will examine the meaning of legal research; the third section will analyse the *"WWHWWW"* principles in legal research writing and documentation and present the practical application; the forth section will focus on academic writing styles, while the fifth section will present a practical guide to legal research writing.

[1] PhD (Manchester); LL.M (Manchester); LL.M (LASU); B.L; LL.B (ESUT); M.Sc (UNN);B.Sc/Ed (UNN); Senior Lecturer, Faculty of Law, Benson Idahosa University, Benin City, Edo State, Nigeria. Email: tumahi@biu.edu.ng, timothy.umahi@gmail.com

Meaning of Legal Research

Academic and legal research is a daunting task at every stage of our academic and career development. Researchers and students get more worried at each stage because the outcome of the research is likely to constitute a great part of the final result, if not the main determinant of our academic pursuit. The situation gets more worrisome once researchers and students start perceiving that supervisors are not being of great help in managing their emotions, panic state and content development. There is no need to be worried as no one is alone in this dilemma; researchers are all caught up in this same confusion as to what is the right approach or right structure for a piece of legal research. It is right to state here that there is no stereotypical approach or structure that will be consistent with legal research, except that we need to understand what we are embarking upon and to strategise upon how to achieve our purpose in order to convince your audience and achieve a high grade. This idea is in line with the argument that "the supreme objective of a brief is to convince the judicial mind."[2]

Suffice to note at this point that academic and legal research writing is not and should not be seen as only an assessment tool, but training geared towards encouraging wider reading, critical thinking, and improving communication skills. It should help us to develop a higher level of competence and professionalism for contemporary and future Nigerian lawyers. Therefore, this chapter enjoins the reader to pay attention to its entire sections and subsections as a guide to structured legal research and documentation.

What is research?

The word "research" is used in various contexts to mean various things. However, a student of law faced with definitional problems may resort to dictionaries, statutes, judicial decisions and opinion of learned authorities. In this context therefore, research has been defined as:

---

[2] J. W. Davies, *The Argument of an Appeal*, 26 A.B.A.J. 895 (1940) inF. Trowbridge vom Baur, "*The Art of Brief Writing,*"' *The Practical Lawyer,* Vol. 22/No 1 (1976), 1 – 16, p. 1.

> A careful study of a subject, especially in order to discover new facts or information about it; to study something carefully and to try to discover new facts about it.[3]

Obeagu[4] notes that research is a careful study or examination of the subject matter, aimed at discovering the truth about a fact through interpretation; that it is systematic and has to be carried out in a most objective manner. He also quotes the definition according to Leedy as:

> The manner in which we attempt to solve problems in a systematic effort to push back the frontiers of human ignorance or to confirm the validity of the solutions to problems others have presumably solved. Ultimately, research is a way of thinking. It is a way of looking at accumulated fact so that those data become meaningful in the total process of discovering new insights into unsolved problems and revealing new meanings... Research is the thrill that comes with the making of a new discovery.[5]

Research has distinct purposes, forms and recognised structures, clarity and accuracy. Academic writing is expected to demonstrate an objective approach and explore the subject matter thoroughly, resulting in a careful analysis.

Academic writing demands being critical and being critical involves:

- Showing an understanding and knowledge of theory.
- Demonstrating an awareness of what has been written or said about the subject.
- Taking into consideration different points of view.
- Using reason to make a judgement.
- Not accepting ideas until they have been examined closely (and then maybe rejecting them).
- Coming to your own conclusions.
- Using your own voice.[6]

However, in the context of this chapter, research means the process of looking for and choosing sources so as to assist one in presenting or

---

[3]Oxford Advanced Learner's Dictionary, *Oxford Advanced Learner's Dictionary of Current English,* 6th ed., (Oxford: Oxford University Press, 2000), 999.

[4]C. C. Obeagu, *The Theory and Technique of Writing Research Papers and Dissertations in Law* (Enugu: Celex Printer & Publisher, 2009), 7-8.

[5]P. D. Leedy, *Practical Research: Planning and Design,* 3rd ed., (New York: Macmillan Publishing Company Inc., 1980), 3.

[6]A. Gillett, A. Hammond and M. Martala, *Successful Academic Writing* (Essex, England: Pearson Longman, 2009), 3.

structuring a good essay, thesis, dissertation, or article, which will enable one's work to stand out. It is on this basis that the questions raised by the *"WWHWWW"* principles come in handy for achieving a justifiable end for our research work. These principles are used as headings or sections in the chapters of our research work and there is the need to identify them, demonstrate them and implement their use during the research process.

Understanding the *"WWHWWW"* Principles of Legal Research Writing

The *"WWHWWW"*[7] principles as have been noted are those questions that guide a good piece of research and each of the acronyms will be reviewed in order to find out where it fits and how it can enhance our research work.

What?

A researcher starts with the first question of, what do I want to research? When you meet your fellow students or supervisor, the first question you should anticipate is, what do you want to research? Getting an answer is usually not an easy one, but you can start tinkering within your area of legal interest or amongst the courses you have studied. At this point a researcher must be as practical as possible; the "what" questions are in tandem with the basic approach in the work of Andy Gillett and others,[8] and the following must be addressed:

- What kind of assignment are you doing (e.g. essay, thesis, dissertation)?
- What does the assignment expect you to do (e.g. carry out an evaluation, an analysis, a critical review, a comparative study, a case study)?
- What is the assignment worth, when is its deadline, what is its minimum and maximum length, what is its referencing style?

The answers to these questions are of great importance because the type of assignment will determine the structure to be adopted and how you will organize your work. It will also determine what must be part of your research work to make it credible and authoritative. For example, a thesis that does not contain references will definitely not attract high marks,

---

[7] Known as the *"what, why, how, where, who, when."*

[8] Gillett, Hammond, and Martala, *Successful Academic Writing,* 30-37.

because the examiners cannot see the sources of the materials used and therefore the final outcome will not be authoritative and credible.

At the point you decide to embark on academic research your mind must focus on the topic you want to research. It must be observed at this stage that while a research topic must not be chosen as a matter of convenience or chosen arbitrarily, there is no unique approach for choosing a suitable research topic, no special skill, and no special wisdom is required. However, an academic research topic must be born out of the need to address a research problem(s) or answer a research question(s). Once a research topic does not seem to have a question or problem it may address, the obvious response of a supervisor is that the topic is not researchable or that it will be overtly descriptive. This presents the need to do some preliminary readings and discussions before choosing a research topic, and read a chapter or an article in your area of interest to see what ideas flow into you.[9]

To avoid exhausting your gunpowder at the middle of a crucial battle, especially an academic research battle which is time-constrained, a good researcher, in choosing a research topic, must consider carefully some issues that might constrain the successful completion of a research work. These include:

- Availability of materials.
- The timeframe for completion of the research.
- The complexity or simplicity of the subject matter.

Why?

Academic research is an important requirement of the National University Commission for the award of Bachelor's degrees in any recognised Nigerian university. Therefore, any student of law would be right to state that academic research is part of the requirement for him to graduate from university. However, it goes beyond that because, though research is an important activity in any study, not just law, it also helps develop your learning and knowledge of your subject.[10] Research is interested in the ability of the researcher to address a research problem or answer a research question. What this means is that you must state in clear terms your research problem(s) or question(s), which will be the yard stick

---

[9] H. Hutchison, *Writing Essays and Dissertations* (Coventry: The McGraw-Hill Companies, Inc, 2007), 38.
[10] Gillett, Hammond and Martala, *Successful Academic Writing,* 40.

for judging the final research document. It is important to note that a sentence cannot and will not suffice for a research problem or question. A research question must be phrased as a question with words like what, how, where, when and why, or to what extent, and have a question mark (?) at the end. For example:

- To what extent does patent right prevent access to essential medicines in developing countries?
- What are the causes of non-availability of essential medicines in developing countries?

Also, the "why" principle is aware that the final document is not entirely an idea from your head and therefore, the sources of the materials used for your research must be stated and stated in the correct format and style agreed by your institution. The sources we use perform several functions like providing background information and support for your argument, as well as evidence and authority for your research. The proper use of research questions in legal research will be demonstrated in the subheading under research documentation.

How?

A good piece of research must clearly identify and state how the research is to be conducted. The focus is on the methodology and the methods that will be used in conducting the research. Your research must state from the outset the methodology and methods that will be used in conducting the research. It is important to note that a piece of research will be judged on the fact that the stated methodology and methods were employed in conducting the research.

Ultimately, three types of methodology can be employed for a piece of legal research:

- Quantitative or empirical.
- Qualitative or doctrinal.
- Hybrid (combination of quantitative and qualitative).

In the same vein, the research method involves the actual systematic techniques that would be used by the methodology. This would include:

- Use of books, journals, online sources.
- Tables, graphs and pictures.
- Published research.

- Existing studies.
- Interviews (structured, unstructured or oral).
- Questionnaires.
- Surveys.
- Fieldwork, etc.

Where?

The "where" principle refers to where the research will be conducted and this may be seen from two perspectives; first, the location for the research and second, how you will arrange you work and what will be done in each part. Our interest at this point is the latter and not the former and this refers to the research structure. A piece of research must identify and state what will be done in each chapter and in the entire work; it must identify and state the number of chapters that will be covered and what will be done under each chapter. It must name the chapter number, the chapter title and what will be considered within each chapter, and this will be demonstrated in the section on research documentation.

Who?

The "who" principle of legal research involves deciding which sources to use and rely on for your research. The decision as to which sources to use requires careful judgement as to what is relevant and what is not and once this decision is made, you have to bring your own ideas into the writing, making sure that you use your own words. The "who" principle sees you as the chairman of a round-table discussion on the subject; which expert would you invite to join you at the table to discuss your subject matter? This at all time remains the decision of the researcher and a researcher may seek guidance from their supervisor as to the resources that may be helpful and useful to the piece of work.

When?

The final principle is the "when" principle, which is the research plan. As a researcher, you need to be guided by a plan as to what you will accomplish and when you hope to accomplish this within you timeframe. The research plan shows how long the research is expected to last, what you expect to cover within the research period (for example in one month, three months, six months, etc), and state when the final chapter and documentation will be done. The research plan guides both the researcher and the supervisor as to the progress of the work and the need to be more focused.

Academic Writing Styles

Academic writing styles for legal research works may involve the following:

- Essays: these will discuss and explore a topic in-depth looking at history, advantages, disadvantages, impact and your opinion on the topic.
- Critique/review: this looks at summary, analysis and evaluation. It seeks to critically appraise a piece of work.
- Report: this is a written account of a situation, event or series of events, investigation or study. It is aimed at getting the practical experience of the student involved in it.
- Case study: this is an in-depth analysis of a situation so as to draw some general conclusion that could be applied elsewhere.
- Research proposal: this is a suggestion for future study. A proposal must be justified with an explanation of how the work will be conducted, what the work is expected to show and the timeframe for conducting the research.
- Thesis or dissertation: this is an organized and structured work or investigation with stages, targets and deadlines. It must provide details of the sources used for the work.

Every legal researcher should always strive to achieve two basic fundamentals in the final documentation of the work:

- The learning outcomes.
- Satisfying the criteria for assessing the learning outcome.

The learning outcomes for legal research in Nigeria generally want to assess students' ability to:

- conduct independent research,
- to analyse arguments,
- to communicate ideas,
- to understand different concepts and theories; and
- to state the various sources of their material.

Attaining these criteria would need an expository of what examiners look out for in your research work. The examiners test the extent of your knowledge and intellectual abilities for:

- Ordering material effectively to form an argument;
- Applying an appropriate methodology;
- Expressing your own ideas and judgements;
- Providing detailed sources for your information;
- Presenting information clearly and accurately.

Presenting your work involves the use of an academic writing style, but achieving a good research outcome involves an understanding of the "instruction" words used in academic research.

For a piece of academic research to address the research questions and satisfy the assessment criteria, the "instruction" words and their meanings as explained by Gillett and others[11] must be adhered to:

- Analyse: Consider all the relevant factors and answer in a methodical and logical way.
- Compare: Discuss the similarities and differences. Write a balanced (fair, objective) answer.
- Criticise: Point out the strengths and weaknesses. Write a balanced answer.
- Discuss: Give both points of an argument, with implications, before reaching a conclusion.
- Explain: Give detailed reasons for a situation.
- Outline: Give the main points in a concise manner. Leave out details.
- Summarise: Give the main points in a concise manner. Leave out detail.
- Account for: Give reason for.
- Assess: Examine the value of the subject, looking at the positives and negatives before reaching a decision.
- Comment on: Give your opinion. Back up your views with evidence from your reading.
- Consider: Give your opinion. Back up your views with evidence from your reading.
- Contrast: Discuss the difference between subjects.
- Define: Explain the meaning of the concept concisely.
- Demonstrate: Use examples to show something.
- Describe: Explain how something works or what it is like.
- Evaluate: Examine the value of the subject, looking at the strengths and weaknesses before reaching a decision.

[11] Gillett, Hammond and Martala, *Successful Academic Writing*, 19-20.

- Explore: Examine the topic thoroughly and consider it from a variety of viewpoints.
- Identify: Recognise and list.
- Illustrate: Show with examples.
- Justify: Give reasons for or against an argument.
- Prove: Show a proposition is true through evidence.
- Review: Examine the topic critically and consider whether it is adequate or accurate.
- State: Express relevant points briefly and clearly without minor details.
- Trace: Outline the development of a theme in a logical or chronological order.[12]

The decision to copiously express these instruction words is based on the fact that most students have shown a total lack of understanding of the meaning and use of the instructional or operational words. Students or researchers must express what they want to do at every stage of their thesis or dissertation, using the instruction or operational words, since theses and dissertations are structured and organized pieces of work.

Practical Guide to Research Documentation

All the explanations that have been made above remain part of the theory of legal research methodology; both staff, professionals and students understand the theory and even make good grades in examination, but when it comes to putting theory to practice they do not show any understanding of what legal research and methodology is all about. In short, the tail at this point starts wagging the dog, and the fun of writing starts fading and grumbling becomes the order of the day. Filling the pages without acknowledgement might become the rule rather than the exception, which will turn out to be plagiarism. Epstein and others note that "plagiarism is the most serious and least forgivable of academic sins,"[13] so try to avoid it.

Please note that the number of chapters will depend on what you are writing on and the outcome of the contact you have with your supervisor. Most theses and dissertations are between five to eight chapters, but there is no hard and fast rule on this; rather it is dependent on the supervisor and the internal policy of the various Faculties of Law in Nigeria.

---

[12] *Ibid*, 7, 19-20.

[13] D. Epstein, J. Kenway and R. Boden, *Writing for Publication,* (London: SAGE Publishing Ltd, 2005), 17.

This section will water down the theory and provide a standard practical guide for both students and supervisors on the questions that may arise from research projects, theses and dissertations for undergraduate and postgraduate legal research works.

Chapterisation

Legal research focuses on the structure of the research, known as chapterisation. This is important because it provides the pointer or guide for accomplishing the research work. Chapterisation is a reflection of the table of contents of the final work and is typified in the subheadings below.

Preliminary Pages

A typical thesis or dissertation should contain these basic headings under the preliminary pages (the institutional requirement may include more subheadings):

- Title page or cover page
- Certification
- Approval
- Dedication
- Acknowledgement
- List of Abbreviations
- Table of Statutes
- Table of Cases
- Table of Contents
- Abstract

Chapter Content/Arrangement

CHAPTER 1 INTRODUCTION

A good research work needs to have a general introduction typified by the first chapter and every other chapter must have its own introduction of what will be done in the chapter. A typical first chapter must contain the following subheadings and contents as stated below; however, researchers, in agreement with their supervisors, may include additional subheadings as need be.

Introduction

- Make clear what the work/research is going to do, using the instruction words.
- Present a brief synopsis of your topic and make clear your main argument.
- The introduction should not be a dumping ground for background information that does not fit anywhere in the research.
- Focus in quickly on the area of your research and announce its main themes and problems.
- Focus on the particular aspects of the issue which you plan to address.
- In the entire essay or dissertation, your introduction should be specific, accurate and focused on what will be done rather than the content, concepts and theories of the work.
- The introduction must be simple and brief—as a rule of thumb, no more than one and half pages—and must say what you want to do.
- Avoid making sweeping statements or generalisation(s) about public opinion.
- Most importantly, the introduction is not for definitions or analysis of judicial decisions.
- Avoid dictionary or internet definitions in the introduction of a piece of legal research.

Topic: A critical analysis and assessment of the evidential rule of facts under the Nigerian judicial system.

Example of Introduction:

This study seeks to examine the peculiar existence of the judicial system in Nigeria and determine whether the "evidential rule of proof of facts," applies to the judicial system in Nigeria.

Criminal law is concerned with public wrongs, matters deemed by society to be so serious that in the event of a person transgressing a legal rule, it is society itself which must punish the offender. Since criminal cases have the possibility of penal sanctions, the evidential rule of proof of facts is strict. In this case the prosecution is required to prove that the accused has committed the offence. The degree of proof required in this regard is proof beyond reasonable doubt. Until this is done, the defendant is presumed innocent.

In so far as evidence primarily preoccupies itself with the existence and proof of facts, it is usually more difficult to determine the circumstances in which the law in one area may bind another area. Proof may grow more difficult because law with respect to the issue of fact does not depend on judicial reasoning and activism. It must be proved by strong evidence.

Research Questions

A piece of research must state clearly the research question(s) and end with a question mark (?):

- The number of question(s) to be addressed.
- It is advised that you limit yourself to no more than three questions.
- Identify other minor questions along the line of your research.

Example of Research Questions:

This research seeks to answer two fundamental questions:
1. How adequate is the legal framework for evidential rule of proof of facts under Nigerian law?
2. What are the challenges and resolutions relating to "Evidential rule of proof of facts" in the Nigerian Judicial System?

Research methodology

The researcher must state the methodology and methods that will be used.

Example of Research methodology:

This research will use the qualitative research methodology. Materials such as journals, contemporary books, newspapers, Internet sources and decided cases and statutes will be used for the research methods.

Research Structure

The researcher must present the structure of the research in a clear and coherent manner. The researcher must:

- State the number of chapters that make up the entire research.
- Name the chapters, the chapter title and what will be considered within each chapter, i.e. state what you will do under each chapter.
- Remember, this structure will guide the entire research.

Example of Research Structure:

> The research will be made up of five chapters. Chapter One provides a background introduction of the study, and specifies the research questions, research methodology and the research structure. Chapter Two provides a review of various related literature. The literature review is aimed at promoting the research position by building a case from credible evidence based on previous research. It also provides the context and the background about the current knowledge of the topic under review and lays out a logical case to defend the position of the study under review. Chapter Three assesses the legal framework for evidential rule of proof of facts under Nigerian law. Chapter Four analyses the evidential rule of proof of facts under Nigerian law as well as the challenges and resolutions from decided cases and statutes relating to "evidential rule of proof of facts" in the Nigerian judicial system. Chapter Five provides a conclusion and recommendations for the study.

In conclusion, every chapter in a thesis or dissertation needs an introduction which must first state what the research wants to do, present the argument(s) and end with the outline structure of the chapter. This must be brief, concise and clear and the need for the use of the 'instruction' words or 'operational' words becomes imperative at this point. Please note that the first research chapter sets out the entire work and is the yardstick for measuring the student's research progress. In most cases, the first chapter is actually the revised proposal for the research and a guiding tool for students, supervisors and examiners.

The next chapter is the literature review, and some institutions or faculties of law may structure this chapter into chapter one. There is no problem with this arrangement, but the content is important and must be known and followed practically.

CHAPTER 2 LITERATURE REVIEW OR THEORETICAL FRAMEWORK

A literature review according to Machi and Brenda "is a written argument that promotes a thesis position by building a case from credible evidence based on previous research."[14] It is also defined as:

> A written document that presents a logically argued case founded on a comprehensive understanding of the current state of knowledge about a

[14] L. A. Machi and B. T. Mcevoy, *The Literature Review* (California: Corwin Press, 2009), 4.

topic of study. This case establishes a convincing thesis to answer the study's question.[15]

Generally, a literature review provides the basis for the following:

- The context and the background about the current knowledge of the topic
- It lays out a logical case to defend the thesis position taken.
- It involves a literature search, and you must preview, select and organize the date for study and arguing successfully.
- It helps organize the relevant data into a body of evidence that explains what is known about the topic.
- It teaches students how to engage with published works on a particular discipline.
- It covers the theoretical basis of your work.
- It involves summarizing a number of publications and discussing how these support or contradict one another.
- It presents a spectrum of views from a variety of scholars and sources.
- It establishes the boundaries of the discipline or theory.
- It explores the topic from a different perspective.
- It is a theorized discussion of the terminology used in the discipline.
- A literature review does not call for your own judgement on the subject, although you can evaluate the vigour and import of the text you explore.
- To teach how to find, digest and evaluate scholarly literature in the field.
- It shows if your sources are up to date.
- It shows your line of argument.

CHAPTER 3 ANALYSIS (STATE THE CHAPTER HEADING)

After the literature review, chapter three and even four should analyse your research questions, while chapter four should present the proffered solutions to the identified problems. It is suggested that the research should start with an appreciation of the research problem which should be in-depth, clear and concise. Therefore, this chapter should:

---

[15] *Ibid.*

- Identify the research problem(s) or question(s)
- Always present the two sides of the argument
- Draw up the analysis, weighing up which side is best
- Make sure the question(s) identified are put in a logical and organized perspective.

Example of Introduction to Chapter Three:

> This chapter will analyse the effect of the criminal justice system in Nigeria and discuss the problems and its implication for ex-convicts. The chapter argues that societal crime would reduce if the criminal justice system was improved and the problems militating against it addressed. The chapter will be organized into three sections; the first section will analyse the criminal justice system in Nigeria, the second section will review the problems with the Nigerian criminal justice system and the final section will conclude the chapter.

The subheadings and sub-subheadings should be stated as follows:

Title of sub-heading here
Title of sub, sub-heading here
Title of sub, sub-heading here
Title of sub-heading here
Conclusion

CHAPTER 4 ANALYSIS OF THE SOLUTION (STATE THE CHAPTER HEADING)

This chapter should proffer solutions to the identified problems. It is suggested that the research should be in-depth, clear and concise. Therefore, this chapter should:

- Proffer solutions to the research problem(s) or question(s)
- Present both recommended and new solutions to the problem
- Make sure the solutions are put in a logical and organized perspective.

Example of Introduction to Chapter Four:

> This chapter is dedicated to the analysis of the requirement of the "evidential rule of proof of facts" in the Nigerian judicial system with respect to civil and criminal cases, the role of judges and jury in the issue of the "evidential rule of proof of facts" and the identified challenges and

solutions relating to the "evidential rule of proof of facts" in the Nigerian judicial system.

The subheadings and sub-subheadings should be stated as follows:
Title of sub-heading here
Title of sub, sub-heading here
Title of sub, sub-heading here
Title of sub-heading here
Conclusion

CHAPTER 5 CONCLUSION AND RECOMMENDATION

Conclusion

Some students and researchers demonstrate tiredness or laziness at the point of concluding a piece of research and this manifests itself in a shoddy end of any piece of work, which will negatively affect the marks for the entire piece. To fail to answer the question is the best way to fail an assignment and the easiest way to achieve this is to avoid writing a conclusion, to write a hazy conclusion, or to write a conclusion that is not obvious. The conclusion is the final verdict of an essay, thesis or dissertation; it is the last chance to make the point of your essay, thesis or dissertation crystal-clear.

Again, some students try to avoid writing a conclusion because of the thinking that they will reach a wrong conclusion and therefore lose marks. The fact is that the reverse is the case; you will lose the marks meant for the conclusion if you do not state the conclusion, rather than giving a flawed or incorrect conclusion. In addition, in legal research, examiners are not interested in testing the correctness of your research outcome or your ability to state the correct answer, but instead your ability to master the method of presenting your argument. This method is your ability to understand that there are two sides of the same coin, two sides of an argument; therefore your ability to introduce the argument, marshal the main points and draw a conclusion is important. What this meant is that there is no right or wrong answer, but the right method to be associated with legal research and the last part of the method is to conclude the work.

"The thing that a conclusion must do is to conclude."[16]A conclusion can refer back to points that were made earlier in the work, but this must

[16] H. Hutchison, *Writing Essays and Dissertations* (Coventry: The McGraw-Hill Companies, Inc, 2007), 85.

be brief and not a reworking of what has been done. As a rule, the conclusion is not and should not be used to introduce a new idea. Do not hold back your main points for the conclusion; rather the conclusion should point out how the evidence that has been given answers the questions that was stated.

A good research work needs to have conclusions for the various chapters and a final conclusion for the entire research work. For every conclusion, there is a need to avoid engaging in new quotations, new authorities, new ideas, new evidence, forgotten points, another side of the argument, an unexpected ending (which is for detective novels); just conclude the conclusion.

- The conclusion should summarise the issues raised by the research.
- It should signal the general points that can be drawn from the research.
- It should signal that the research is finished and the purpose achieved.

Recommendation

The recommendation simply demands of suggestions from the researcher as to what is good or sensible from your perspective on the topic you have researched on. It is an approval of one's opinion for improvement and needs to be stated in a piece of research.

Referencing

Referencing and bibliography in a piece of research work asserts the accuracy of the research, reliability and authority of the sources. It shows the source of your idea and allows your readers to check on the accuracy of the source material used in the work. While references refer to the source of information, directing the reader's attention to the sources, the bibliography provides a list of books, articles and online sources consulted, and it appears at the end of the work.

For the purpose of consistency of final documentation, referencing and bibliography styles used in any Faculty of Law are the internal policy of the Faculty Board; however, the style to be used will come from a variety of referencing styles. Most Faculties of Law demand that either the "author-date" system or "author-title" system is practiced. It is important that every student must contact the supervisor or Faculty of Law on the approved referencing style for their Faculty, but note that the "author-date" system of citation in footnote and bibliography remains an accepted standard in most Faculties of Law in Nigeria.

Kinds of Reference Styles

There are various kinds of referencing or citation styles. The forms of citations generally subscribe to one of the accepted citation systems. These styles include the Oxford,[17] Harvard, MLA, American Sociological Association (ASA) American Psychological Association (APA) and others that are known and easily interpreted by the reader. All the citation patterns have their advantages and disadvantages and thus are chosen relative to the needs of the types of publication being crafted.

However, generally in three Commonwealth jurisdictions, legal citations come under the following:

- The Bluebook is a citation system used in American academic writing. It is also used by the courts. Presently, academic legal writings are always footnoted but the courts use lines citations.
- The legal citation styles used almost universally in Canada is based on the Canadian Guide to Uniform Legal Citation (McGill Guide), published by McGill Law Journal.[18]
- British Legal Citation almost universally follows the Oxford Standard for Citation of Legal Authorities (OSCOLA).

Irrespective of the referencing style adopted by your Faculty of Law in Nigeria, the citation style still depends on the source of the material. This is exemplified below:

References in the body of the text

Where reference is put in the body of the text, whether it is a book, article or any other kind of source, the author-date reference is in brackets in the main body of the text. The format is as follows:

(Authors surname, date of publication) For example:
(Umahi, 2012)

---

[17]Oxford Referencing Systems

[18]Canadian Guide to Uniform Legal Citation, McGill Law Journal, updated October 2008.

If there are two authors, state both surnames:
(Umahi and Akpoghome, 2012)

If there are more than two authors, like Umahi, Akpoghome and Idehen, state the first name and then add, *et al* in italics:
(Umahi *et al.,* 2012)

If a quotation is directly from the text, also state the page number:
(Umahi, 2012, 8)

Where significant words and phrases are lifted directly from a source always use quotation marks for them when it is three lines or less; if it is more than three lines, it should be indented without quotation marks, e.g.:

> The in-roads made by economists and policy makers into patent law have resulted in the use of economic theories to explain the effects of patent law on the global and national economies (Gifford, 2004; Arrow, 1962; Mansfield, 1986). This is so because the patent system operates through harnessing market-based incentives: it is the expected value of the patented invention that provides the incentive to undertake the R & D which leads to product manufacture. Some argue that "invention like other economic activities is pursued for gain" (Schmookler, 1996).This idealized representation is almost a consensus in most theoretical work concerning the economics of patents (Levin, 1986; Landes, 2003). This thesis does not intend to recast these theories (Arrow, 1962), but the incentive to invent and the implications for developing countries is an argument that brings to fore the negative effect of the utilitarian justification on patent system on developing countries.

If an author is cited twice in different publications of the same year, differentiate the citations with a, and b, etc. in the reference list: e.g.

(Umahi, 2012a)
(Umahi, 2012b)

Secondary references

Secondary reference is the citation made from another citation. In this case it must be made clear that the citation is coming from another source and that this is permissible, but you must use the phrase "cited in" to show where the information is coming from, e.g.:

Umahi and Akpoghome (2012) Legal Research Methodology in Nigeria (cited in Nwano, 2008).

It is permissible, but should not be used too often, to avoid the suspicion that you have resorted to second-hand information or that you have not read widely. Therefore, you are encouraged to track the original source of the information.

Books

The reference of book titles must be in italics or underlined, but you must be consistent with whichever you choose. The format for books is as follows: authors(s), title of book (in italics), place of publication, publisher, year of publication. Note if the citation is in the footnote, the page(s) must be included, e.g.:

Umahi, O. T., *Legal Research and Methodology in Nigeria*, (Benin: Ambrose Ali University Publishers, 2012).

Where a book has two authors, list the surnames and the initials as they appear on the book, e.g.:

Umahi, O. T. and Akpoghome, T. U., *Reading the Law and Practice,* (Benin: Ambrose Ali University Publishers, 2011).

Chapters in edited books

Titles of chapters or articles in edited books should be in quotation marks. If you reference a book chapter, give the name of the author of the chapter and the publication date, but in the reference list, cite the chapter first, followed by the reference information for the book and the pages of the chapter.

Contributions to edited books: name(s) of contributor(s), title of article, name(s) of editor(s), title of work where the contribution appeared, place of publication, publisher, year, page(s).

Example:

Umahi, O.T., "Intellectual Property in Nigeria." Ohuruogu, C.C (ed.) *Contemporary Legal Issues in Nigeria.* Benin: Ambrose Ali University Publishers, 2012), 56-92.

A reference to a conference paper published in conference proceedings should follow the format for a chapter in an edited book, but the date and place of the conference should be written after the title of the conference proceedings.

Journal Articles

The title of articles should be written in quotation marks, while the title of the journals is written in italics, date/year of publication, before the volume number, issue number and page numbers of the article. Journal: author(s), article title in quotes, journal title, journal volume number and page number(s).

For example:

Umahi, O. T., "Re-visiting Issue of Access to Medicines in Developing Countries," *Journal of Law and Development*, (2012), Vol. 4, No. 2, 13-20.

Electronic journals

All online journals should be cited with the same format as print journals, with the addition of the URL address of the article and the date when the article was accessed. For example:

Umahi, O.T., "Comparing Democracies in Developing Countries,"
Journal of Law and development (2012), 5 (2), 24-36.
http://links.jstor.org/sici20123% [Accessed 14/07/2012]

Where the online article has a Digital Object Identifier (DOI), you should quote the number; this is a mark of authenticity and repute for academic journals.

Websites

For online materials that are not published in a journal, you should provide as much information as is possible, ranging from author (date), "title of article," title of web publication, edition, the URL/Web address, date of publication, place of publication: publisher. [Access date]. For example:

Umahi, O.T., "Intellectual Property and Innovation" in http://www.emerald.com/php/works.php?UID=155648 [Accessed 14 July 2012]

Newspaper articles

Newspaper and magazine articles citation follow the same format similar to journal articles: Author (date) "title of article." *Title of newspaper,* date of publication, page number(s)

Example:

Umahi, O. T., "Can Government Stop Terror?" *The Guardian,* (Nigeria, 20 July 2012), 12.

Cases

Party names in italics, year in parenthesis, the Law Report, part where applicable. Example:

John v. James (1979) I NWLR (Pt.780) 335
Page v. Smith (1996) AC 155 (HL)
Omorodion v. Judy (2010) 51 EHRR 10

Research Pitfalls

- Plagiarism
- Spelling errors
- Slangs/jargon
- Personalising with I
- Punctuation errors
- Avoid repetition
- Failure to properly cite sources
- Inconsistency in paragraphing (indented and block)

Conclusion

Demystifying legal research writing and documentation for Nigerian researchers, students, lecturers, and others who engage in the art of writing and documentation of legal work with a practical focus is the objective of this chapter. Understanding the rubrics of the *WWHWWW* principles and the use of instruction words or the operational words to drive legal research writing is explained and demonstrated in the practical guide with appropriate use of references.

However, this chapter is not and should not be a substitute to reading widely on legal research and methodology as the old adage still applies in this respect that "practice makes perfect" and legal research and documentation is not immune to the same saying. Therefore, the author urges you to practice the principles enunciated in this chapter.

CHAPTER ELEVEN

REGULATION OF THE LEGAL PROFESSION IN NIGERIA

NKECHI HUOMACHI WORLUH-OKOLIE[1]

Introduction

The word "ethics" is derived from the Greek word *'ethos'* (character) and from the Latin word *'mores'* (customs). Together, they combine to define how individuals choose to interact with one another. In philosophy, ethics defines what is good for the individual and for society and establishes the nature of duties that people owe themselves and one another. Suffice to say that, ethics are moral beliefs and rules about right and wrong.[2]

Legal practitioners in Nigeria are guided by the ethics of the legal profession, which are the moral principles about the right and wrong behaviours that influence the attitudes and philosophy of legal practitioners in Nigeria.[3] In order to maintain the standard of the legal profession, there exist various regulatory laws and organs of the legal profession.

This chapter aims to examine the history of the legal profession in Nigeria, the laws regulating the legal profession in Nigeria and the regulatory organs of the legal profession in Nigeria.

[1] Lecturer, Faculty of Law, Benson Idahosa University, Benin City, Edo State.

[2] Legalpedia Pro, Law Dictionary.

[3] See: The Rules of Professional Conduct for Legal Practitioners, 2007.

Historical Overview of the Legal Profession

The legal profession in Nigeria derives its origin from the English legal system and legal profession, which were introduced into this country in the second half of the nineteenth century.[4] The Nigerian legal profession is examined here in three historical perspectives:

a. 1876-1914
b. 1914-1962
c. 1962-2013

1876-1914

In 1876, the Supreme Court Ordinance was enacted to regulate the legal profession.[5] The Ordinance provided for three categories of people who would be admitted to practice law, namely:

a. **Those entitled to practice in Great Britain or Ireland** –the Supreme Court Ordinance of 1876[6] provided for the admittance of barristers and solicitors. Such persons as shall be admitted barristers or advocates in Great Britain or Ireland, and shall have been admitted as solicitors or writers to the signet in any of the courts of London, Dublin or Edinburgh, provided always, that the Chief Justice may upon due cause, refuse to admit any person as a barrister or as a solicitor, notwithstanding whether he may have all of the aforesaid qualifications.[7]

b. **Those who have served as articles** – Section 73 of the Ordinance provides for the admission as solicitor of the Supreme Court any person who have served as articles i.e. persons who have served five years continuously in the office of a practicing barrister or solicitor residing within the court's jurisdiction and who have taken and passed

---

[4] J. O. Orojo, *Professional Conduct of Legal Practitioners in Nigeria*, 3rd ed., (Lagos: Mafix Books Limited, 2008), 3.

[5] The Supreme Court Ordinance (hereinafter referred to as S.C.O.) No.4 of 1876

[6] In S.71 empowered the Chief Justice to approve, admit and enrol barristers and solicitors.

[7] The first Nigerian barrister was Christopher Alexander Sapara-Williams, who was enrolled in England as a barrister in 1879 and later returned to Nigeria to be enrolled in 1880. See S. O. Imhanobe, *Lawyer's Deskbook*, 2nd ed., Vol. 2, (Abuja: Rehoboth Publishing, 2010), 1144.

such examinations on the principles and practice of law before such persons as the Chief Justice may appoint from time to time.

c. **The Local Attorneys** – Section 74 of the Ordinance provides that, in the case that there are not sufficient number of barristers, solicitors and proctors within the colony qualified in the manner hereinafter prescribed, it shall be lawful for the Chief Justice to admit temporarily so many fit and proper persons to appear and act in the capacity of barristers, solicitors and proctors as may appear necessary, subject to such conditions and regulations as may be prescribed by rules of court.

To qualify, the Local Attorneys were required to sit for an examination to test their general education and knowledge as well as the principles and practice of law; they were to be of good character, attested to by a Judge or two District Commissioners.[8] They were licensed to practice for six months and their license was subject to renewal by the Chief Justice, if they were of good moral conduct. Thus as of 1908 when the last Local Attorney was licensed, there were only 30 persons enrolled in the country as legal practitioners; these included Britons, West Indians and Nigerians.[9] However, in 1913, in response to the protest of professionally qualified lawyers, no further Local Attorney was appointed. The last, J. Osho-Davies, had his application refused by the Chief Justice and on appeal, his appeal was dismissed by the full court on the grounds that the Chief Justice's discretion in that respect had been properly exercised.[10]

1914-1962

In 1943, the Supreme Court Ordinance of 1876 was repealed and replaced with the Supreme Court Ordinance, No. 14 of 1943. Although the new Ordinance did not make provisions relating to legal practitioners, the rules made under it, namely the Supreme Court (Civil Procedure) Rules of 1945 did.[11]

---

[8] S. O. Imhanobe, *Lawyer's Deskbook*, 2nd ed., Vol. 2, (Abuja: Rehoboth Publishing, 2010), 1143.

[9] J. O. Orojo, *Professional Conduct of Legal Practitioners in Nigeria*, 3rd ed., (Lagos: Mafix Books Limited, 2008), 15.

[10] S. O. Imhanobe, *Lawyer's Deskbook*, 2nd ed., Vol. 2, (Abuja: Rehoboth Publishing, 2010), 1143-1144.

[11] J. O. Orojo, *Professional Conduct of Legal Practitioners in Nigeria*, 3rd ed., (Lagos: Mafix Books Limited, 2008), 15.

Order 16 Rule 1 of the Supreme Court (Civil Procedure) Rules provided, inter alia, as follows:

> The Chief Justice may, in his discretion, approve, admit and enrol to practice as a Barrister and Solicitor in the Court:
> a. any person who is entitled to practice in England or Ireland or as an advocate in Scotland who:
> i. Produces testimonials sufficient to satisfy the Chief Justice that he is a man of good character;
> ii. Has read in the chambers of a practicing barrister or advocate of more than five years standing for at least one year , or has practiced in the Court of the Country in which he has been called or admitted for, at least two years subsequent to his call or admission; or
> iii. Has subsequent to his call to the Bar or admission as an advocate read in Nigeria in chambers of a practicing barrister of more than ten years standing for, at least two years; or
> iv. Has practiced as a barrister[12] or solicitor[13] in the courts of a British colony or protectorate for at least two years…[14]

The foregoing were the conditions for admission to practice law in Nigeria from 1945-1962.[15]

This arrangement proved to be inadequate because the foreign-trained lawyers were not grounded in the Nigerian statute laws or the Nigerian customary laws. It was against this background that the government began to consider the need for an indigenous system of legal education capable of responding to the peculiar needs of Nigeria's indigenous community. Thus in 1960, the British government appointed a committee on Legal Education for African Students. Headed by Lord Denning, the committee was asked to review the suitability of the legal training offered in the Inns of Court vis-à-vis the needs of African Commonwealth countries. After acknowledging the inadequacies of the existing training programmes, the

---

[12] For one to practice as a barrister, you must have been called to any of the four Inns of Court (such as the Middle Temple, Inner Temple, Lincoln's Inn and Greys Inn) in England. The educational qualification required was the West African School Certificate (W.A.E.C.).

[13] In England the Law Society is the regulatory body and it provides that an aspiring solicitor must be articled for a minimum of four years to a firm of solicitors; and must pass the solicitors part 1 and solicitor's final examination set by the Law Society - US Department of State, *Legal Education in Nigeria*; http://www.nigeria-law.org/index.html, accessed on 28/08/2012.

[14] See the Supreme Court (Civil Procedure) Rules 1948.

[15] US Department of State, *Legal Education in Nigeria*; http://www.nigeria-law.org/index.html, accessed on 28/08/2012.

Committee recommended expanding the course contents in order to accommodate the peculiar needs of African countries. Particularly noteworthy is the recommendation of the Committee to introduce a substantial period of practical training for African students.[16]

Earlier in 1959, the colonial government in Nigeria had appointed its own Committee on the Future of the Nigerian Legal Profession, which was under the chairmanship of E.I.G. Unsworth, Q.C.,[17] with a mandate "to consider and make recommendations for the future of legal profession in Nigeria with particular regard to legal education and admission to practice,[18] the right of audience before the courts and the making of reciprocal arrangements in this connection with other countries."[19]

The Committee's report was published in 1959[20] with the following recommendations:

i. That Nigeria should establish its own system of legal education;
ii. That a faculty of law should be established at the University College, Ibadan and other subsequent universities—academic stage;[21]
iii. That a university degree should be a necessary prerequisite to practice in Nigeria;
iv. It recommended a fused profession for Nigeria;
v. That a Council of Legal Education be established in Nigeria;
vi. That a Nigerian Law School be established in Lagos—professional stage.[22]

To give effect to the Committee's recommendations, the Legal Education Act of 1962[23] and the Legal Practitioners Act of 1962[24] were

---

[16] *Ibid.*

[17] Mr. E.I.G Unsworth was the then Attorney-General of the Federation.

[18] US Department of State, Constitution, Government and Legislation, http://jurist.law.pitt.edu/world/nigeria.htm accessed 28/05/2013.

[19] US Department of State, *Legal Education in Nigeria*; http://www.nigeria-law.org/index.html, accessed on 28/08/2012.

[20] E.I.G. Unsworth, Q.C. Committees report. Members of the Committee include: E.I.G. Unsworth, Q.C., Chief F.R.A. Williams, M.O. Ajegbo, G.K.O. Amachree, L.M. Lewis, Alhaji Jibiril Martin, C.A.H. Obafemi, Asuquo, Okon, J.M. Udochi, Dr. F.A Ajayi, C.O. Nwokedi, see S. O. Imhanobe , *Lawyer's Deskbook*, 2nd ed., Vol. 2, (Abuja: Rehoboth Publishing, 2010), 1146.

[21] This recommendation was not accepted. The first Faculty of Law in a Nigerian University was the University of Nigeria, Nsukka established in 1961; see S. O. Imhanobe, *Lawyer's Deskbook*, 2nd ed., Vol. 2, (Abuja: Rehoboth Publishing, 2010), 1143-1147.

[22] *Ibid* p. 1147.

passed. The former provides the guidelines for the training of persons desiring to become legal practitioners in Nigeria, while the latter regulates the practice of the profession in Nigeria.

1962-2013

Three categories of persons are entitled to practice as a barrister and solicitor in Nigeria today. They are as follows:[25]

a. Those entitled to practice generally, whose names are on the roll

A person shall be entitled to practice generally if, and only if, his name is on the role of legal practitioners kept by the Chief Registrar of the Supreme Court of Nigeria.[26]

A person shall be entitled to have his name on the roll if and only if he has been called to the Nigerian Bar by the Body of Benchers and produces a certificate of call to the Bar to the Registrar.[27]

A person shall be entitled to be called to the Bar if he is a citizen of Nigeria;[28] if he produces a qualifying certificate to the Body of Benchers and if he satisfies the Benchers that he is of good character.[29]

Production of Qualifying Certificate

The issuance of a qualifying certificate stating that a person is qualified to be called to the Bar is the responsibility of the Council of Legal

---

[23] The Legal Education Act of 1962 has been repealed and replaced with the Legal Education (Consolidation, etc.) Decree 1976, which revised and consolidated the previous Act and Amendments, formerly known as CAP 206 LFN 1976, now CAP L10 LFN 2004.

[24] The Legal Practitioners Act of 1962 was repealed in 1975 and replaced by the Legal Practitioners Decree of 1975, which was a consolidating Decree, which revised and consolidated the previous acts and amendments, formally called L.P.A. CAP 207 LFN 1990 now L.P.A. CAP L11 LFN 2004.

[25] Section 2 of the Legal Practitioners Act of 1962, now CAP L11 Vol. 8 LFN, 2004.

[26] Section 2 (1) LPA 2004.

[27] Section 7 (1) LPA 2004.

[28] Citizenship may be acquired by three ways: (a) by birth; (b) by registration; and (c) by naturalization.

[29] See Section 4 (1) L.P.A. as amended by the Legal Practitioners (Amendment) Decree No.9 of 1992.

Education. Two conditions are prescribed by Section 5 of the Legal Education Act for issuance of the certificate; they are:

i. Nigerian citizenship;
ii. Successful completion of a course of practical training in the Nigerian Law School, lasting for a period fixed by Council as an academic year.

Under Section 1 of the Legal Education (Consolidation, etc) (Amendment) Act, 1992, a non-citizen may now be entitled to have a qualifying certificate issued to him by the Council stating that he is qualified to be called to Bar, subject to the Council's direction.

Exemption from producing the qualifying certificate

The Council of Legal Education can exempt some Nigerians from the course at the Nigerian Law School before issuing a qualifying certificate.[30] All applications for exemption are screened by a Committee of the Council of Legal Education, which may grant full or partial exemption.[31] Under the regulations, there are two categories of persons exempted from the requirement of producing the qualifying certificate:

a. Persons in active legal practice

The Council in the exercise of this power may exempt a person from going through the course at the Law School if:

i. He is a Nigerian Citizen
ii. He is qualified to be admitted to the Nigerian Law School
iii. His qualifying subjects for admission to the Law School include all the core subjects prescribed by the Council of Legal Education; and
iv. At the time of the application for exemption, he satisfies the council that he has acquired knowledge and experience over a period of at least 5 years in the practice of law in a common law country, fitting him for enrolment;

---

[30] See: The Professional Bodies Special Provisions Act 1972 and the Professional Bodies (Legal profession) Exemption Order 1973.
[31] Section 2 (b) of the professional Bodies (Special Provisions) Act, CAP P33, Vol. 14 LFN, 2004.

v. The applicant did not attend the Nigerian Law School for reasons beyond his control;
vi. The applicant has been attached to chambers approved by council for a period of at least six calendar months and completed his dinner obligations;
vii. That it will be unreasonable, having regard to all the circumstances, to require him to go through the Law School.

b. Law Teachers

i. Graduates trained in common law countries who have been teaching law for five years or above in a Faculty of Law of a Nigerian University, can be exempted from Bar Part I Course; and
ii. Graduates trained in non-common law countries who have taught law in a Faculty of Law of a Nigerian University for ten years and above, can be exempted from Bar Part I Course.[32]

c. Those entitled to practice by warrant issued by the Chief Justice of Nigeria for the purpose of any particular proceeding

If a person is entitled to practice as an advocate in a country where the legal system is similar to that of Nigeria, he may apply to the Chief Justice of Nigeria and upon approval, pay the practicing fees.[33]

d. Those entitled to practice in Nigeria by virtue of office i.e. ex officio

A person for the time being exercising the function of any of the following offices that is:

a. the Office of the Attorney-General, Solicitor-General or Director of Public Prosecutions of the Federation or of a state,
b. such office in the civil service of the federation or of state as the Attorney General of the Federation of a State, as the case may be, may

---

[32] *Ibid.*
[33] S.2 (2) (a) & (b) LPA 2004; However, in the case of *Awolowo v. Minister of Internal Affairs* (1962) 1 All NLR 178, the provision of s. 2 (2) LPA received a restrictive interpretation to the effect that the applicant must be a person who is entitled to enter into Nigeria as of right. The court in this case held that the right of a citizen to be defended by a lawyer of his own choice is subjected to practical limitation that the legal practitioner of his own choice must not be subject to restriction or disability.

be order specify, shall be entitled to practice as a barrister and solicitor for the purpose of that office.[34]

Laws Regulating Legal Practice in Nigeria

a. **The Legal Education Act[35]** – the Act provides, inter alia, for the establishment, composition and functions of the Council of Legal Education;[36] responsibility for continuing legal education;[37] issuing the qualifying certificates for the purpose of call to Bar;[38] appointment and matters related to the tenure of staff and the Director-General;[39] Financial matters including the keeping of accounts[40] and repeal of some previous Acts.[41]

b. **The Legal Practitioners Act[42]** - this is the major Act which regulates the legal profession at present in Nigeria. It contains 25 sections and two schedules.[43] The Act deals with the following matters: the General Council of the Bar;[44] practice as a Legal Practitioner;[45]

---

[34] S.2 (3) LPA 2004.
[35] Chapter L 10 in the Laws of the Federation, 2004.
[36] Section 1-2 of the Act.
[37] S. 3 of the Legal Education Act (L.E.A).
[38] S. 5 of the L.E.A.
[39] S. 6-7 of the L.E.A
[40] S. 8-9 of the L.E.A
[41] J. O. Orojo, *Professional Conduct of Legal Practitioners in Nigeria*, 3rd ed., (Lagos: Mafix Books Limited, 2008), 27.
[42] Chapter L 11 in the Laws of the Federation, 2004.
[43] The first schedule provides the table of precedence for legal practice while the second makes supplementary provision to the disciplinary committee, e.g., the quorum, the power of the Chief Justice of Nigeria etc; see the Legal Practitioners Act 2004.
[44] S.1 of the L.P.A.
[45] S. 2-14 of the L.P.A. This covers such matters as the entitlement to practice as a Legal Practitioner, call to the Bar and enrollment, the Body of Benchers, conferment of the rank of senior advocate of Nigeria, etc.

Legal Practitioners remuneration;[46] safeguard for clients[47] and general provisions.[48]

Subsidiary legislation under the Legal Practitioners Act include

a. Standing Orders of the General Council of the Bar, 1963;
b. Legal Practitioners Account Rules, 1964;
c. Legal Practitioners (Disciplinary Committee) Rules, 1965;
d. Legal Practitioners (Special Facilities to practise in Nigeria) Regulations, 1968;
e. Senior Advocates of Nigeria (Privileges and Functions) Rules, 1979;
f. Body of Benchers Regulation, 1983;
g. Legal Practitioners (Remuneration for Legal Documentation and Other Land Matters) Order, 1995;
h. Entitlement to practise as Barristers and Solicitors (Federal Officers) Order, 1992
i. Entitlement to practise as Barristers and Solicitors (National Assembly Office) (Legal Practitioners) Order, 1995;
j. Entitlement to practise as Barristers and Solicitors (Federal Housing Authority) (Legal Practitioners) Order 1995;
k. Entitlement to practice as Barristers and Solicitors (Federal Road Safety Commission) Order, 1997;
l. Legal Practitioners (Bar Practising Fees) Notice, 2002; and
m. Rules of Professional Conduct for Legal Practitioners, 2007.[49]

Rights of a legal practitioner

In explaining the rights of a legal practitioner, it is important to understand who a legal practitioner/lawyer is. A lawyer is a person that

---

[46] S. 15- 19 of the L.P.A. This covers the scale of charges, the recovery and taxation of charges.

[47] S. 20 of the L.P.A. This covers the proper keeping of accounts, record for clients money and trust account.

[48] S. 22-25 of the L.P.A. This covers offences and punishment under the Act, maintenance of the roll, payment of practising fee, the exclusion of civil proceedings and interpretation.

[49] The RPC for legal practitioners 2007 commenced on the 2nd of January 2007. It provides the rules a legal practitioner must adhere to, and shall be examined in the course of this work on the duties owed by a legal practitioner.

has been trained in the law and certified to give legal advice or to represent others in litigation.[50]

The rights of a legal practitioner include:

a. Representation of litigants in any proceeding in all courts of Nigeria (except a Senior Advocate of Nigeria who cannot appear in lower courts) and preparation of documents in relation to proceedings in court.[51]
b. Incorporation of companies;[52]
c. Only legal practitioners are statutorily empowered to prepare conveyance documents;[53]
d. Preparation of documents for probate or letter of administration;[54]
e. Only a legal practitioner can be appointed as a judge to a superior court with the exception of the Sharia Court of Appeal and the Customary Court of Appeal;
f. Only a legal practitioner can be appointed an Attorney General either at the federal or state level of government.

Restriction on the rights of a legal practitioner

a. Non-payment of practicing fee - where a legal practitioner fails to pay his practicing fees, he would not be granted a right of audience in any court in Nigeria; he shall also not sign documents, pleadings, affidavit, depositions, applications, instruments, or process or file such documents as a legal practitioner.[55]
b. A member of the Nigerian Bar, whilst a servant or in a salaried employment of any kind, shall not appear as an advocate in a court or

---

[50] *Ali Safe v. Northern States Marketing Board* (1972) 1 All N.L.R 61; *Safe v. Northern States Marketing Board* (1972) 1 S.C. 19.
[51] Section 22 LPA 2004; *Uzodinma v. Police* 1982 1 NCR 27.
[52] Section 35 (3) Companies and Allied Matters Act CAP 20, Vol. III, LFN 2004.
[53] Section 22 (d) LPA 2004.
[54] Supra note 53.
[55] Section 8 (2) LPA 2004, Rule 9 RPC 2007 and Article 19 of the NBA Constitution 2001; Please note that nine-tenths of the money collected is paid to the Nigerian Bar Association for it to run its affairs and non-payment of this practicing fee is a breach of professional ethics. The fee must be paid not later than 31st of March each year and in the case of a new lawyer, within a month of enrolment.

judicial tribunal for his employer, except where the lawyer is employed as a legal officer in a government department.[56]

c. A lawyer, having once held public office or having been in public employment, shall not after his retirement accept employment in connection with a matter in respect of which he had previously acted in a judicial capacity or on the merit of which he had advised or dealt with in such office or employment.[57]

d. A judicial officer who has retired shall not practice as an advocate in any court of law or judicial tribunal in Nigeria, nor sign any pleading in any court.[58]

e. A legal practitioner who is a public officer shall not engage in private practice;[59]

f. A Senior Advocate of Nigeria cannot appear before any Superior Court of record except with a junior counsel or another Senior Advocate in civil cases; he may however appear alone in criminal cases;[60]

g. A legal practitioner shall not practice at the Bar and simultaneously practice any other profession,[61] without the authority of the General Council of the Bar or engage in any trade or business declared by the Bar Council to be incompatible with practice as a lawyer or which tends to undermine the high standing of the profession.[62]

h. Section 292 of the Constitution of the Federal Republic of Nigeria 1999 provides that any person who has held judicial office shall not on ceasing to be a judicial officer for any reason whatsoever thereafter appear or act as a legal practitioner before any court of law or tribunal in Nigeria.[63]

Duties of a Legal Practitioner

Upon call to the Nigerian Bar, a legal practitioner owes the following duties:

---

[56] Rule 8 of the Rules of Professional Conduct 2007.

[57] Rule 6 (2) of the R.P.C 2007.

[58] Rule 6 (3) & (4) of the R.P.C 2007.

[59] Section 1 part 1 of the 5th schedule of the 1999 Constitution of Nigeria.

[60] Section 5 (8) LPA 2004.

[61] The term 'other profession' refers to all forms of trading including the sale or purchase of commodities personally or as commission agent.

[62] Rule 7 of the R.P.C 2007

[63] See: *Atake v. Afejuku* (1994) 12 SCNJ1

a. A duty to the court

a. Not to obstruct, delay or adversely affect the administration of justice;[64]
b. Respect for the court;[65]
c. Not to conduct himself in a manner calculated to gain favour from a judge;[66]
d. A lawyer must deal with the court candidly and fairly;[67]
e. Honour and respect his undertaking to the court;[68]
f. To be fully prepared to go on with the case and not seek unnecessary adjournment;[69]
g. To conduct his cases in logical sequence to enable the court to follow the case with ease.

b. A duty to the state

a. Duty to act within the law;[70]
b. Duty to uphold and observe the rule of law.[71]

c. A duty to the profession

a. Duty not to instigate litigation;[72]
b. Duty to uphold and observe the rule of law, promote and foster the cause of justice, maintain a high standard of professional conduct and not engage in any conduct unbecoming of a legal practitionership;[73]
c. Not to knowingly do an act or conduct designed to lead to the admission into the legal profession of a person who is unsuitable for

---

[64] Rule 30 of the RPC 2007
[65] Rule 31-35 of the RPC 2007, *Magna Maritime Services Ltd & Anor v. S.A. Oteju & Anor.* (2005) ALL FWLR (Pt. 270); 6 S.C. 92
[66] Rule 34 RPC 2007, *Aladetoyinbo v. Adewunmi* (1990) 6 NWLR (pt. 154) 98
[67] Rule 32 RPC 2007
[68] Rule 37 (2) RPC 2007
[69] Rule 16 (b) RPC 2007
[70] Rule 15 (2)(a) RPC 2007
[71] Rule 1 RPC 2007
[72] Rule 47 (1) RPC 2007
[73] Rule 1 RPC 2007

admission by reason of his moral character or insufficient qualification;[74]

d. Not to aid a non-lawyer in the unauthorized practice of the law;[75]

e. Duty to treat opposing counsel with utmost courtesy;[76]

f. Duty against soliciting professional employment;[77]

g. Duty not to allow his services to be controlled or exploited by any agency, personal or corporate, which intervenes between him and his client.[78]

d. A duty to his client

The duties of a lawyer to his client are contained in the Rules of Professional Conduct for Legal Practitioners 2007 in Rules 14–25. A legal practitioner owes a duty to his client to:

a. Be dedicated and devoted to the cause of his client;[79]

b. Represent his client within the bounds of the law;[80]

c. Represent his client competently;[81]

d. Not to conflict his interest with that of his client;[82]

e. Agreement with his client as to his fees;[83]

f. Not to betray the confidence of his client,[84] subject to the exceptions as provided in Rule 19 (2) of the RPC2007;

g. Not to act in any contemplated or pending litigation as a witness for his client, subject to the exceptions as provided in the rules;[85]

h. Not to abandon or withdraw from an employment with a client once assumed except for a good cause;[86]

---

[74] Rule 2 RPC 2007

[75] Rule 3 (1)(a) RPC 2007

[76] Rule 27 RPC 2007

[77] Rule 39 (3) RPC 2007

[78] Rule 4 RPC 2007

[79] Rule 14 RPC 2007, *Queen v. Imadebhor Eguabor* (1962) 1 All NLR 287

[80] Rule 15 RPC 2007

[81] Rule 16 RPC 2007, *Rondel v. Worsley* (1969) 1 AC 191

[82] Rule 17 RPC 2007, *Onigbongbo Community v. Minister of Lagos Affairs and Ors* (1971) LPELR-SC271/1971

[83] Rule 18 RPC 2007

[84] Rule 19 RPC 2007

[85] Rule 20 RPC 2007, *Elebanjo v. Tijani* (1980) 5 NWLR Pt.46, p.954.

[86] Rule 21 RPC 2007

i. Not to call at clients' houses or place of business, except in special circumstances;[87]

j. Not abuse, use or mix clients' property or money with his;[88]

k. To accept any brief brought to him by a client except where special circumstances justify his refusal;[89]

l. Investigation of facts and production of witnesses on behalf of his client.[90]

Regulatory Bodies of the Legal Profession in Nigeria
Council of Legal Education

The Council of Legal Education was established by the Legal Education Act 1962.[91] It is a body corporate with perpetual succession and a common seal. It can sue and be sued in its own name.[92]

It consists of the following members:

a. A Chairman[93] to be appointed by the President on the recommendation of the Attorney-General of the Federation;

b. Attorneys-General of States or, where there is no Attorneys-General, the Solicitors-General of the State;

c. A representative of the Federal Ministry of Justice to be appointed by the Attorney–General of the Federation;

d. The Head of the Faculty of Law (accredited) of any recognized University in Nigeria whose course of studies is approved by the Council as sufficient qualification for admission to the Nigerian Law School;

e. The President of the Nigerian Bar Association;

f. 15 persons entitled to practice as Legal Practitioners in Nigeria of not less than ten years standing and selected or elected by the Nigerian Bar Association;

---

[87] Rule 22 RPC 2007

[88] Rule 23 RPC 2007

[89] Rule 24 RPC 2007

[90] Rule 25 RPC 2007

[91] Note: the Act has been replaced by the Legal Education (Consolidation, etc.) Act 1976 CAP. L10, LFN 2004

[92] See: S. 1 (2) of the Legal Education Act CAP L10 LFN, 2004; *Okonjo v. Council of Legal Education* FAC/L16/78 March 12, 1979.

[93] The Chairman and two authors hold office for four years and can be reappointed for another four years unless they are removed or resign. Council members are not entitled to remuneration.

g. The Director–General of the Nigerian Law School;
h. Two persons who must be authors of published learned works in the field of law, to be appointed by the Attorney-General of the Federation.[94]

Under Section 4 of the Act, the Attorney-General of the Federation may give to the Council directions of a general character with regards to the exercise of the Council of its functions and it shall be the duty of the Council to comply with such direction.

Functions of the Council include

a. Legal education of persons seeking to become members of the legal profession,[95]
b. Assumes responsibility of the Nigerian Institute for Continuing Legal Education for legal practitioners;[96]
c. Sets standards for the law faculties in the universities through the accreditation programme;[97]
d. Incidental matters, such as conditions which a University Faculty of Law must comply with before its students are given admission to the Law School;
e. To ensure that aspirants are fit and proper persons.[98]

Body of Benchers

The Body was first established in 1974 by the Legal Practitioners (Amendment) Decree, which is now re-enacted as S.3 (1) of the LPA 2004.[99] This provides that:

---

[94] Section 2 (1) of the Legal Education Act, CAP L10 LFN, 2004.

[95] The Council is charged with the primary responsibility for training prospective members of the legal profession. In April 1963, the Council established a school known as the Nigerian Law School for the purpose of providing "practical training in the work of a barrister and of a solicitor." Only those who have successfully completed the one-year of practical training offered by the school are issued a qualifying certificate and admitted to the Nigerian legal profession by the Council.

[96] Section 3 LPA CAP L11 LFN 2004.

[97] S. O. Imhanobe, *Lawyer's Deskbook*, 2nd ed., Vol. 2, (Abuja: Rehoboth Publishing, 2010), 1172.

[98] Section 1 (2) & 5 of the Legal Education Act, CAP L10 LFN, 2004.

[99] It is the equivalent in Nigeria of the Benchers in the Inns of Court of England. It was first thought of in 1967 by the Council of Legal Education so as to bridge the

There shall be a body of Legal Practitioners of the highest distinction in the legal profession in Nigeria to be known as the Body of Benchers.

The Body of Benchers is a body corporate with perpetual succession and a common seal.[100] To become a member of the Body of Benchers, candidates must be of highest distinction and possess a minimum requirement of 15 years post-call standing.

Members of the Body include

a. The Chief Justice of Nigeria[101] and all Justices of the Supreme Court;
b. The President of the Court of Appeal;
c. The Attorney General of the Federation;
d. The Presiding Justice of the Court of Appeal Divisions;
e. The Chief Judge of the Federal High Court;
f. The Chief Judge of the Federal Capital Territory, Abuja
g. The Chief Judge of the States of the Federation;
h. The Attorneys-General of the States of the Federation;
i. The President of the Nigerian Bar Association;
j. The Chairman of the Council of Legal Education;
k. Thirty legal practitioners nominated by the Nigerian Bar Association;
l. And such number of persons not exceeding ten, who appear to the Body of Benchers to be eminent members of the legal profession in Nigeria of not less than 15 years' post-call standing.[102]

Under this Body, there is no statutory Chairman. The Chairmanship of the Body rotates between the Bench and the Bar in such a manner that when the Chairman is from the Bench, the Vice-Chairman comes from the Bar; the Vice-Chairman automatically becomes the Chairman in the succeeding year and his vice a member of the Bench.[103] The Body has powers under its regulations to confer membership of the Body for life on

---

gap between the students of the law school and senior members of the Bench and the Bar and to learn professional etiquette.

[100] Regulation 3(2) of the Body of Benchers Regulations of 1983.

[101] By virtue of office, the Chief Justice of Nigeria is a Life Bencher.

[102] Section 3(1) of the L.P.A., CAP L11, LFN 2004.

[103] S. O. Imhanobe, *Lawyer's Deskbook*, 2nd ed., Vol. 2, (Abuja: Rehoboth Publishing, 2010), 1156-1157.

any person who would otherwise not be a member,[104] and to appoint honorary members.[105]

The Body of Benchers is responsible for

a. The formal Call to Bar of persons seeking to become legal practitioners in Nigeria;[106]
b. The exercise of disciplinary jurisdiction over members of the profession and over students seeking to become legal practitioners;
c. Taking measures which appear to it to be necessary or expedient for maintaining at all times the traditional values of the Legal Practitioners;
d. Prescribing fees to be paid by legal practitioners pursuant to the provisions of this Act after consultation with the Association.[107]

Privileges accorded to Benchers include

a. They have the same privileges as a law officer;
b. They can mention their cases first when listed for mention;
c. They sit in the inner row or front row.[108]

Legal Practitioners Privileges Committee

The Legal Practitioners Privileges Committee (L.P.P.C) is established pursuant to Section 5(3) of the L.P.A and consists of the following:

---

[104] Reg. 2(2) of the Body of Benchers Regulations of 1983.
[105] *Ibid*, Reg. 1(2).
[106] In performing these functions, the Body has prescribed three requirements for persons seeking to become legal practitioners in Nigeria, such as:
a. Keeping dinner terms (the importance of which is for the aspirants to the Bar to meet eminent members of the Profession, learn some of the unwritten rules of the profession, etc.)
b. Sponsorship of aspirants to the Bar by two Benchers
c. The person seeking to become a legal practitioner must be a fit and proper person.
[107] *Ibid*, S. O. Imhanobe, 1177.
[108] Note that these privileges accorded to a Bencher are accorded only for the period that he is a Bencher. Benchers have no elaborate ceremony on conferment and are difficult to identify as a result of the fact that they do not wear any special gown or wig, unlike Senior Advocates who are identified by the silk gown they wear.

a. The Chief Justice who shall be the Chairman
b. The Attorney General of the Federation
c. One Justice of the Supreme Court
d. The President of the Court of Appeal
e. Five Chief Judges of the States
f. The Chief Judge of the Federal High Court
g. Five legal practitioners who are Senior Advocates of Nigeria.[109]

Section 5 (4) of the L.P.A further provides that:
"The members of the committee under paragraphs (c), (d) and (g) of Sub-section 3 of this Section shall be appointed by the Chief Justice in consultation with the Attorney General of the Federation."

Functions of the Legal Practitioners Privileges Committee include

a. The L.P.P.C is responsible for the conferment on a legal practitioner the prestigious rank of Senior Advocate of Nigeria.[110]
b. The L.P.P.C with the approval of the Body of Benchers makes rules as to the privileges to be accorded to Senior Advocates of Nigeria. [111]

Requirements for the conferment of the rank of Senior Advocate of Nigeria

Section 5 (2) of the LPA empowers the LPPC to confer the rank of Senior Advocate of Nigeria on a legal practitioner, upon application to the Registrar of the Supreme Court of Nigeria. A person shall be conferred the rank of SAN upon application, provided he has:

a. been qualified to practice as a legal practitioner in Nigeria for no less than 10 years and has achieved distinction in the legal profession;
b. The applicant must provide 10 particulars of contested cases which he has handled, which he believes to be of particular substance, complexity or particular difficulty or sensitivity handled by the applicant.[112]

---

[109] The Chief Registrar of the Supreme Court is the Secretary to the Committee.
[110] Section 5 (1) of the L.P.A
[111] Section 5 (7) of the L.P.A
[112] The 10 contested cases shall consist of 3 cases from the Supreme Court of Nigeria, 3cases from the Court of Appeal and 4 cases must have been decided by a

c. Payment of a non-refundable fee of two hundred thousand Naira for each application upon submission, payable to the Chief Registrar of the Supreme Court of Nigeria "SAN ACCOUNT"; cheques are drawn in Nigeria Naira from the Nigerian Bank. Acknowledgement of receipt of application shall be received by the applicant within 14 days of receipt of his application and payment of the prescribed fee.[113]
d. Physical inspection of the applicant's chamber and library to ensure that in the opinion of the committee, it meets the high standard in terms of staff and legal materials.

Legal Practitioners Remuneration Committee

The Legal Practitioners Remuneration Committee is established by virtue of Section 15 (1) of the L.P.A., and consists of:

a. The Attorney-General of the Federation, who shall be the chairman of the Committee;
b. The Attorney-Generals' of the States;
c. The President of the Nigerian Bar Association and
d. Three other members of the N.B.A.

The Legal Practitioners Remuneration Committee has the major function of making orders regulating the charges of legal practitioners.[114] The current charges of the Legal Practitioner are regulated by the Legal Practitioners (Remuneration for Legal Documentation and Other Land Matters) Order, 1991.

The General Council of The Bar

Section 1 (1) of the LPA provides for the establishment of the General Council of the Bar, which is also referred to in the Act as 'the Bar Council.'[115] The Bar Council consists of:

High Court or an Arbitral Tribunal – Guidelines for the Conferment of SAN, Rule 3 (7) 1; The citation of the law report is to be provided, but otherwise the applicant is to provide certified hard copy as well as electronic PDF version. Applicants are encouraged to provide particulars of recent cases to demonstrate current engagement in full time practice and that the applicant is abreast with current developments in the law.

[113] R.3(2) Part 1 of the Guidelines for the Conferment of SAN 2007.

[114] Section 15 (3) of the L.P.A.

[115] Section 1(1) LPA.

a. The Attorney-General of the Federation, who shall be the President of the Council;
b. The Attorneys-General of all the States; and
c. Twenty members of the Association (of which not less than seven must be legal practitioners of not less than ten years post call standing).[116]

The Bar Council is charged with the following functions

a. To make the rules of professional conduct.[117]
b. To make rules for keeping accounts and records of clients' money by a Legal Practitioner;[118]
c. To determine what business is incompatible with the status of a legal practitioner;
d. Any other function as may be conferred on the Council by the Constitution of the Nigerian Bar Association.

The Nigerian Bar Association

The Nigerian Bar Association, established in 1958, is a corporate entity; thus the NBA through its registered trustees can sue and be sued. The NBA comprises of all legal practitioners in Nigeria. Membership is automatic upon being called to the Nigerian Bar. Members are expected to pay their annual practicing fee,[119] default of which, such a member cannot appear in court.

Functions of the Nigerian Bar Association include

a. To maintain the integrity and independence of the Bar and the defence of the Bar in its relations with the Judiciary and Executive arms of Government;
b. To promote the improvement of the system of administration of justice;
c. To establish an endowment fund for the proper discharge of its functions;

---

[116] Section 1(2) LPA.
[117] Section 12 (4) of the LPA (as amended by Section 10 of the Legal Practitioners (Amendment) Decree No. 21of 1994).
[118] Section 20 LPA.
[119] On or before 31st of March every year.

d. To ensure the highest standards of professional conduct;
e. To promote legal education and law reform;
f. To promote good relationships among members of the Association.[120]

Legal Practitioners Disciplinary Committee

The Legal Practitioners Disciplinary Committee is established by virtue of Section 11 of the LPA as amended.[121] The Committee is charged with the duty of considering and determining any case where it is alleged that a person who is a member of the legal profession has misbehaved in his capacity as such or should for any reason be the subject of proceedings under this Act.[122]

The Disciplinary Committee consists of

a. A Chairman who shall not be the Chief Justice of Nigeria or a Justice of the Supreme Court;
b. Two Justices of the Court of Appeal, one of whom shall be the President of the Court of Appeal;
c. Two Chief Judges;
d. Two Attorneys-General, who shall be either the Attorney-General of the Federation and the Attorney-General of a State or two State Attorneys-General; and
e. Four members of the Nigerian Bar Association who are not connected with either the investigation of a complaint or the decision by the Association to present a complaint against a legal practitioner for determination by the disciplinary committee.[123]

---

[120] Constitution of the Nigerian Bar Association, clause 2 (a) – (f).
[121] By virtue of Section 9 of Decree No.21 of 1994 which introduced substantial amendments to the LPA (The LPA, CAP L 11, LFN, 2004 omitted this substantial amendment introduced by the Decree).
[122] Categories of unprofessional conduct: infamous conduct in a professional respect; conviction of an offence incompatible with the status of a legal practitioner; fraudulent enrolment and misconduct not amounting to infamous conduct but incompatible with the status of a legal practitioner. See: Section 12 (1) & (2) of the LPA (as amended).
[123] *Ibid*, Section 11 (2).

On the importance of the Legal Practitioners Disciplinary Committee, Hon. Justice Umaru Eri, OFR, Chairman of the Legal Practitioners Disciplinary Committee, in *N.B.A v. Odiri*[124] stated that:

> Most professions, if not all, provide in-house machinery to suspend or expel from the practice of a professional standard. The Bar is no exception. The central means by which the Bar itself controls the conduct of legal practitioners and jealously guards the reputation for the maintenance of high professional standards is the application of disciplinary sanctions of its code of conduct.[125]

Reference of complaints to committee

The procedure for the reference of complaint to the committee is set out in rules 3 and 4 of the Legal Practitioners Disciplinary Committee Rules, which state that a complaint by any person against a legal practitioner shall be forwarded in writing by the complainant to any of the following persons: the Chief Justice of Nigeria; the Attorney-General of the Federation; the President of the Court of Appeal or any Presiding Justice of the Court of Appeal; the Chief Judge of the High Court of a State or the Chief Judge of the Federal Capital Territory; the Attorney-General of a State; the Chairman Body of Benchers and the Chairman of the Nigerian Bar Association, or the Chairman of a State Branch of the Nigerian Bar Association.

A complaint received by any of the above persons is to be forwarded to the Nigerian Bar Association which shall cause the complaint to be investigated to find out if there is a *prima facie* case or not. If there is no *prima facie* case, the complaint would be cancelled; if there is, the Nigerian Bar Association shall forward a report of such a case to the Legal Practitioners Disciplinary Committee, together with all the documents considered by the Nigerian Bar Association and a copy of the charges[126] on which the Nigerian Bar Association is of the opinion that a *prima facie* case is shown.

---

[124] (2007) 8 NWLR (pt. 1035) 203.

[125] *Ibid*, S. O. Imhanobe, 1190.

[126] With regard to what amounts to a charge in this regard, it was held in *Okike v. L.P.D.C & 3 Ors*. (2005) 15 NWLR (pt. 949) 471 that a charge of professional misconduct is not by any standard a criminal charge but civil in nature and is akin to a charge for conversion of clients fund by a legal practitioner which is a clear professional misconduct.

On the direction of the Chairman of the committee, upon the satisfaction that a *prima facie* case does exist, the Legal Practitioners Disciplinary Committee Secretary shall fix a date, time and place for the hearing of the matter and communicate this to the parties. The proceedings shall be held in private but its findings and directions shall be announced in public. When a decision is given, the committee will cause a notice of the direction to be served on the person to whom it relates and submit to the Body of Benchers a report on the findings which resulted in the issuance of the notice. A person to whom a direction relates may, at any time within 28 days from the date of service on him of the direction, appeal against the direction to the Supreme Court.[127]

The directions which the committee or the Supreme Court may give include:

a. Ordering the Chief Registrar to strike that person's name off the roll;[128] or

b. Suspending that person from practice by ordering him not to engage in practice as a legal practitioner for such period as may be specified in the direction;[129] or

c. Admonishing that person;[130]

d. Restoration of names to the roll.[131]

Conclusion

The laws regulating the Nigerian legal profession by their provisions together with the regulatory bodies of the profession promote the ethics of the profession and maintain a relatively high standard when compared to other professions as exemplified by the cases earlier referred to in the body of this chapter. Legal practitioners must therefore in their best interest adhere to the rules guiding the profession or otherwise face the consequences for their failure.

---

[127] *Ibid*, Section 11 (7).

[128] This is reserved for the most serious misconduct; see the case of *Re Martin* (1843) 6 Beav. 337, 49 E.R. 856; *Re Abuah* (1962) 1 All NLR 279, p. 285.

[129] This will be ordered where the misconduct is not of such a serious nature as to warrant striking off; see the case of *Re Cyril v. Rogers Wright* 7 WACA 17.

[130] See the case of *Re: Certain Legal Practitioners* 5. F.S.C. 233, *Ikpeazu v. African Continental Bank Limited* (1965) NMLR 374.

[131] *Ibid*, Section 12 (1) (c) (i)-(iii); See the Case of *Re A. C. Abuah* (1962) 1 All NLR 279, p. 285, *Adesanya v.Attorney-General of the Federation* S. C. (1964) 130.

CHAPTER TWELVE

ADVOCACY AND MOOTING SKILLS

ONYEKA OSUJI[1]

Chapter Aims

The aims of this chapter are to:

(1) Explain the meaning of advocacy
(2) Explain the meaning of mooting
(3) Link advocacy and mooting
(4) Outline advocacy skills
(5) Highlight the importance and benefits of advocacy and mooting skills to law students
(6) Outline practical tips for success in mooting
(7) Outline the common mooting judging criteria.

Advocacy and Mooting: Concepts and Implications

Advocacy: Meaning and Reach

Advocacy is the art of persuasion. In the courtroom context, advocacy involves persuading the judge to accept one's arguments or discredit the opponent's case. Advocacy requires compliance with applicable rules and conventions. It is a core component of the work of legal practitioners who appear before the court. However, law students can practise advocacy in mooting and mock trials. Advocacy requires the application of a bundle of skills which will be identified and discussed later.

As a bundle of skills, advocacy can be learned, acquired, practised, improved and polished. It may be helpful to read books and other

---

[1]PhD (Manchester), BCL (Oxford), LL.B (Hons) (Nigeria), Senior Lecturer, University of Exeter, United Kingdom.

materials, observe proceedings in the court or elsewhere, or watch videos of top advocates in performance. However, constant practice and rehearsals are essential even for the most experienced advocate. Learning, no matter how advanced, cannot displace the need for practising advocacy.

Mooting: Meaning

Mooting is the simulation of arguments of legal issues in the imagined setting of an appellate court. Mooting mirrors the real court environment and requires the argument of points of law raised by hypothetical cases in accordance with the rules of the legal profession. The parties in a moot case are the appellant and the respondent. The appellant attempts to persuade an appellate court to reverse the decision and/or overrule or reject the reasoning of the lower court which the respondent supports.

Mooting and the Real Courtroom

Mooting and professional legal advocacy share the same objective of persuading the court of the correctness of one's arguments. Both generally follow similar conventions and professional rules of ethics and conduct. Nevertheless, mooting differs from the real court in certain ways.

Firstly, mooting involves students while professionally qualified advocates present before the real court. However, both student mooters and legal practitioners are required to be aware of and comply with the rules and conventions of the legal profession. Secondly, mooting is often designed to be set before an appellate court but legal practitioners appear before both trial and appellate courts. Thirdly, the facts in the moot problem are assumed to be true and advocates are not expected to contradict such facts. In the real court, however, factual evidence is required during trials and in certain situations may be allowed with the permission of the court in hearings before the appellate court.

Mooting and Mock Trials

Mooting can be distinguished from mock trials although they are both simulations of courtroom cases. Mooting tests the applicable law and legal principles in hypothetical cases. However a mock trial examines the handling and presentation of evidence (facts) and includes examination, cross-examination and re-examination of witnesses. A mock trial is often designed as a first instance trial and focuses on the evidence and testimonies required to prove a case. Therefore advocacy at mock trials is aimed at proving the facts of a case and the applicability of the law to such facts.

Mooting and Debating

Similarities: Mooting and debating share some similarities which include:

Public speaking

Both mooting and debating require one to speak in front of a public audience. The speaker in mooting and debating is the focus of the attention of the audience when he or she is speaking.

Communication

In mooting and debating, speakers attempt to communicate ideas and arguments. Therefore, clarity of language and expression is important in both contexts.

Persuasion

Mooting and debating share a similar goal of persuading judges that their arguments and points are better than the opponent's. In other words, mooting and debating may present opportunities for the speaker to demonstrate advocacy skills.

Rules and conventions

Usually rules and conventions govern mooting and debating events which speakers are expected to be aware of and comply with. Mooting and debating are therefore not occasions for people to speak or behave in any manner they like.

Timed speech

Although mooting and debating require speeches from the participants, such speeches are usually timed. It is therefore important for speakers to be aware of the time constraints of a mooting or debating event and prepare their speeches accordingly.

Responding to the points raised by opponents

In both mooting and debating it is not enough for one to prepare one's case or argument. It is also important to anticipate and understand the points raised or to be raised by opponents and respond to them appropriately.

Contest

A mooting or debating event is usually a contest between two sides. However, the desire to win should not dispense with the need to comply with applicable rules of the competition and behave fairly toward rivals.

Differences

There are significant differences between mooting and debating. These differences relate to the nature of the rules and conventions, the nature of the topic and the relevance of professional standards.

Issues/Topics

Mooting is restricted to an argument on legal issues but the subject of a debate can in fact be any matter including law, politics, economics, science, fashion and sports.

Rules

Participants in mooting are required to follow the rules and conventions of the legal profession. No such requirement exists in debating which is not constrained by the need to mirror the legal professional standards and the real courtroom. Debating organizers can design any rules they find suitable and are not constrained by professional legal requirements.

Advocacy and University Education

Law students often undertake their academic education in universities where the emphasis is on critical reasoning. University education enables one to start 'thinking as a lawyer'. In most universities advocacy is not formally taught because it is assumed that the Law School which provides the professional legal training incorporates advocacy into its programme.

However, students who are expected to demonstrate advocacy in moot court hearings and mock trial events, for example, need to acquire certain advocacy skills to succeed as law students. These skills are also required for life after education. It may be too late if students wait until the Law School stage or professional legal practice to start paying attention to advocacy skills.

Advocacy Skills

An advocate learns and acquires a number of skills which are useful for the art of persuasion. These skills, which are required before, during and after presenting one's case before the court, are useful for identifying legal issues, preparing and making submissions and complying with the rules and conventions of the legal profession and society.

Planning

Planning is usually central to the success of advocates. It requires organisational skills and the ability to anticipate and deal with future matters and resolve difficulties in advance. Planning helps advocates to allocate roles and organize research, presentation and rehearsals.

Research

Research is important for advocacy. It enables advocates to learn and understand the area of law they are arguing as well as the social, ethical and other non-legal issues related to the case. Research helps advocates to become 'experts' in what they are doing and be more persuasive in their submissions.

Inter-Disciplinary Research

Advocacy may involve research of fields other than law in order to effectively prepare for cases and presentation. For example, a criminal law matter involving the use of a prohibited drug which caused death or grievous bodily injury will require the investigation of the nature and consequences of administering the drug. Fluency of presentation requires the advocate to demonstrate this technical scientific or medical knowledge in addition to knowledge of the substantive and procedural laws surrounding the matter. The advocate has to know how the drug works, its properties and its indications and contraindications. In fact, the history of the drug's development, clinical trials and regulatory approval may be helpful in some cases.

Reading

Law requires a lot of reading whether one is a student or a practitioner. Relevant statutory provisions, cases, administrative reports, scholarly commentaries and news materials may sometimes be voluminous. It is also not unusual for opposing counsel to refer to an extensive range of materials. An advocate is expected to read materials referred to by opposing counsel in addition to their own materials in order to prepare well for court cases. This helps an advocate to anticipate and respond to the opponent's case and also avoid being a victim of unpleasant surprises.

Writing

Writing is a component of advocacy and is required, for instance, for briefs and skeleton arguments. An advocate is expected to demonstrate clarity and conciseness of expression in their writing. An advocate is required to be formal when writing briefs or skeleton arguments and to comply with the rules of grammar as well as the legal professional etiquette. A sloppy piece of writing or one full of grammatical errors and inconsistencies does not do any good to the image of an advocate.

Analysis

Analysis is the process of investigating or breaking down the constitutive elements of materials such as legislative provisions, judicial opinions and scholarly commentaries.

A central component of advocacy is the ability to interpret legal and other materials. An advocate is expected to identify aspects of the materials that help his or her case and distinguish the ones which seem to weaken the advocate's case and support the opponent's case.

Conciseness

A good advocate is concise in both speaking and writing. Verbosity can affect time and space management. It can distract the audience from the message in a speech or piece of writing. Long-winded presentations and writings can lose advocates their audience.

Critical Reasoning and Engagement

An advocate should at all times demonstrate the ability to critically reason and engage with the law, and the facts and issues surrounding a case. Critical thinking is core to the practice of law.

Persuasion

Persuasion is central to advocacy. An advocate is expected to speak well, maintain eye contact with the judge and employ gestures and other speaking aids to persuade the judge of the correctness of his or her arguments.

Confidence

An advocate is expected to demonstrate confidence in public speaking. Confidence is required of advocates even when judges and opposing counsel employ undermining tactics.

Listening

Advocacy is said to be the art of public speaking. However, advocacy requires one to be a good listener. An advocate ought to listen to judges in order to respond appropriately to queries. An advocate who does not listen to opposing counsel is unlikely to understand the arguments of that counsel and prepare effective responses.

Professional Ethics and Conduct

An advocate is a legal professional. Whether in real professional practice or in student mooting, an advocate is expected to follow the rules and conventions of the legal profession including the ethics and proper conduct towards the judges, counsel, court officials, clients, and the public.

Language

Advocacy requires the use of formal language. It is not the same as having a conversation at home or on the street. The use of colloquial expressions and slang should be avoided unless it is directly relevant to the case before the court.

Appearance

An advocate has to follow the professional rules of dressing and maintain a sober appearance. An advocate should avoid any type of dressing, accessories and other items that may attract undue attention. A good image is critical to a lawyer, since it will command respect, while an untidy appearance undermines the ability of the advocate to persuade others that he or she has a good case.

Decorum

Advocacy involves public speaking and therefore advocates are expected to be aware of the public nature of their presence and presentations and comply with the professional and social rules for public behaviour. For example, it does not help at all if an advocate is aggressive, condescending or abusive towards opposing counsel, judges or the audience. It is also disrespectful to the court to use a mobile phone while in court.

Problem-Solving

Advocacy is a problem-solving skill. It requires the identification of relevant issues and controversies plus the solutions and responses to such problems. An advocate in legal practice or student mooting is expected to disentangle difficult legal questions and make suggestions to the court on how to resolve such difficulties in accordance with the law and legal principles.

Patience and Tolerance

An advocate is expected to be patient towards judges, opposing counsel, clients and the public even in difficult situations. Advocacy requires tolerance of differences among people including the social backgrounds, language and mannerisms of other people.

Stress Management

Public speaking can be stressful but a good advocate is able to deal with the stress-related difficulties arising from case preparation and presentation. Dealing with stress depends on the individual concerned and what is good for one advocate may not be helpful for another. It is for individual advocates to find out what can calm them and avoid actual and potential stressors.

Time Management

An advocate is expected to demonstrate good time management skills. An advocate ought to be aware of and comply with deadlines such as the time for submitting briefs of argument or skeleton arguments. The length of speeches should not be excessive or too brief.

Teamwork and Collaboration

Advocates in legal practice and student mooting work in teams and are therefore expected to demonstrate the ability to work as part of a team. Collaboration requires the sharing of information, discussion of ideas and agreement on tactics and strategies.

E-Resources

The legal practice environment is increasingly surrounded by digital and electronic resources. Modern advocates ought to be aware of and exploit such resources in research, preparing cases and presenting their cases.

Application of Advocacy Skills

Advocacy presents a useful set of skills. Advocacy skills are often required to be demonstrated in wide ranging circumstances including professional legal practice environments, during study, and in pre- and post-employment situations.

Legal Practice

A barrister is expected to be aware of and apply advocacy skills in his or her work. A 'good' barrister is actually one who is able to demonstrate and effectively apply the bundle of advocacy skills required in preparing and presenting cases before the court.

Student Mooting

Since mooting mirrors the professional legal practice, it enables students to acquire and at the same time demonstrate advocacy skills.

Study

Advocacy skills are also required for one to be a successful student. For example, a good student needs to conduct good research, write and present ideas well in a concise and clear manner, and also be a good manager of time and materials.

Job Interviews

An interviewee usually attempts to persuade potential employers of his or her suitability for a post. A successful interview may require one to demonstrate a range of advocacy skills such as research, confidence, stress management, clarity and conciseness of expression, and problem solving.

Employment Situations

Advocacy skills may help one to excel in the workplace. This does not need to be in a law office. For instance, stress management and time management are likely to be useful in different public and private working environments.

Other Situations

It is possible for advocacy skills to be useful in other situations such as participation in debates, legislative proceedings, administrative hearings, public petitions, public and community relations, stakeholder engagement and management, and diplomacy.

Practical Advocacy in Mooting

Advocacy is central to mooting. It is important to reiterate that mooting provides a strong platform for law students to acquire and demonstrate advocacy skills. Success in mooting is often judged by the level of the expression of advocacy skills. A mooter should always remember to think and behave like a lawyer.

Mooting Participants

Participants in mooting vary from one mooting event to another. However, mooting requires a minimum of four types of participants including two mooters for each side, a court clerk, a judge and the master/mistress of the moot.

a. Mooters (Advocates)

The appellant and the respondent are usually represented by two mooters, a senior advocate and a junior advocate often known as the leading and junior counsel respectively. The terms ‘senior’ and ‘junior’ are not a mark of superiority but in fact refers to the order of speeches. Senior counsel normally speaks before the junior counsel. The order of speeches is usually as follows:

Senior Counsel for the Appellant
Junior Counsel for the Appellant
Senior Counsel for the Respondent
Junior Counsel for the Respondent

b. Clerk

The clerk of the court is a student whose main role is to be the timekeeper. The clerk also announces the arrival and departure of the judge and acts as the intermediary between the judge and the advocates who are not normally expected to approach the court directly.

c. Judge

The judge presides over the proceedings, asks questions for the mooters, and announces the judgment and result of the moot. The judge can be a student, an academic, a legal practitioner or a serving judge.

d. Master/Mistress of the Moot

The master or mistress of the moot is a student who is responsible for organising a mooting event. In some institutions, two students play the role.

Preparation for Mooting

Mooters are expected to prepare individually and as a team. Collective preparation for mooting may involve a series of meetings. Mooters ought to meet and to discuss individual and collective preparation, identify relevant issues from the moot problem, agree on the method of research and agree on tentative and final roles for team members. The frequency of meetings may depend on the nature of the mooting event and the convenience of the mooters.

Legal Research

Research is essential to mooting. The main sources of legal research are statutes, cases, statute books, law reports, textbooks, practitioner books, scholarly commentaries and journal articles.

There are various reasons for legal research which may include:

Clarification of issues- Research enables one to gain deeper understanding of the legal issues raised by a moot problem.

Application of legal principles to facts- Research helps one to identify the law that applies to the facts of a moot problem.

Finding authorities for arguments- Research is useful for locating authorities to support one's arguments.

Refutation of opponents' case- Research can help one to discredit or weaken the opponent's points or case.

Distinguishing cases- Research is essential for distinguishing cases that appear to weaken or undermine one's case or points.

Authorities

A key ingredient in legal arguments is the citation of authorities. Authorities are of different classes including statutes and subsidiary legislation, cases, scholarly commentaries and opinions. In citing authorities, as much detail as possible should be given. For instance, to cite a case it is important to refer to the names of the parties and the year, volume and page of the law report.

A mooter has to be aware of the status of applicable authorities. The ranking system which should determine the priority given to authorities is usually as follows:

1. The Constitution
2. Statutes and subsidiary legislation
3. Cases
4. Scholarly commentaries and opinions

Cases

Status and Priority

The status of cases depends on a number of factors, including:

1. The **doctrine of precedent**: The position of the deciding court in the hierarchy of courts is important. Under the common law tradition and in accordance with the provisions of the Nigerian Constitution a judgment of a higher court is normally binding on a lower court. A decision of a lower court can only have a persuasive effect for a higher court.

2. ***Ratio decidendi* and *obiter dictum***: The doctrine of precedent applies only to the *ratio decidendi* (reasoning) in judgments and not to *obiter dictum. Obiter dicta* are statements by judges which are not part of the reasoning of the judgment. However, the remarks can be strongly persuasive if they have been made by a higher court, for example the Supreme Court, in very clear and emphatic circumstances.

3. **Unanimity of judgment**: A unanimous decision of a panel of judges may appear stronger than a judgment that contains majority and minority opinions. Sometimes a minority opinion in a lower court judgment can be more persuasive to a higher court because of the reasoning it contains.

4. **Age/Date of judgment**: Although older cases can be regarded as *locus classicus* in some instances, more recent cases are likely to be more persuasive to the court, particularly where the conclusion and reasoning in older and recent cases are in conflict. It is, for example, assumed that more recent cases take later changes in legislation and other legal developments into consideration.

Distinguishing cases

It is sometimes useful in advocacy and mooting to distinguish cases which may appear to be against one's case or submissions. Methods of distinguishing cases include:

Doctrine of precedent

The doctrine of precedent which permits a higher court to ignore the decision of a lower court can be used to distinguish cases. It can also be relied on in distinguishing a case by proving that the case has been overruled or reversed by a superior judgment.

Reason and obiter distinction

A closer analysis of a judicial opinion can determine whether the statement forms part of the reasoning for the judgment in which case the doctrine of precedent applies. If the statement is merely *obiter* it can be distinguished and may not be hugely influential for the decision of the court in a current case.

Different facts

Cases can be distinguished by highlighting material differences in the facts of those cases and the one currently before the court. The law is applied to facts and differences in facts of cases could be significant.

Differences or changes in laws/legislation

A case could be distinguished by proving that it was decided under an old law. For instance, the differences between the 1979 and 1999 Constitutions can be used to distinguish cases decided under either constitution.

Supremacy of subsequent legislation

Statutes rank higher than cases. Therefore, a later legislation can override a judicial decision. Such decisions can be distinguished from cases which appear before the court after subsequent legislative interventions.

Wrong concession and pleading by counsel

Previous cases can be distinguished by proving that counsel in such cases wrongly conceded points of law to their opponents. A case can also be distinguished by demonstrating that the decision was affected by wrong pleading or a lack of pleading by counsel.

Policy reasons

It is possible to cite policy grounds such as national security, public order, public health and welfare and public interest as the basis for distinguishing cases.

Contexts/practical reasons

An older case can be distinguished by demonstrating the differences in its context and the current case, which may make the principles of the older case impractical in the modern circumstances.

Skeleton Argument

A skeleton argument is usually a brief document which contains the summary of the case of a mooting team. It serves similar purposes as the briefs of arguments at an appellate court but the length is often a one-page document.

Form

A skeleton argument is often divided into parts including a heading, introduction, submissions, conclusion, and signature.

Conciseness and clarity of presentation

A skeleton argument ought to be concise, direct and clear. It captures the essence of a party's case without providing too much detail. Details are given when cases are orally presented before the moot court.

Argument

Skeleton arguments contain legal arguments. Therefore counsel makes submissions and is not expected to proffer opinions in a skeleton argument.

Opponents' case

The arguments in a skeleton argument should incorporate or respond to the opponent's case. It is therefore important for counsel to try and anticipate the points or arguments of the opponents and deal with them in the skeleton argument.

Authorities

Skeleton arguments contain authorities for arguments they express. Authorities are often listed immediately under the arguments that rely on them. Authorities may also be required to be contained on a different page.

Length

A party to a mooting session should be aware of the particular rules which apply. Skeleton arguments are often not required to be more than a page long.

Names and Signature

A skeleton argument should indicate the identity of the mooters who prepared and submitted it.

Submission and Exchange

It is normally required that parties to a mooting event submit their skeleton arguments by a certain deadline. Parties are also usually required to exchange their skeleton arguments before the hearing date.

Sample Skeleton Argument

A skeleton argument may look like this:

IN THE SUPREME COURT OF NIGERIA

A v B

SKELETON ARGUMENT OF THE APPELLANT
Background [Brief statement of the facts]

First Ground of Appeal
Submissions [Brief statement of counsel's argument on the first ground of appeal]
Authorities [List of statutes, cases etc relied on for submissions]

Second Ground of Appeal
Submissions
Authorities

Names of Senior and Junior Counsel
Counsel for the Appellant

Presentation and Conduct in Mooting

Participants should at all times be aware that mooting mirrors the real courtroom. This means that the rules and conventions of the legal profession and the real courtroom apply to mooting events. While in the moot court, one is expected to comply with the dress code, show good manners, and avoid using mobile phones and having loud conversations.

Order of Presentation

The order of presentation and addresses is by party (appellant first) and by counsel (senior first) as listed below:

Parties: 1. Appellant; 2. Respondent
Counsel: a. Senior; b. Junior Counsel

Presentation Style

The presentation style should be thoughtful and not aggressive. A mooter ought to maintain good demeanour, stance and eye contact with the judge. Being an oral presentation, the voice pitch, pace of delivery and tone of delivery should be moderate and engaging. A conversational style of presentation is often useful in mooting.

Argument

Oral presentations in mooting consist of the argument of counsel. Counsel therefore makes submissions and does not provide testimonies or opinions which may be the role of witnesses in trials and mock trials.

Authorities

Oral presentations usually rely on authorities referred to in the skeleton arguments. Mooters are normally prohibited from relying on any legal authority, law report or other literature not cited in the list of authorities contained in the skeleton argument of either team. However, mooters may be free to rely on any legal authority or other literature, whether it has been cited in the lists of authorities in the skeleton argument or not, when dealing with any judicial intervention.

Timing

Time management is important in mooting because mooting speeches are normally timed. It is therefore necessary for mooters to prepare and make submissions within the stipulated time. The length of speeches should not be too long or too short.

Language

The language of mooting ought to be formal and professional. Colloquialisms, inflammatory language and abusive expressions should be avoided. It is also important for one to be aware of the legal professional conventions and etiquette in addressing the court and counsel.

Listening and Note taking

Mooters ought to speak well and also listen well when members of their team, judges and opposing counsel are speaking. A bad listener may not understand the judge's questions and provide good answers to them.

Note taking is also essential for counsel in mooting, particularly when the opposing counsel is speaking. This may enable counsel to respond to the opponent's arguments during his or her presentation or do a rebuttal if the rules of a mooting event so permit.

Teamwork

Mooting is often done in pairs. It is therefore important for mooters to work well as a team both before and during presentations. For example, both the senior and junior counsel ought to be aware of each other's submissions. It is not a positive performance if counsel does not respond to the judge's questions and instead refers the judge to the other counsel's submissions.

Bundle

Rules of mooting competitions often require parties to submit 'bundles' to the court before making presentations. A bundle contains full copies of any authorities that counsel may wish to rely on. These are usually authorities cited in the skeleton argument.

Judicial Interventions

Mooters should expect and deal with judicial interventions. A judge is at liberty to interrupt presentations, ask questions or direct submissions on particular points or issues.

Judging Criteria for Mooting

Mooting events usually indicate their preferred judging criteria. However it is often the case that the judging criteria are: **law, presentation, etiquette and response to judicial intervention**. Judges in reaching their decisions may take into account the following matters:

(a) the arrangement and quality of each team's summary argument in the skeleton and relevance of legal authorities and literature cited;

(b) the presentation, pace, volume, accuracy, clarity and relevance of each advocate's speech, including whether each speech (or aspects of it) was too long or too short, bearing in mind the confines of the mooting;
(c) analysis and integration by each advocate of legal authority or other literature cited;
(d) the ability of each advocate to respond to and undermine opponents' arguments;
(e) the ability of each advocate to comprehend and analyse theoretical issues;
(f) the ability of each advocate to deal with the judge's interventions, particularly to maintain the logical position in the face of undermining strategies;
(g) the court room manner and etiquette of each advocate; and
(h) the ability to work as a team.

CHAPTER THIRTEEN

EXAMINATION SKILLS AND STRATEGIES

OKECHUKWU TIMOTHY UMAHI[1]
AND COLLINS CHIKAODILI AJIBO[2]

Introduction

The aim of this chapter is to give practical suggestions to help students prepare for examinations and to gain knowledge of skills which assessors are looking out for. The chapter is based on personal experience, training and practice. In Nigeria, we have had the opportunity to counsel students that were asked to probate, withdraw or repeat a class, but only very few law teachers or law text books see good reason to make information on study skills and examination strategy readily available to students. The focus has always been on the contents of any law course, with the general assumption or presumption that students should know how best to succeed.

Success is good for every student, but it must be planned and carefully executed for a desirable end result. Examinations are known events and the Nigerian universities are guided by the National University Commission's regulations which provide for the course system and stipulate the minimum benchmark for courses. The course system allows students to be examined on a 30 percent continuous assessment and 70 percent written examination. Therefore, this chapter will provide emphasis on how to succeed as a law student in three sections. The first section will identify the course content and structure. The second section will focus on

[1]PhD (Manchester); LL.M (Manchester); LL.M (LASU); B.L; LL.B (ESUT); M.Sc (UNN); B.Sc/Ed (UNN); Senior Lecturer, Faculty of Law, Benson Idahosa University, Benin City, Edo State, Nigeria. Email: tumahi@biu.edu.ng.
[2]LL.M (Manchester), LL.B (Nigeria), B.L., PhD Candidate, The University of Manchester, United Kingdom. Email: chikaodili.ajibo@postgrad.manchester.ac.uk.

preparations for examination and the examinations proper, noting the key skills and the application of the skills in answering both the continuous assessment and the examination questions. The third and final section is the conclusion.

From the start of the semester

Education in Nigeria is increasingly becoming a nightmare for both parents and students. This fact can be observed with the increasing pressure on the faculties for legal education in Nigerian universities and the Nigerian Law School that provide for practical legal education. Therefore, law teachers must start performing above board in their chosen career and stop assuming or presuming what the student should know by making available and communicating this information. It is no longer acceptable for faculties of law to ask students to probate, withdraw, or repeat a class for performing below expectation or even rusticate students for attempting to pass at all costs. This in no way amounts to condoning indolence and/or malpractice amongst students. There is a need for law teachers and administrators to improve the knowledge of examinations, preparation skills, success strategies and to communicate on student's progress to their parents/guardians.

The following may be instructive for a student's career development:

1.Every course leader or lead lecturer must provide students with the course outline, which must state the philosophy, objective, method of teaching and the method of evaluation for the course as well as the recommended books. As a student of law, endeavour to make the course outline a working document to guide you for the course and the exams. Good universities and faculties of law also produce their academic programme which stipulates when the mid-term test will be conducted and follow up with monitoring the feedback process for the students. You are advised to make use of the feedback system to guide your career development plan and correct any identified errors.

2.Every student desirous of success must endeavour to have the right instructional materials used for the course. This may include the lecture notes, seminar notes and relevant or recommended textbooks. In addition, students should make a summary note of any of these materials showing understanding of the important and salient points in the private notes. Always identify the principles, the statutory provisions and the judicial decisions in the notes.

3.Course outlines are arranged into main topics and sub topics and the delivery of lectures strive to cover the topics and sub topics before the end of the semester. In the same vein, assessments are designed to test students' understanding of the various topics and sub topics. Therefore, having a total and comprehensive knowledge of one topic and knowing nothing about other topics and sub topics would be a recipe for failure in an examination.

Preparations and Examinations

At the start of the academic year, a student's success story starts with attending every lecture and being part of every lecture. Again, law lecturers and administrators must put in place a system that can monitor class attendance and the records from class attendance should be used promptly to follow up on deviant students. At the end of every day and week, every student must settle down to private study; this is the only way to appreciate the topics or sub topics covered during the day or week. Strategize to succeed along the following:

1. Produce a personal reading timetable at the start of every semester. We are aware of the difficulty in strictly following a reading timetable, but not having one remains a conscious effort to fail or perform badly in a highly competitive programme like law.
2. Organize group discussions amongst your friends. Avoid long group discussions; rather, get involved in small group discussions that cover one topic or sub topic at a time. This encourages comprehension and retention of the topics discussed and remains the surest way to convince yourself of your understanding and ability to state what you understand. Care should be taken in the formulation of a discussion group to include at least one exceptional student to checkmate the incidence of inadvertent misleading discussion. In Nigeria, a seminar class is an agreed norm, but a rare occurrence in most faculties of law. The Universities have the responsibility of recruiting graduate teaching assistants who can coordinate the seminar classes and contribute to improving the system.

Students need to understand the required examination skills and apply them to a specific question. Generally, law examinations come in two parts, namely essay questions and problem questions. Essay questions demand two things from the students; first, knowledge or mastery of the subject matter, and second, conveying the information in accordance with the demands of the question. Every question wants the student to satisfy the assessment criteria, which is an understanding of the instruction/command words and their meanings. This as explained by Gillett *et al*[3] as stated below:

- ❖ Analyse – Consider all the relevant factors and answer in a methodical and logical way.
- ❖ Compare – Discuss the similarities and differences. Write a balanced (fair, objective) answer.
- ❖ Criticise – Point out the strengths and weaknesses. Write a balanced answer.
- ❖ Discuss – Give both points of an argument, with implications, before reaching a conclusion.
- ❖ Explain – Give detailed reasons for a situation.
- ❖ Outline – Give the main points in a concise manner. Leave out detail.
- ❖ Summarise – Give the main points in a concise manner. Leave out detail.
- ❖ Account for – Give reason for.
- ❖ Assess – Examine the value of the subject, looking at the positives and negatives before reaching a decision.
- ❖ Comment on – Give your opinion. Back up your views with evidence from your reading.
- ❖ Consider - Give your opinion. Back up your views with evidence from your reading.
- ❖ Contrast – Discuss the difference between subjects.
- ❖ Define – Explain the meaning of the concept concisely.
- ❖ Demonstrate – Use examples to show something.
- ❖ Describe – Explain how something works or what it is like.
- ❖ Evaluate – Examine the value of the subject looking at the strengths and weaknesses before reaching a decision.
- ❖ Explore – Examine the topic thoroughly and consider it from a variety of viewpoints.
- ❖ Identify – Recognise and list.
- ❖ Illustrate – Show with examples.
- ❖ Justify – Give reasons for or against an argument.
- ❖ Prove – Show a proposition is true through evidence.
- ❖ Review – Examine the topic critically and consider whether it is adequate or accurate.
- ❖ State – Express relevant points briefly and clearly without minor details.
- ❖ Trace – Outline the development of a theme in a logical or chronological order.[4]

---

[3] Gillett, Hammond and Martala, *Successful Academic Writing* (Essex: Pearson Education Limited, 2009), 7.

[4] *Ibid.*, pp. 7, 19-20.

Understanding an essay question and what is required enables you proffer the right solution, and to get the right and desired score in an examination. As a law student and a lawyer, understanding these command words remains the key to examination success, therefore you need to master them, practice them and use them at any given opportunity.

Mastering these command words is the starting point, which must be carefully built up in arguments that are accurate, relevant and concise and must be organized as introduction, the body and the conclusion. The write-up has to be supported with relevant authorities, including legal principles, statutory provisions and judicial decisions.

The other question pattern for law examination is the problem question. Problem questions are so important to the law programme because of the understanding that it is a caricature of the reality that faces a law graduate. It tends to present a real life situation and seeks to prepare students on the reality ahead of them. We have to bear in mind that most of the students that gain admission into the universities to read law are from secondary school or at best graduates of other programmes where this question pattern is not the norm. Therefore, law lecturers should appreciate this fact and incorporate law examination skills and strategies into a first year course like the legal method.

Problem questions require analysis of some fictitious fact-situation, identifying the legal issues and liabilities they create and advising the parties in line with the questions that are asked. Most problem questions involve a sequence of events, involving few or several people, containing both relevant and irrelevant issues which at times may not concern all the parties that are mentioned or may become relevant when linked with something else that may appear later in the question. The questions at times may be too long winded and even the story line may be unrelated, but students must focus on what is expected of them, such as "Discuss the legal issues," "Advise the parties or a named party," "identify the legal issues and advise the parties as to their rights and liabilities," etc. There is no universally agreed approach to answering problem questions, but a good answer will flow from the knowledge of the principles, the relevant statutes, judicial decisions and adopting a systematic approach to the question.[5]

Students are advised to adopt a systematic approach and practice it as well. I have always advocated for a mapping approach that helps students

---

[5] J. Holland and J. Webb, *Learning Legal Rules,* 6th ed., (Oxford: Oxford University Press, 2006), 96.

to systematically address the question, and this will involve the following steps:

- Identify all the parties mentioned in the question. This is in line with law reports where the parties must be identified.
- Identify all legal issues raised in the question.
- For every legal issue identified apply the law to the party it concerns, state and describe the principles of law concerned, the relevant statutory provision (acts, edict, bye-law) and the judicial decisions (decided cases). This must be done for all the legal issues and the parties mentioned. Based on the authorities' advice to all parties, and following the line of the question, note who should be the claimant and the defendant.
- Draw the conclusion.

Evaluation of Academic Performance

University education has been in Nigeria for the past five decades and law education has not been left out in the development process. The National Universities Commission (NUC) provides for two types of evaluation: continuous assessment (conducted through mid-term test or take-home essay) and final examination (conducted at the end of the semester).

The continuous assessments are a significant part of the final evaluation, accounting for 30 percent of the final examination, so prepare for them in the same way as you prepare for the final examination. At present, some Nigerian universities are considering an upward review of the weight attached to the continuous assessment and a downward review of the weight attached to the final examination. This is part of the strategy to discourage students from getting involved in examination malpractice. Whether the reviews become actualised or not, every student must put in his/her best during the continuous assessment as it is a significant part in the final result outcome.

The final examination usually consists of 70 percent of the total assessment and comes with the attendant stress, desperation and temptation by some students to pass at all costs. This is not necessary if one has planned for success from the start of the semester and part of the success plan would involve assessing oneself with past examination questions which are kept in the law library. Examinations test your learning and understanding of the course and are an accepted format for grading the progress of students. They are used to assess the skills, knowledge and intelligence of students ranging from memory, the understanding the course contents, appreciation of the questions and timing. Generally, examinations assess a range of skills which include but are not limited to:

- Correct identification of the issues which the question(s) raise or demand.
- Test student's ability to present an argument and support this argument with relevant legal principles, legislation and judicial decisions.
- Show evidence of critical thinking and understanding.
- Present a well-structured piece of work with legible writing.
- Present evidence of organisational skill and independent research and ability to apply the acquired knowledge and understanding to the question correctly
- Most importantly, ability of present logical answers within the given time.
- Ability to manage yourself, avoiding overworking on the night of the exam day, controlling your nerves and being at the right exam venue at the right time, with the right materials.[6]

Remember, success comes with planning to succeed and every student must endeavour to:

- Plan time allocation and follow it strictly.
- Read and follow all instructions.
- Read the questions carefully and choose the questions carefully.
- Plan answers carefully.
- Answer the required number of questions.
- Write legibly and comply with the instructions.
- Leave at least ten minutes of the exam time to revise answers for spelling, grammar and missing links before submitting your answer script.
- Finally, avoid post-exam dissection/discussion of finished exams as it can upset you and affect your next exam.

---

[6] S. Hanson, *Legal Method, Skills and Reasoning,* 3rd ed. (Oxon: Routledge-Cavendish, 2010), 361.

Grading Requirement

The National Universities Commission (NUC) provides the benchmark for assessing/grading students answer scripts. These are the minimum standard that guides the marking schemes and the final marking.

While students' academic competence for the award of degrees is determined thorough script/examination assessment, competence or adequacy in other non-academic benchmarks can be determined through assignments, projects, moots, law clinics, tutorials, work placements, students-led court visits and extra-curricular activities. These **attainment levels** are stated below for students to have a good idea of how the scripts are graded, and these include:

First Class scripts must be exceptionally good and reveal:

- Comprehensive and accurate coverage of areas;
- Critical evaluation;
- Clarity of argument of materials;
- Depth of insight into theoretical issues; and
- Originality of exposition or treatment.

Second Class Upper scripts should:

- Be generally accurate and well informed;
- Be reasonably comprehensive;
- Be well organized and structured;
- Display some evidence of general reading;
- Indicate evaluation of materials, though these materials may be derivative;
- Demonstrate good understanding of the materials, and
- Be clearly presented.

Second Class Lower scripts should display an acceptable level of competence as indicated below:

- Generally accurate;
- Provide an adequate answer to the questions based largely on text books and lecture notes;
- Clear presentation;
- No real development of argument, and
- May contain some major error or omission.

Third Class represents the minimum acceptable standard. The script must demonstrate some knowledge or understanding of the general area but it will be expressed in the following weak ways:

- Descriptive only;
- Does not answer the question directly;
- Misses key points;
- Contains important inaccuracies;
- Covers materials sparsely, possibly in note form, and
- Assertions are not supported by authority or evidence.

Conclusion

This chapter has set out some of the key skills and strategies for examination success. The chapter did not get involved in the big debate as to whether examination is a true test of knowledge or whether one should love or hate examinations, but presents the skills and strategies that will guarantee success. The authors have opened various examinations which used to be the exclusive preserve of very few people and advise that students should get acquainted with them and carefully practice the provisions in order to be guaranteed success, which is the aim of the authors.

CONTRIBUTORS

Celestine Chukwuemeka Okoro. Lecturer in the Faculty of law, Benson Idahosa University, Benin city, holds a Bachelor's degree in law from the University of Nigeria, Enugu campus, Nigeria as well as a Master's degree in Law from University of Benin, Benin city, Nigeria and a diploma in Spanish and European Cultural Studies, University of Lorca, Spain. He is a barrister and solicitor of the Supreme Court of Nigeria and his research and teaching interest is in the areas of law of Torts, Oil and Gas law, Banking, Insurance and Corporate law.

Chijioke C Ohuruogu. Professor and Dean, Faculty of Law, Benson Idahosa University, Benin City. One time Chair, Board of Trustees, Access to Justice, Alumnus of the Universities of Ife and Lagos. Teaching Fellow and Human Rights Scholar at the Human Rights Institute, Columbia University, New York USA (fall 2002 and spring 2003); Holder of Certificate of Honour, Xiamen Academy of International Law, Xiamen China (2009), Alumnus GGP (Public International Law) of the University of Pretoria in South Africa; Alumnus of the International Institute of Human Rights in Strasbourg France and the CIEDHU Programme; Alumnus of the International Institute of Humanitarian Law in San Remo Italy; The Centre for the Study of International Humanitarian Law in Geneva Switzerland; The Salzburg Law School of International Humanitarian Law, International Criminal Law and International Human Rights Law in Salzburg Austria; The Euro Mediterranean Courses on International Law in Castellon Spain, The Forced Migration Course at the American University in Cairo, etc. His areas of teaching and research interests include Public International Law and its branches, particularly International Human Rights Law, International Humanitarian Law, International Criminal Law, Refugee Law, Transitional Justice, Alternative Dispute Resolution, Maritime Law and Constitutional Law.

Chukwuma Famous Ikechukwu. Assistant lecturer in the Department of Public Law, Faculty of Law, Benson Idahosa University. He holds an LL.B from the University of Benin and a B.L from the Nigerian Law School. He is currently undertaking an LL.M program in the University of Ibadan. He is also a member of the Nigerian Bar Association.

Chukwudumebi Okoye. Assistant lecturer in Public Law Department, Faculty of Law, Benson Idahosa University. She holds a Bachelor's degree and a Master's degree from the University of Benin, Benin City and has been called to the Nigerian Bar. Her academic interests are in International Humanitarian Law, International Human Rights Law and Constitutional Law. She is also a member of the Nigerian Bar Association.

Collins Chikaodili Ajibo. Law graduate of University of Nigeria where he obtained his LL.B. He holds LL.M from the University of Manchester (Distinction) and is a Doctoral Candidate at the University of Manchester. His areas of interest include International Trade and Investment Law; Arbitration; Corporate Governance; Corporate Social Responsibility.

Jesuorobo Emmanuel Idugboe. Senior lecturer and Sub-Dean, Faculty of Law, Benson Idahosa University. He hold a Bachelor of Laws degree of the University of Ife, Ile-Ife, now designated Obafemi Awolowo University, and a Master of Laws degree of the University of Jos. He was called to the Bar in 1984. He also served in the Directorate of Army Legal Services where he rose to the rank of Captain before he retired voluntarily in 1996. His teaching areas include Constitutional Law, Law of Contract, Criminal Law and Law of Evidence.

Josephine Omi Obasohan. Lecturer in the Department Private and Property Law at the Benson Idahosa University. She is a contributor in two books, titled *Nigeria Legal System* and *Nigerian Legal Methods*. Her research interest also extends to Company Law, particularly the examination of civil liabilities of corporate bodies in host communities.

Lilian Akhirome-Omonfuegbe. Lecturer in the Department of Private and Property Law, Faculty of Law, Benson Idahosa University. She holds a Bachelor's degree LL.B from Ambrose Alli University Ekpoma and an LL.M from the University of Aberystwyth, Wales, UK. She has also been called to the Nigerian Bar and is a member of the Nigerian Bar Association.

Nkechinyere Huomachi Worluh-Okolie. Assistant lecturer in the Department of Private and Property Law, Faculty of Law, Benson Idahosa University. She holds a Bachelor's degree from Benson Idahosa University. She has also been called to the Nigerian Bar and is currently undertaking her Master's program at the University of Benin. She is a member of the Nigerian Bar Association, and an arbitrator.

Okechukwu Timothy Umahi [PhD, Manchester]. Senior lecturer in Law and Head, Department of Private and Property Law, Faculty of Law, Benson Idahosa University. In addition, Umahi holds LL.M in Intellectual Property Law from the University of Manchester, LL.M in Maritime Law from Lagos State University, LL.B from Enugu State University and B.L. Nigeria. He is a solicitor and advocate of the Supreme Court of Nigeria. Umahi's university teaching experience covers the following subject areas: Intellectual Property Law, Information Communication Technology Law, Commercial Law, Legal Research and Methodology, Tort Law, Contract Law, Legal Methods and English Legal Systems. His research interest is on the impact of intellectual property law on access to drugs, healthcare, innovation in developing countries, and financial regulation for developing economies.

Oyekanmi Idode Adewoye. Lecturer in the Department of Private and Property Law, Faculty of Law, Benson Idahosa University, Benin City. He holds LL.B from the University of Lagos, Nigeria and was called to the Nigerian Law School in 1982. He holds an LL.M Master's Degree from Ambrose Alli University Ekpoma in 1991. His teaching and research interests cover law of Commercial Transactions, Equity and Trusts, Legal Methods and Constitutional law.

Onyeka Kingsely Osuji [PhD]. Senior lecturer in Law at the University of Exeter, United Kingdom. His research interests include corporate social responsibility, corporate governance, social and non-financial reporting, globalization, multinational enterprises and regulation. He is qualified as a barrister and solicitor of Nigeria and a solicitor of England and Wales, and has advised individuals, corporations, and national and international governmental and non-governmental organizations. He holds an LL.B from University of Nigeria, BCL Oxford, LL.M and PhD from the University of Manchester.

Theophilius Chinedu Nwano. Lecturer, Department of Public Law, Benson Idahosa University. He is a solicitor and advocate of the Supreme Court of Nigeria. Nwano holds both the Masters of Laws (LL.M), Bachelor of laws (LL.B) from Lagos State University and Barrister at Law (B.L.) from the Nigerian Law School. Nwano has teaching experience that covers the Nigerian Legal System, Land Law, Criminal Law, Maritime Law, Human Rights Law and International Law. His research interest is on Property and Human Rights Law.

Theresa Uzoamaka Akpoghome [PhD]. Senior lecturer, Department of Public Law, Benson Idahosa University. She is a solicitor and advocate of the Supreme Court of Nigeria. Akpoghome has a teaching experience that covers Law of Contract, Law of Commercial Transactions, Maritime Law, Oil and Gas Law, Business law and Use of Library. She also teaches International Humanitarian Law, International Law, Legal Aspects of ICT and Legal Research. Her research interest and publications is on International Humanitarian Law, War Prisoners and Oil and Gas Development.

INDEX